Muslim Chaplaincy: Handbook
and Voices of Muslim Women
Chaplains in Higher Education

Islamic Studies at Gerlach Press

Colin Turner
The Qurʾān Revealed: A Critical Analysis of Said Nursi's Epistles of Light. With a Foreword by Dale F. Eickelman
ISBN 9783940924285, 2013

Aziz Al-Azmeh
The Arabs and Islam in Late Antiquity: A Critique of Approaches to Arabic Sources
[Series: Theories and Paradigms of Islamic Studies]
ISBN 9783940924421, 2014

Sadik J. al-Azm
On Fundamentalisms
ISBN 9783940924223, 2014

Sadik J. al-Azm
Islam – Submission and Disobedience
ISBN 9783940924247, 2014

Sadik J. al-Azm
Is Islam Secularizable? Challenging Political and Religious Taboos
ISBN 9783940924261, 2014

Sadik J. al-Azm
Critique of Religious Thought. First English Translation of Naqd al-fikr ad-dini. With a New Introduction by the Author
ISBN 978394092444, 2014

Carool Kersten (ed.)
The Caliphate and Islamic Statehood – Formation, Fragmentation and Modern Interpretations (3 Volumes)
ISBN 9783940924520, 2015

Nasrin Rouzati
Trial and Tribulation in the Qurʾān. A Mystical Theodicy. With a Foreword by Colin Turner
ISBN 9783940924544, 2015

Esther Peskes (ed.)
Wahhabism – Doctrine and Development
(Critical Surveys in Islamic Denominations Series, 2 Volumes)
ISBN 9783940924506, 2016

Muhammad Shahrour
Islam and Humanity: Consequences of a Contemporary Reading. First Authorized English Translation of Al-Islam wa-l-insan by George Stergios. With a Foreword by Dale F. Eickelman
ISBN 9783959940184, 2017

Seyfeddin Kara
In Search of Ali ibn Abi Talib's Codex: History and Traditions of the Earliest Copy of the Qurʾān. With a Foreword by James Piscatori
ISBN 9783959940542, 2018

Mahshid Turner
The Muslim Theology of Huzn: Sorrow Unravelled. With a Foreword by Alparslan Açıkgenç
ISBN 9783959940405, 2018

Carool Kersten (ed.)
The Fatwa as an Islamic Legal Instrument: Concept, Historical Role, Contemporary Relevance (3 Volumes)
ISBN 9783959940207, 2018

Nadia Duvall
Islamist Occidentalism: Sayyid Qutb and the Western Other
ISBN 9783959940627, 2018

Sadik J. al-Azm
Occidentalism, Conspiracy and Taboo. Collected Essays 2014-2016
ISBN 9783959940467, 2019

Abdel-Hakim Ourghi
Reform of Islam. Forty Theses
ISBN 9783959940566, 2019

Imène Ajala
European Muslims and their Foreign Policy Interests: Identities and Loyalties
(Islam and International Relations Series, Vol. 1)
ISBN 9783959940603, 2018

Asma Hilali, S. R. Burge (eds.)
The Making of Religious Texts in Islam. The Fragment and the Whole (Pre- and Early Islam Series)
ISBN 9783959940702, 2019

David Cook
Studies in Muslim Apocalyptic
ISBN 9783959941204, 2021

Josef Horovitz
The Earliest Biographies of the Prophet and Their Authors. Edited by Lawrence I. Conrad
ISBN 9783959941068, 2021

Michael Lecker
The "Constitution of Medina": Muḥammad's First Legal Document
ISBN 9783959941242, 2024

Andreas Görke and Gregor Schoeler
The Earliest Writings on the Life of Muḥammad: The ʿUrwa Corpus and the Non-Muslim Sources
ISBN 9783959941266, 2024

Colin Turner
Divine Communication and Revelation: A Contemporary Muslim Theological Approach
ISBN 9783959941907, 2025

www.gerlachpress.com

Muslim Chaplaincy

Handbook and Voices of Muslim Women Chaplains in Higher Education

With a Foreword by Sophie Gilliat-Ray

Edited by Mahshid Turner

First published 2025
by Gerlach Press
Berlin, Germany
www.gerlachpress.com

Cover Design: Frauke Schön, Hamburg
Set by Anne Jeschke, Gerlach Press
Printed and bound in Germany, the United Kingdom and the United States of America

© Gerlach Press and the authors 2025
All rights reserved. No part of this publication may be reprinted or reproduced, or utilised in any form or by any electronic, mechanical, or other means, now known or hereafter invented, including photocopying and recording, or in any other information storage or retrieval system, without permission in writing from the publisher.

British Library Cataloguing in Publication Data.
A catalogue record for this book is available from the British Library.

Bibliographic data available from Deutsche Nationalbibliothek
http://d-nb.info/1336236531

ISBN: 978-3-95994-170-9 (hardcover)
ISBN: 978-3-95994-171-6 (eBook)

Contents

Acknowledgements   vii

Foreword   ix
Sophie Gilliat-Ray

Part 1: Chaplaincy Handbook
Mahshid Turner

1   Introduction   3

2   History of Christian Chaplaincy   7

3   History of Muslim Chaplaincy   9

4   Defining Muslim Chaplaincy   13

5   The Role of Prophets as 'Shepherds of Transcendence'   17

6   The Character of the Prophets   21

7   How Can Muslim Theology be Practiced in Pluralistic Settings?   39

8   What Do Muslim Chaplains Do?   41

9   Theological Reflection   45

10   Critical Reflection, Self-vigilance (*murāqaba*) and Self-accounting (*muḥāsaba*)   53

11   Matters of Concern for Muslim Students and Staff   59

12   Pastoral and Spiritual Care: The Shepherding of Muslim Chaplains   65

     Notes   81

     Bibliography   87

Part 2: Voices

	Introduction	93
1	Ameena Blake (University of Sheffield)	95
2	Syeda Midhat Batool (Loughborough University)	117
3	Amra Bone (University of Portsmouth)	145
4	Mahshid Turner (Durham University)	161
5	Rukia Bi (Keele University)	177
6	Sabiha Iqbal (Roehampton University)	193
	Notes	215
	Bibliography	217

Part 3: Interviews

1	Ameira Abahadur Kutkut (Cardiff Metropolitan University)	223
2	Umm Issa (Manchester Metropolitan University)	231
3	Farhat Yaqoob (Leeds University)	237
4	Concluding Remarks	245
	About the Contributors	247

Acknowledgements

I am deeply indebted to the people who have supported me to finally produce a Muslim chaplaincy handbook.

Most people have not heard very much about the important role that Muslim chaplains play. The aim of Part One of this book has been to provide an outline of what Muslim chaplaincy is all about, so that it may serve as a handbook and guide for chaplaincy work.

The aim of Part Two of this book has been to showcase the chaplaincy work that Muslim women are carrying out in various Higher Education institutions in UK. In this regard I am particularly grateful to Dr Susan Frenk, Principal of St. Aidan's College, Durham University, whose support has been invaluable. Her kind and enthusiastic hosting of a workshop and discussion meetings at St Aidan's, where the contributing authors were able to come together to flesh out their ideas and help me 'landscape' the book, was of inestimable value, and we are all much obliged to her.

I would like to thank Kai Gerlach and Malcolm Campbell at Gerlach Press for their patience, guidance and meticulousness. Gerlach has built up an impressive roster of titles over the past two decades and it is an honour for us to have our book published with them.

I also have to thank my dear husband, Dr Colin Turner, Head of Research at the International Foundation for Muslim Theology, whose support and input has also been invaluable.

Out of respect for the Prophet Muhammad, it is customary to add the words "peace be upon him" or a variant of this blessing after mentioning his name. I assume that the readers insert the words accordingly.

Mahshid Turner, Durham, Autumn 2024

Foreword

Across North America and Europe, Muslim chaplains are increasingly taking up institutional chaplaincy appointments, especially in the health and education sectors. Slowly but surely, Muslim chaplaincy work is beginning to become a recognised career path, and an especially important one for Muslim women wishing to exercise a professional religious vocation. The volume of research associated with this growth is arguably resulting in a distinctive field of 'Muslim Chaplaincy Studies', to which this new volume makes an important contribution.

While there has been a flourishing of research about Muslim chaplaincy in North America, there is so far relatively little empirical research this side of the Atlantic in the UK and Europe. Besides my book with Mansur Ali and Stephen Pattison (*Understanding Muslim Chaplaincy*, 2013) there remains a dearth of research and especially the kind of literature which might guide those who are exploring the possibility of working in chaplaincy. This practitioner-orientated volume will be the answer to their prayers, in so far as it offers a theological grounding for the role, alongside insights about the realities of working as a chaplain. The accounts and pastoral case-studies you will read in this book are honest, reflective, and full of wisdom.

While there is a particular focus on Muslim chaplaincy in the HE context, there is much potential for the advice and perspectives in this book to have cross-transference to other sectors. Issues around mental health and relationship breakdowns, as well as the practical needs of Muslims living or working in an institutional context are relevant across sectors. Any new or aspiring Muslim chaplain will find the advice and practitioner accounts in this book invaluable, while more experienced chaplains will find fresh perspectives and ideas that could increase the rewards and potential of their work.

Within the Islamic tradition, the importance of 'chains of transmission' are crucial. The links between scholars and students across the generations have served to maintain the integrity of Islam across time and space. The reflections in this book are in some senses perpetuating that tradition as knowledgeable and skilled practitioners hold out the hand of experience to those exploring this new religious profession, gently guiding them to understand the complexity, the rewards, and the religious grounding of the chaplaincy role. I am delighted that at long last there is a book that foregrounds the experiences of Muslim women working as chaplains. As well as blazing a trail for their sisters, they are pointing to the potential (and need) for much greater 'pastoral care' provision for and by women within Muslim communities and institutions more widely.

Overall, this book is about so much more than the experiences of female Muslim chaplains in higher education. It shines a light on our human condition and suggests possibilities for the way in which we can flourish and find our potential as responsible Muslims in the modern world as either the givers, or receivers of chaplaincy work, Insha'Allah.

Professor Sophie Gilliat-Ray OBE FLSW FBA,
Director, Centre for the Study of Islam in the UK, Cardiff University,
Cardiff, Autumn 2024

Part 1

Chaplaincy Handbook

Mahshid Turner

1

Introduction

Most Higher Education institutions in the UK have now appointed Muslim chaplains to support Muslim students and staff with their faith needs. Although a few of these chaplains are recruited on a voluntary basis, the majority are in paid employment as there is increasing recognition that they play a vital role in contributing to the well-being of students and staff in their institutions.

However, there is no clear definition of Muslim chaplaincy, what are their tasks and what knowledge and skills are required for their role. The main aim of this handbook is to provide a foundational, contemporarily relevant theological framework in which Muslim chaplains can carry out their care-giving role.

Before discussing Muslim chaplaincy, I will also give a brief account of the history of its Christian counterpart. The examination of the origin of the word 'chaplaincy' will provide a context for discussion on the meaning and purpose of the role. The aim is to show that while the word 'chaplain' has a Christian origin, chaplaincy or 'shepherding' is, and has always been, an integral part of Muslim practical theology.

Ryan provides a broad definition of a chaplain as "an individual who provides religious and spiritual care within an organisational setting".[1] This broad definition does not clarify what constitutes the religious or the spiritual and whether that care is inclusive of all faiths, or whether it caters for the needs of individuals who are not directly 'religious' or 'spiritual'. It is therefore important to examine the theologies upon which the work of the chaplain depends, especially within the context of a pluralistic society.

Although Sophie Gilliat-Ray et. al. are right to point out that there is no concept of 'clergy' as such in Islam, institutionalised 'chaplaincy' – albeit by a different name[2] – has existed, and still does exist, in some parts of the Muslim world.[3] Also, the theology that underpins Muslim chaplaincy has not been adequately addressed. Without a clear theology, Muslim chaplaincy is reduced to only the externals of the faith and the teachings of the five pillars of Islam, with chaplains recruited largely with those aims in mind.

Gilliat-Ray et. al. define Muslim chaplaincy mainly in terms of 'caregiving'.[4] This present book aims to explain the multifarious aspects of caregiving unique to Muslim chaplaincy, which differs from other well-being sectors such as counselling.

Muslim chaplaincy has also been defined in terms of: "the pastoral care of Muslims within institutional settings."[5] However, although pastoral care is the main task of a Muslim chaplain, it does not adequately incorporate the holistic role that Muslim chaplains play. Christian chaplaincy tends to differentiate between pastoral care and shepherding; the first is seen as a means of helping service-users to come to reach important decisions by themselves; the second is understood to be more about the total dependency of the 'flock' on the 'shepherd'.[6] However, he Muslim idea of shepherding is different. Muslim shepherding has always included pastoral care, which is understood in the context of revelation as the empowering of individuals to find themselves. However, for individuals to find themselves, they also need guidance on how to read the signs in creation in order to be able to remove the 'veils of darkness' themselves.

Thus in this chapter, a broad definition of chaplaincy is posited which reflects the inclusion of pastoral care within the act of shepherding, designed for lifting up and supporting individuals in their attempts to reconnect with that innate part of their disposition which craves balance and harmony. This is why examples of prophets, who were tested with the most difficult trials and tribulations, are given in this chapter, as they serve as the major models and templates for Muslim chaplains in performing their roles as shepherds.

This broader definition of chaplaincy also enables Muslim chaplains to carry out their shepherding in pluralistic contexts, for it is arguable that all human beings have been graced with the potential to return to their innate state, regardless of their race, ethnicity or culture. The Quranic concept pairs expounded in Chapter Twelve can be seen as tools for chaplains to use in the shepherding of their diverse communities.

The main commonality between Muslim chaplaincy and counselling is the attempt to help individuals examine their thought processes and change their behaviours accordingly. Muslim chaplaincy differs in the sense that it suggests lasting solutions to often profound existential problems and questions. This is what sets it apart from Cognitive Behavioural Therapy (CBT), which is limited in its scope, with no locus for the offering of solutions which go beyond the material and into the vast and eternal domains of metaphysical and spiritual space. Having said that, CBT is in a sense a Quranic concept by default, revealed over 1400 years ago, since it is concerned with the changing and development of human souls. While CBT encourages individuals to change their thought processes in order to be able to examine their experiences in a different way, it does not offer permanent or foundationally meaningful solutions to human existential problems or crises. By contrast, revelation points both to itself and to the 'book of the cosmos', replete with signs for all to read and to be guided.

In the absence of literature on Muslim reflective practice, Muslim chaplains tend to follow either the secular or Christian models. However, the Quranic concepts of self-vigilance (*murāqaba*) and self-accounting (*muḥāsaba*) serve as an excellent framework for Muslim reflective practice as well constituting a conceptual backdrop against which chaplaincy work can be carried out. Part One of this Handbook has therefore been devoted to the use of this concept pair in order to devise a unique Muslim behavioural change model (MBCM) for chaplains to use in their shepherding, as well as for self-reflection. This method will also be valuable for Muslim chaplains in other institutions, as it provides a unique, six-step Muslim counselling model which they can easily incorporate in their particular shepherding role.

Despite the profusion of Christian chaplains in many institutions and the community, and notwithstanding the increasing acknowledgement of the important role of Muslim chaplains, there is actually still no agreement on what the role of a Muslim chaplain is or should be. Similarly, there is no consensus regarding the qualifications one should have for this role and the qualities and motivations that are necessary.[7] Moreover, there is no general agreement as to whom a Muslim chaplain is ultimately accountable from an organisational perspective. There is also very little opportunity for professional development for Muslim chaplains, and where there are opportunities, most of the literature and training methodologies utilised reflect a predominantly Christian framework. Part One of this book provides a framework that will be of inestimable utility for all Muslim chaplains in Higher Education, as well as other institutions, as it provides a unique and authentically Quranic framework which has hitherto been conspicuous by its absence from the discourse.

Most Higher Education institutions, which are predominately Christian, have very little understanding about the difference between the role of imams and Muslim chaplains. Often imams, particularly when in clerical garb, are deemed to outrank chaplains, even though for the most part, the scope of an imam's engagement with his institution is limited almost exclusively to the leading of congregational and/or Friday prayers. A major difficulty encountered by Muslim chaplains is the fact that most Muslims are unaware of what a Muslim chaplain is and what his or her role entails. Consequently, much time is spent by Muslim chaplains on raising awareness among the Muslim community in order to gain their trust. In Part One of this book, an attempt will be made to clarify the points of convergence and divergence between the functions of Muslim chaplains and imams, and to highlight the crucial role played by Muslim chaplains in institutions of higher education.

It is important to note that Part One of this book has been written to address a longstanding and hitherto neglected need, and that is the production of a handbook for Muslim chaplains in general, and for those working in higher education in particular. As a work of guidance and reference, this handbook will focus significantly on the pastoral principles that grow organically out of the six articles of faith in Islam, namely belief in one God; belief in angels; belief in prophethood and messengership; belief in the Divinely-revealed books and scriptures; belief in the Day of Judgment and the existence of an eternal afterlife; and belief in the ubiquity of Divine Determining. These articles of belief and, more importantly, how they were engaged with and utilised by prophets and messengers in their shepherding roles, are thus the conceptual pillars upon which this handbook has been constructed.

The handbook – i.e. Part One of this work – also includes real-life examples of case studies in order to showcase and illustrate the multifarious tasks which Muslim chaplains undertake as educators, mediators, advocates and general bridge-builders, connecting people and departments in their respective institutions.

Much of the work done by Muslim chaplains contributes significantly to the mental well-being of the student and staff community, nurturing positive values which benefit them not just in their university setting, but also in their lives beyond the confines of university. Another set of case studies provides a small window through which some of the work of Muslim chaplains in this area can be glimpsed.

Part Two of the current work consists of a number of narratives provided by female Muslim chaplains working in higher education contexts in the United Kingdom. Traditionally, the position of imam is held by men; however, in the case of Muslim chaplaincy, both men and women can fulfil this role. While the primary duty of an imam is to lead congregational prayers and provide Friday prayer sermons, the primary function of the Muslim chaplain is to shepherd and to give pastoral care. Muslim chaplaincy requires particular skills and training in mental health, professional ethics, counselling and, broadly speaking, Muslim theology. Part Two of this book provides an opportunity for Muslim women chaplains to showcase their work and their particular skills, and how their roles contribute to the well-being of students and staff. Their stories also include accounts of both the advantages they may meet as Muslim chaplains who happen to be women, together with the challenges that they may encounter as females in the role.

2

History of Christian Chaplaincy

The word 'chaplain' comes from the Latin word *cappellani*, which means cloak. It dates back to the fourth century and the story of St Martin, the third bishop of Tours, whose compassion upon seeing a beggar clad only in rags compelled him to cut his cloak in two so that he could share it with him. Later, a priest kept Martin's half-cape as a relic. Over time, as other relics were added, priests were appointed to guard them, appointed by royalty and acquiring the title 'chaplain' in the process.[8] As well as being guardians of the relics, these chaplains also gave advice on ecclesiastical and other matters. In the West, the practice of appointing chaplains spread throughout Christendom and of course still exists today.[9] Christian chaplaincy can thus be viewed from two aspects: its institutional side, including its connections to royalty; and its pastoral side, which is about 'taking care of the flock' in order to bring about transformation at both the individual and societal levels.[10] These two aspects are not, one should add, mutually exclusive.

Pastoral care is also associated mainly with Christianity because of its historical context and its association with the role of pastors, who strived to emulate Jesus as "the good shepherd". In the late eighteenth century, practical theology emerged in the German Protestant tradition, with the aim of applying specialist theological principles to practice.

The origins of pastoral care in the United States can be traced back to the philosopher William James, whose Gifford Lectures emphasized the importance of personal religious experience and the observation and study of such phenomenon.[11] Influenced by James's ideas on the importance of the function of religious belief and the study of human experience, Anton Boisen, described as the founder of clinical pastoral education in the United States, believed that many forms of mental illness are related to religion rather than to medical problems; consequently, he asserted, they require theological interpretations.[12] Seward Hiltner also emphasised the importance of pastoral theology and argued that it should be considered as a separate and legitimate discipline, largely on account of its contribution to the understanding of the 'shepherding perspective', which he describes as the healing effect of theology in practice.[13]

According to Pattison and Woodward, in the contemporary British experience, pastoral theology and practical theology are considered to be more or less the same thing.[14] Atkinson and Field stress that all theological thinking is in fact practical, since "theology arises from practice, moves into theory, and is then put into practice again".[15] Paul Ballard adds that it is not possible to give a clear definition of British pastoral/practical theology since it is a discipline that is continually developing in various directions.[16] A broad definition of practical theology is provided by Forrester as "The theological discipline which is primarily concerned with the interaction of belief and behaviour".[17]

Ben Ryan questions the pastoral model of chaplaincy, stating that "simply caring for others is rather a limited vision of the role".[18] However, it depends how the concept of 'caring' is understood. Looking at it from a Muslim perspective, if caring includes manifesting God's presence, then it would need to include not just God's love but all of His other attributes too, such as wisdom, mercy, justice and the like, since all human beings are "a symbol of the Creator within creation."[19] In order to consciously manifest those names and attributes by acting in accordance with them, chaplains would need theological knowledge and understanding. While knowledge is to an extent measurable, thus allowing employers, for example, to ascertain whether certain qualifications for entry into chaplaincy have been met, understanding, conviction and the extent to which a chaplain is personally committed to God are clearly unquantifiable. However, the changes that each chaplain brings as a result of their devotion and commitment, together with their particular skills or, more importantly, the unique way they manifest God's names, can potentially contribute to considerable transformations in individual lives and in the lives of the institutions in which they operate. While such results resist quantification, they can be seen and experienced, which is what counts.

3

History of Muslim Chaplaincy

According to Gilliat-Ray et al., there is no formal, structured hierarchy of religious professionals in Islam. While it is true that there is no clergy to administer sacrament as there is in Christianity, an informal hierarchy of religious leaders has always existed in the Muslim world.[20] Although the terms pastor, clergy and chaplain have a Christian origin, similar roles have existed in Muslim communities, albeit under different guises, e.g. *ḥakīm* (philosopher), *mutakallim* (scholastic theologian) and *shaykh* (Sufi master). All of these roles, and more, generally come under the collective term *'ulamā* (lit. 'those who know'), which is a catch-all term that is sometimes mistranslated as 'clergy', but which in actual fact is used to signify anyone with a background in learning and teaching, and in particular those versed in the exoteric disciplines such as law and legal theory.

The *ḥakīms* of the medieval age were versed not only in philosophy but also in medicine, mathematics, ethics, metaphysics and many other disciplines. Consequently people at all levels looked to them for help with their spiritual problems.[21] In order to raise awareness and reach a larger audience, key figures such as Ibn Sina (980-1037)[22] and al-Kindi (801-873) wrote epistles on particular metaphysical/spiritual problems and how to solve them in a language accessible to the general public.[23] It is also important to note that it was mainly down to al-Kindi's elevated position as scholar and his close connection to the caliphs al-Ma'mun (813-833) and al-Mu'tasim (833-846) that he was able to secure his position as *ḥakīm* and to oversee and supervise the work of the translation movement.[24]

While the approach of the medieval Muslim philosophers to matters of faith stressed the importance of 'reason' as a priority, Sufi shaykhs concurred with the scholastic theologians (*mutakallimūn*) on the primacy of the Quran and hadith. However, they also emphasized the importance of the 'purification of the soul' in understanding the revelatory messages. One such example is Abu Ḥāmid al-Ghazālī (1058-111) whose magnum opus *The Revival of the*

Religious Sciences (Ihyā'ulūm al-dīn), and in particular parts three and four, can be described as a book of practical wisdom or pastoral theology since it concerns the inner life of the soul, its vices and how to confront them.[25] Ghazālī, described variously as a Muslim philosopher, theologian and jurist, and sometimes as a mystic, was appointed by the Seljuq grand vizier, Nizām al-Mulk (d. 1092), as an official of the Seljuk court, holding the prominent position of professor of Muslim law and theology at the Nizāmiyya madrasa. Later in his life, of course, he famously decided to abandon his prestigious office, certain that his striving in this life should be purely for the hereafter and not for worldly gain.[26]

Today the title of *ālim* (religious scholar) is given to anyone who has followed a certified Islamic studies course in seminaries such as Al-Azhar University in Cairo. Similar seminaries exist in South Asia and in Britain, with women now able to attend.[27] However, these courses are not externally validated and have been criticised for, among other things, not offering pastoral care skills as part of their curriculum.[28] Moreover the courses tend to lean heavily on *ahkām* (Islamic law), with very little emphasis on the spiritual aspects of the faith.[29]

Although the Muslim community is familiar with the title of imam (prayer leader) and *ālim* (religious scholar), there is less familiarity with the concept of Muslim chaplain. Muslims became involved in hospital and prison chaplaincy in the 1970s, when they were referred to as 'visiting minsters' and were mainly sought out from the community on a mostly ad hoc basis. In the UK prison system, it was not until 2003 that such individuals were given the title of 'chaplain' and were employed formally, with the same terms of employment as their Christian counterparts.

Within the British educational sector, the tendency traditionally was for Muslim staff already working at a particular institution to take on the extra task of tending to the 'religious needs' of Muslims in that institution, again on a largely ad hoc basis. Today, the vast majority of Muslim chaplains in UK educational institutions hold mostly part-time positions. However, many of them do not have any formal and recognised chaplaincy qualifications; they are employed largely on the basis of their experience in the Muslim community as religious leaders or advisors.[30]

In most institutions, chaplaincy in general is Christian-led, the tendency being for the chaplaincy to seek *ālims* or religious leaders in communities such as imams to address the practical religious needs of the institution's Muslim service users. This includes, but is not restricted to, giving advice on appropriate places to pray, the location of ablution areas, issues concerning halal food, whether or where Friday prayers are held, and so on. This is despite the fact that most of the information pertaining to orthopraxy and the legal-juristic matters of the faith can these days be accessed via the plethora of books that have been written on the subject, both in print as well as online.[31] Moreover there appears to be no consistency concerning the requisite qualifications for Muslim chaplaincy; where criteria are actually mentioned, there seems to be little or no requirement for a thorough theological-spiritual understanding of the faith. Examples of the practical repercussions of this oversight abound, such as the occasion a Muslim man was recruited by his institution as Muslim chaplain simply because he had been observed praying in the university prayer room.[32]

4

Defining Muslim Chaplaincy

The Difference between Chaplains and Imams

The term chaplain remains under-appreciated within the Muslim community, as it is regarded to be a Christian term owing to its etymology and original usage. Muslim chaplains are, however, the 'external face of Islam' and the 'voice of Muslims' in their institutions – in prisons, hospitals and universities – for they are more than just spiritual caregivers: Muslim chaplains also play significant roles as advisers, counsellors, advocates, teachers, administrators and religious service advisors and/or facilitators. They also cater for a multi-faith, multicultural and global community. Mark Newitt describes the role of chaplains as people who do "not tell people what to think" but people who help individuals "explore and think for themselves".[33] Moreover, while there is generally a requirement for mosque imams to be males, Muslim chaplaincy is open to qualified female candidates.

Imams provide an important service for their communities. Their main duty is to lead the five daily prayers, especially the Friday congregational service, and conduct other religious duties such as officiating at marriages and leading Quran reading classes for children and adults. However, most of them lack training with regard to the more challenging social issues such as youth alienation, problems of identity, domestic violence, drug addiction and mental health.[34]

Their training mainly involves an understanding of the technical-juristic underpinnings of religious practice, and thus typically they work within the congregational setting of mosques. Chaplains, however, tend to have broader qualifications and training, and have usually experienced greater exposure to diverse faiths and cultures. Thus while chaplains are happy to work within a multifaith and multi-denominational context, imams generally work with people from the same denomination.[35]

Theological Framework for Muslim Chaplaincy

Farhad Khosrokhavar, in his study of Muslim prison chaplains in France, refers to four kinds of Muslim prison chaplains: those who solely support individuals with external needs and rituals; those who engage in occasional dialogue with Muslim prisoners; those who also give support with regard to existential problems; and the "opportunistic chaplains" whose main aim is to bolster their own public image. He argues that even though most Muslim prisoners seek some kind of spiritual support at some time, Muslim prison chaplains are far fewer in number than those included in the first category. He adds that the mindset of these chaplains is such that they equate knowledge of religion solely with the knowledge of jurisprudence.[36] While the provision of such services is indeed very important to service-users, practical needs should not be separated from the needs of the spirit. It is in fact the spiritual aspect that feeds into the practical, giving it energy and purpose and thus rejuvenating practice and making it more meaningful.

Contemporary Muslim scholarship tends to conflate theology with jurisprudence, resulting in faith support being offered mainly in terms of advice and support pertaining to practical and legal-juristic issues, which historically has been less of a problem.[37] Muslim philosophers and scholars such as al-Ghazālī, Miskawayh (932-1030), Balkhī (849-934) and al-Rāzī (846-925) all echo the sentiments of al-Kindī (800-870) with regard to the importance of spiritual needs.[38]

Practice without a firm foundation in belief runs the risk of degenerating into a mere robotic physical exercise, and the likelihood that it will fizzle out is high. Muslim chaplaincy training has an urgent need to be grounded in a theological framework which takes spirituality and the ethics of chaplaincy seriously. Since theology informs both orthopraxy and methodology, it is important to identify a broad definition for Muslim theology and a systematic framework upon which practice can be based. The concept of *kalam*, which literally means "speech", tends to be conflated with theology. However, within the broader theological framework, it relates to "the study of Divine Speech,"[39] and it is in connection to this definition that Nguyen defines theology as encompassing "the totality of one's being."[40] As the six articles of faith are an integral part of all of the prophets' teachings and lived experience, this definitional framework will be used for Muslim chaplains to follow in their practice.

Definition of Muslim Chaplaincy

Islam is not an ideology; rather, it is considered to be the default setting of the created universe, or the way things are innately, which is expressed colloquially as 'a whole way of life'. The triliteral Arabic root *s-l-m* and its derivates connote many things which pivot around peace and surrender. The word *salām*, of course, forms part of the Muslim greeting of peace, with other derived verbal nouns being 'submission', 'surrender' and 'being in a state of safety'.[41] Submission, therefore, can be seen as a state in which one is in harmony within oneself as well as with the rest of creation. Since the central task of chaplains is to support individuals in their search for peace and harmony, or to assist the return of harmony to the life of an individual, a broader definition of chaplaincy can, I contend, be expressed as: *the support a chaplain gives to people in order to facilitate their return to their innate 'Adamic' nature.*

Our Adamic Nature: The Human Story

Contrary to certain secular materialistic ideas that human beings have no free will but are merely puppets controlled by laws of physics,[42] Muslims believe that they have been given the ability to either accept the right criterion for living, which is believed to accord with their innate being, or to reject it.

The primordial covenant, referred to in the verse below, is the promise that every human being is believed to have given to God before entering this world, namely the promise to use the gift of free will in order to bear witness to God's creation:

> *And when your Lord brought forth from the children of Adam, from their backs, their descendants, and made them bear witness against their own souls: Am I not your Lord ['alastu bi rabbikum]? They said: Yes! we bear witness. Lest you should say on the day of resurrection: Surely we were heedless of this.*[43]

This "*alast* covenant" was part of the 'Trust' (*amāna*), convened between God and human beings before we entered this world. The agreement was that we as human beings would honour our part of the Trust by attesting to the existence of our transcendent Lord and manifest consciously all of God's names and attributes. Indeed, this is what distinguishes humankind from the rest of the created beings. However, although human beings had promised to fulfil the primordial covenant and to refrain from usurping God's names, God has pre-eternal knowledge of the fact that humans would inevitably become dazzled by the glitz and glamour of worldly life, and that many, if not most, would become lured away from their good intentions and become lost in a world of temptation and attraction.

Thus, since all human beings have accepted the primordial covenant, and since they are the only beings who were taught all of the names and attributes of God, they all manifest those Divine qualities, whether consciously or unconsciously. This ability to appreciate, yearn for and manifest consciously the names of God – names such as knowledge, wisdom, beauty, justice, order and the like – is an innate ability present in all human beings. And this ability is something that Muslim chaplains can take benign advantage of, for it forms a shared experience and a common ground on which chaplain and client can engage in meaningful conversations that resonate profoundly with both parties.

5

The Role of Prophets as 'Shepherds of Transcendence'

In the Muslim tradition, those figures to whom revelatory missions were given by God are referred to as messengers (*rasūl*), while those who called others to God using the framework of an existing revelation are referred to as prophets or bringers of news (*nabī*). Collectively, however, they are all generally referred to in English as prophets. And teaching others how to read the 'signs' (*āyāt*) in creation, in accordance with the criteria outlined in revealed scripture, has been the primary duty of all of the prophets. Prophets, therefore, serve as the interpreters and instructors who teach others how to understand the 'language' of God's revelations to, and communications with, humankind:

> *Just as We have sent among you a messenger from yourselves reciting to you Our verses and purifying you and teaching you the Book and wisdom and teaching you that which you did not know.*[44]

There is no notion of proselytization in Islam. God is the only One who truly guides, and He has no partners to share in this task. There is no-one or nothing in the world able to shield or protect anyone against God, since He is the only Protector (*walī*) and Helper (*naṣīr*).[45] The role of the prophets, then, is essentially to direct people and to support them in their search for meaning and understanding, and in submitting to the message and guidance of God.[46]

As is stated in the Quran, there is nothing in creation that does not glorify God and recite His praises; in other words, everything is a sign pointing to its Maker. Furthermore, the Quran makes it clear that every messenger was sent to help people keep hold of the "firm rope" of belief and not to stray away from the right path by helping them to read the Divine signs in the correct way:

> *And how could you disbelieve while to you are being recited the verses of Allah and among you is His Messenger? And whoever holds firmly to Allah has [indeed] been guided to a straight path.*[47]

This shepherding role of prophets is further confirmed in Prophetic sayings (*hadith*) through the analogy of the literal grazing of sheep and the idea of guiding to the straight path:

> "Allah did not send any prophet but shepherded sheep." His companions asked him, "Did you do the same?" The Prophet (ﷺ) replied, "Yes, I used to shepherd the sheep of the people of Mecca for some Qirāts."[48]

However, shepherding is not considered to the responsibility of prophets alone: everyone has a responsibility of care in accordance with their role and context:

> *Every one of you is a shepherd and is responsible for his flock. The leader of people is a guardian and is responsible for his subjects. A man is the guardian of his family, and he is responsible for them. A woman is the guardian of her husband's home and his children, and she is responsible for them. The servant of a man is a guardian of the property of his master, and he is responsible for it. No doubt, every one of you is a shepherd and is responsible for his flock.*[49]

Prophets, therefore, were sent to support lost souls and prevent them from harm by elucidating and interpreting the signs in both the Quran and in creation through example, explanation and instruction. The way prophets were instructed to help people to remain on the straight path was linked to their role as *mubashshir* (bearers of good news) and *mundhir* (warners):

> *Mankind was [of] one religion [before their deviation]; then Allah sent the prophets as bringers of good tidings and warners and sent down with them the Scripture in truth to judge between the people concerning that in which they differed.*[50]

The role of Muslim chaplains, therefore, is to emulate the prophets, Muhammad, as the final prophet, in particular. Their role is to support individuals through example, explanation and instruction, without any expectation of results. For as the Quran clarifies, ultimately the outcome of all actions is under God's control.[51]

However, in order to go beyond the exoteric aspects of the faith, the four stations attained by all the prophets need to be taken into consideration. These are:

1. Sacred laws (*shari'a*)
2. Sacred path (*tariqa*)
3. Divine reality (*haqiqa*)
4. Gnosis of God (*ma'rifa*)

The sacred laws (*shari'a*) are there for those who accept God's unity and submit to His rule, so that those things which are permissible and forbidden in the juristic sense can be distinguished. These laws are there in general in the Quran and have been explained in greater detail by Prophet Mohammad via the corpus of hadith. The sacred path (*tariqa*) is the station at which devotees attribute all things, including the creation of human actions, to God. Divine reality (*haqiqa*) is the station at which one seeks God and God alone through recognition of the Divine names and attributes. And finally, knowledge of God (*ma'rifa*), is the station at which one seeks to attain God-consciousness in every action and state.

Explaining the hadith "The Holy Law is my words, the Way is my acts and Reality is my states",[52] Nasafi says that to reach the station of a leader, one must accept what the messenger has said in order to be recognised as the 'people of the law'; one must do what the messenger did in order to be recognised as the 'people of the way'; and one must see what the messenger saw in order to be one of the 'people of reality'. Furthermore, he explains the purpose of these stations:

> *The purpose of the Holy Law, the Way and the Reality is that humans become truthful speakers, truthful in their actions, and become wise and adorned with good character traits.*[53]

6

The Character of the Prophets

The Quran describes the character of Prophet Mohammad as kind (*ra'ūf*) and merciful (*raḥīm*), as well as emphasizing his ability to empathize with the human condition:

> *There has certainly come to you a Messenger from among yourselves. Grievous to him is what you suffer; [he is] concerned over you and to the believers is kind and merciful.*[54]

The Quranic approach to shepherding is clearly defined in the above verse. It reassures the reader that the Prophet is not an angel, but a human being who has himself experienced many trials and tribulations and is thus able to understand and empathize with the difficulties that believers encounter. As the foundation of creation is based on the concepts of *raḥmāniyya* (compassion) and *raḥīmiyya* (mercy), prophets are also the manifesters of those names. These attributes of empathy, kindness and mercy are characteristics that Muslim chaplains must also adopt in their care-giving role.

Adam as Archetype for Human Beings

As theology in its broadest sense is very much tied to understanding one's identity and purpose in life, and is what distinguishes one from other creatures, it will be useful to look at the story of Adam, the archetype for all human beings. The significance of Adam's being given the knowledge of all God's names will be examined in connection to Muslim theology or 'God-talk'. More about this will be said shortly.

As discussed earlier, everything we experience in creation and everything that happens to us in our day-to-living over our whole lives is a 'sign', a direct communication from the Creator to be acknowledged and responded to. This acknowledgement signifies acceptance of God's Oneness and the reality of human servanthood. This ability to 'read', identify and reflect all of Divine attributes was given to Adam, the first human male, the first of Islam's prophets and the archetype for human beings. The Quran talks about God 'teaching Adam all of the names', and it is Adam's knowledge of the names which, according to 'Allama Tabātabā'ī (1904-1981),[55] distinguishes him from all other created beings. It is this knowledge of the names which, together with other qualities, qualifies him as Divine *khalīfa* or vicegerent. Other creatures also have knowledge or apperception of some of the names – angels, for example, know only those Divine names connected with their specific duties – but human beings are unique in the sense that they are able to recognise and understand all of God's names without exception.[56]

> *Behold, thy Lord said to the angels: "I will create a vicegerent [khalifah] on earth [ard]." They said: "Wilt Thou place therein one who will make mischief therein and shed blood? – whilst we do celebrate Thy praises and glorify Thy holy (name)?" He said: "I know what ye know not."*[57]

> *And He taught ['allama] Adam the names [al-asmā] – all of them. Then He showed them to the angels and said, "Inform Me of the names of these, if you are truthful."*[58]

> *They said: Be glorified! We have no knowledge saving that which Thou hast taught us. Lo! Thou, only Thou, art the Knower, the Wise.*[59]

All humans, therefore, as creatures created in God's image, have been taught all of the names and attributes, and thus have the potential to reflect them consciously. Al-Qushayrī (d.465/1072)[60] says that the fact the jinn and angels are informed about the vicegerency of Adam, and asked to show deference by prostrating, shows that all other creatures are created to be subservient to humankind and their needs.[61]

The Quran tells us that while Adam was in a temporary state of forgetfulness, he was tempted by Iblīs to taste the fruit of a tree – the tree of eternal life – that God had forbidden to him. Seduced by Iblis, Adam ate of the fruit and consequently fell from paradise. Although Iblis was also cast down to earth, the difference in his case was that he found himself banished from paradise forever, with no possibility of return. This eternal damnation was the result of his refusal to bow down to Adam as God had commanded. His stubbornness was born out of overreliance on his own limited powers of reasoning. Adam, on the other hand, became aware of his momentary lapse, later repenting and asking forgiveness. As a result, he was given the potential to reach the highest state possible for a created being, higher even than that of the angels.⁶² This juncture marks the point at which free will was given to human beings, which means that human beings were now able either to accept the truth or to refuse to acknowledge it. As Muhammad Iqbal (1877-1938) states, "Man's first act of disobedience was also his first act of free choice".⁶³

What we learn about the human character from the story of Adam is that forgetfulness is a human weakness. The verbal root of the word human (*insān*) is *n-s-y* and is linked to a range of words meaning 'to forget'. This was a title given to Adam due to his momentarily lapse and the fact that he neglected to obey God's command.⁶⁴ We also learn that humans have the potential to reach the very highest level in creation (*aḥsan-i taqwīm*) by accepting their servanthood (*ubūdiyya*).⁶⁵ We should not forget, however, that they also have the potential to fall to lowest level (*asfal al-sāfilīn*)⁶⁶ if they persist in exhibiting the personality traits of Iblīs, who was arrogant and who used his own limited reasoning to justify going against his innate disposition towards obedience and servanthood. The fall of Adam also shows that Iblīs's seduction of Adam would not be a one-off, as he was given permission to be the means for the continuous testing of all of humankind:

> [Satan] said, "Because You have put me in error, I will surely sit in wait for them on Your straight path.⁶⁷

Another human weakness is our tendency not to use our own faculties of discernment, but, through haste, to follow others blindly, in just the same way that Adam followed Iblis, even though he later repented for his mistake.⁶⁸ One of the most comforting lessons in the story of Adam is the extent of God's compassion towards his creatures. For just as He forgave Adam his lapse, God has promised to forgive all individuals for their wrongdoings so long as they offer sincere repentance (*tawba*).⁶⁹

The concept of *tawba* (repentance), which is literally 'a return', is linked to the primordial covenant and the confirmation of humankind's open acknowledgment of both God's Lordship and their own servanthood. Hence in this world, all human beings have the potential to see beyond form by realizing that everything is a 'sign' which needs to be read, understood and internalized. However, we also have a tendency to be easily distracted, and thus we run the risk of focusing on the signposts rather than on the truths and realities to which the signposts are pointing.

Chaplaincy is about offering hope and reminding individuals that the light of guidance is ubiquitous and thus never turned off at source; it also about reassuring people that it is normal to sometimes loose the path and wander aimlessly in the shadows. This realization has the potential to dispel the despair that individuals may be experiencing, allowing chaplains to better assist their attempts to come out of the darkness and back into the light. Furthermore, chaplains are thus able to reassure people who, on account of profound feelings of guilt concerning the past, cannot move forward, that God will totally wipe their slate clean if they are able to offer sincere repentance and make every attempt not go back to their former state.[70] And therefore mistakes and difficult situations are not necessarily bad if they offer one the opportunity to turn to one's Lord in repentance and ask for forgiveness. In fact, it was Adam's fall, together with his conscious acceptance of God's Lordship and his own servanthood, that resulted in the opportunity for him to attain a position in creation that was even higher than his original, angelic state.

The main thing that distinguishes Adam from all other creatures is his comprehensive knowledge of the Divine names. This means that despite differences in human beings, all individuals have the potential to understand the 'signs'. In other words, as Ghazālī says, hiding behind every created form is a message waiting to be read, and "those whose eyes never see beyond the world of phenomena are like those who mistake servants of the lowest rank for the king."[71] Therefore we need to look beyond the externality of phenomena in search for meaning and purpose. The prophet Abraham's cosmological journey, which will be discussed next, shows how he read 'signs' in creation, and serves as a blueprint for all such pursuits of meaning.

The Cosmological Journey of Abraham

The Quran describes Abraham as a: model or example *(uswa)*; as someone devoutly obedient to God *(ḥanīf)*; and as one who does not ascribe partners to God:

> Abraham was indeed a model [uswa], devoutly obedient to Allah [ḥanīf], (and) true in Faith, and he joined not gods with Allah.[72]

The word *ḥanīf* comes from the verbal route *ḥ-n-f*, the derivates of which connote uprightness. According to Ṭabātabā'ī, it means inclination away from excess and deficiency towards the middle *(wasaṭ)* and within the right balance.[73] We know from the Quran that Abraham was already a believer in one God, but that he wished to increase his knowledge to the level of certainty.[74] Al-Qushayrī explains that knowledge has different levels and stations, and that 'knowledge of certainty' (*'ilm al-yaqīn*) is conditional on demonstrative proof *(burhān)* and belongs to the masters of intellects *(arbāb al-'uqūl)*, while the 'eye of certainty' (*'ayn al-yaqīn*) depends on clear evidence (*bayān*) and belongs to the masters of different types of knowledge (*aṣḥāb al-'ulūm*). The highest level of certainty, he says, is the 'truth of certainty' (*ḥaqq al-yaqīn*), which is communicated through direct witnessing (*'iyān*) and belongs to the masters of deeper knowledge (*aṣḥāb al-ma'ārif*)".[75] Abraham therefore wished to reach the highest level of certainty, while his metaphysical journey as a whole serves as a model for others who seek answers to their existential questions. In a sense the word *uswa* invites those searching for permanence and meaning to embark on a similar quest:

> *(Remember) when Abraham said unto his father Azar: Takest thou idols for gods? Lo! I see thee and thy folk in error manifest. Thus, did We show Abraham the kingdom of the heavens and the earth that he might be of those possessing certainty: When the night grew dark upon him he beheld a star. He said: This is my Lord. But when it set, he said: I love not things that set. And when he saw the moon uprising, he exclaimed: This is my Lord. But when it set, he said: Unless my Lord guide me, I surely shall become one of the folk who are astray. And when he saw the sun uprising, he cried: This is my Lord! This is greater! And when it set he exclaimed: O my people! Lo! I am free from all that ye associate (with Him).*[76]

The fact that there are different stations of knowledge signifies that the journey towards monotheism is a life-long commitment.[77] Also, Abraham's journey serves as a model for the process of unveiling by reading the signs (*āyāt*) in creation:

> *Indeed, in the creation of the heavens and earth, and the alternation of the night and the day, and the [great] ships which sail through the sea with that which benefits people, and what Allah has sent down from the heavens of rain, giving life thereby to the earth after its lifelessness and dispersing therein every [kind of] moving creature, and [His] directing of the winds and the clouds controlled between the heaven and the earth are signs for a people who use reason.*[78]

Thus the type of knowledge Abraham uncovered entailed his going beyond the exoteric (*ẓāhir*) aspect of phenomenon in the search for the inner (*bāṭin*) truths and realities of things. Al-Attas (b. 1931) describes this type of knowledge as the "the arrival of meaning in the soul".[79] In order to acquire this type of knowledge, all that is required is sincerity, the use of the *'aql* (intellect) as well as the *qalb* (the heart).[80] Ghazālī identifies the heart as being the highest level of the intellect and also serving as the means for self-knowledge and knowledge of God:

> *Whosoever does not know his [own heart], so that he might oversee it and guide it, and [yet] observes [the stars] from among the storehouses of the malakūt that gleam upon him and within him, is one of those about whom God – be He exalted – said, 'they forget God, and so he causes them to forget themselves. Those are the iniquitous ones (al-fāsiqūn)'.*[81]

Abraham is also described in the Quran as a *ḥanīf* (friend of Allah) because of his two important qualities, namely his total submission to God and his being a 'doer of good' (*muḥsin*). According to a hadith, *iḥsān* "is to worship Allah as if you see Him".[82] Therefore the state of the *muḥsin* is the state of one who has attained the level of God-consciousness at all times and in all circumstances, and is able to appreciate the Divine mercy manifested in the universe as a whole, as well as in particulars. This means accepting and submitting to the fact that chance and accident have no part to play in creation; that it is through God's universal lordliness (*kullī rubūbiyya*) that all created beings are nurtured; and that it is through His particularised lordliness (*juz'ī rubūīya*), that God's mercy and compassion come to the aid of individuals in a particular fashion, in accordance with their individual capacity, context and needs.[83]

Chaplains can also follow the Abrahamic model of shepherding and 'reading the signs.' This method can be used to encourage individuals to examine every event in their lives in order to be able to make sense of the meaning of the 'signs' being conveyed. The fact that knowledge of Divine attributes such as beauty (*jamāl*), justice (*'adl*), compassion (*raḥmāniyya*) and mercy (*raḥīmiyya*) has been imparted to all human beings without exception means that this method can be applied within a diverse and pluralistic context.

Joseph

According to the Quran, in order to not be 'at a loss', one must possess faith; one must perform deeds of righteousness; and one must counsel truth and patience to others:

> *By (the token of) time (through the Ages), Verily Man is in loss, Except such as have faith, and do righteous deeds, and (join together) in the Mutual teaching of Truth, and of patience and constancy.*[84]

The word *khusr* is from the triliteral root *kh-s-r* which means 'to wander from the straight path'. The story of Joseph shows what happens to those who wander away from the path of truth. It is also about separation, loss, temptation, patience, passion, compassion and much more. It demonstrates also that prophets were tested to the utmost so that they could manifest their state of servanthood (*ubūdiyya*) at the highest level.[85]

Joseph's experience of loss began at a very young age. He lost his mother, he lost the caring love of his father and his aunt, and finally he lost his freedom. He was separated from his loved ones when, out of jealousy, his brothers threw him into a well. There, alone in the darkness, he cried out to his brothers to help but they did not respond. He then cried to his Lord to help him; eventually, his prayer was answered when travellers passing the well suspended a bucket into the well to draw water, unaware that the well had had dried out. To their surprise, however, the well yielded a handsome young boy whom they decided to sell as a slave. Attracted by his pleasing features and outward manner, the chief minister (*'azīz*) of Egypt purchased him from the slave market and took him to his great mansion. Joseph's kind, just and caring personality had a great impact on the people who worked for the Aziz, while the Aziz himself, impressed by Joseph's good character, made him the personal attendant of his wife, Zulaykha.[86] However, the promise of a safe refuge[87] was broken by Zuleikha, who over the years had become attached to him and attempted to seduce him. Jāmī (1414-1492), the fifteenth century Persian poet,[88] describes Zulaykha's scheme for seducing Joseph and how she entraps him by enticing him through seven doors, locking each door after them. Realizing the danger, Joseph puts his trust in God and as he makes a run for it, the locked doors are flung open for him miraculously, enabling him to escape Zulaykha's trap. These stories allude to the belief that for someone who trusts in God, there will always be a rope, an open door or some other such means of deliverance whereby one is able to escape the depths of darkness. They also show that there is absolutely no need for despair.

Despite the fact that Joseph's shirt was ripped from the back was proof of his innocence, to preserve the reputation of the palace, the Aziz pinned the blame on Joseph and had him imprisoned. However, incarceration proved to be a blessing for Joseph as he felt it provided more safety for him than the comfortable mansion where he once resided.[89] Joseph spent many years in the Pharaoh's dungeons, but his stay there served a purpose. For just as he was a perfect role model *(uswa)* while living in the household of the Aziz's, his compassion and honesty also influenced his new community of prison inmates, whom he invited to Divine unity and helped to find their way towards the straight path.[90]

Joseph regarded both his times of difficulty and his times of wealth and abundance as tests from God, as well as signs that needed to be to read and responded to accordingly. The state of servanthood that he attained in all circumstances enabled him to remain on the straight path, and he encouraged others to follow his example. It was essentially those internal qualities of manifesting Divine mercy and compassion that attracted people to him wherever he went, allowing him to gain the trust even of the most ardent criminals. Chaplains can use the story of Joseph to reassure their clients that there is always an open door for those who genuinely seek guidance from God.

Jonah (Yunus)

Following the same path as previous prophets, Jonah's mission was to shepherd the people of Nineveh towards the right path. On one occasion when he was carrying out his duty as 'the bearer of good news' (*mubashshir*) and 'warner' *mundhir*, to the people of that town, they turned away and refused to listen to him. Feeling frustrated that he had not accomplished his task of convincing people, he stormed off and boarded a ship, hoping that he might escape from what he perceived as his failure.

Now all of the prophets were tested with the greatest trials and Jonah was no exception. He was tested by walking into a much bigger storm than the one he felt in his heart. Facing an incredibly turbulent sea, the crew of the ship had to make the difficult decision of lightening their load. This had to be done not only by getting rid of cargo but also sacrificing at least one member of the crew. So they drew lots and it was Jonah's fate to draw the short straw; accordingly he was thrown overboard and was later swallowed by a huge fish. It was in the dark and lonely stomach of the whale that Jonah beseeches the Creator, the Causer of all causes, with the following supplication:

> *There is no deity except You; exalted are You. Indeed, I have been of the wrongdoers.*[91]

God answered Jonah's prayer for salvation and duly the fish opened its mouth and spat Jonah out onto the shore. His liberation from a very dark and forbidding place was the outcome of his taking refuge in his Creator. Thus it is only through the light of Divine unity and oneness that people can find relief from the dark times in their lives. As Said Nursi (1876-1960)[92] explains, it is the reliance on material causes to transform our lives and our expectations – rather than on the Causer of all causes – that results in much pain and despair:

> *The night, the sea, and the whale were united against him. Only one whose command might subdue all three of these could bring him forth on the strand of salvation. Even if the entirety of creation had become his servants and helpers, it would have been*

of no avail. For causes have no effect. Since Jonah saw with the eye of certainty that there was no refuge other than the Causer of Causes, and unfolded to him was the meaning of Divine Oneness within the light of Divine Unity, his supplication was able suddenly to subdue the night, the sea, and the whale. Through the light of Divine Unity he was able to transform the belly of the whale into a submarine; and the surging sea, which in its awesomeness resembled an erupting volcano, into a peaceable plain, a pleasant place of excursion. Through the light of Unity, he was able to sweep the sky's countenance clear of all clouds, and to set the moon over his head like a lantern. Creation that had been pressing and threatening him from all sides now showed him a friendly face from every direction. Thus, he reached the shore of salvation, where beneath the creeping-gourd tree he observed this favour of his Sustainer.[93]

In fact, as Nursi says, we are all in danger of being swallowed by a whale – the whale symbolising for Nursi the caprices of the soul. Without belief in the hereafter, the future appears dark, and the spinning of the globe seems much more frightening than the stormy sea into which Jonah was thrown. Since we are all in the same dependent and apparently precarious state as Jonah, we too need to take refuge directly in the 'Causer of causes':

To understand with full certainty that it is only He who can repel from us the harm of the future, this world, and caprice of our souls, united against us because of our neglect and misguidance. For the future is subject to His command, the world to His jurisdiction, and our soul to His direction.
What cause is there other than the Creator of the Heavens and Earth who can know the most subtle and secret thoughts of our heart; who can lighten the future for us by establishing the Hereafter; who can save us from the myriad overwhelming waves of the world? No, outside that Necessarily Existent One, there is nothing that can in any way give aid and effect salvation except by His consent and command.[94]

Thus, the story of Jonah implies that Muslim pastoral care becomes redundant if it is not rooted in Divine Unity. Trusting in one's Maker takes away the burden of guilt and responsibility, as the focus is on doing the right thing with sincerity and wise precaution, irrespective of the outcome. This story also serves as a reminder to chaplains themselves that they are first and foremost servants of God and thus answerable in the first instance to their Creator. With this in mind, chaplains would hopefully see their caring role not just as something that benefits their institution or, worse still, their own egos. Nor would it be seen as just a job, a means of financial gain. To counsel others for the sake of God rather than for the sake of the self or material advancement would, one trusts, be the most conducive means of achieving the best possible outcome.

The Story of Ayyūb (Job)

Ayyūb was a descendant of the Prophet Abraham. He was blessed with wealth and a large family and a community who respected him as a leader. Ayyūb's possessions were to become the very object of the Divine trial visited upon him to test his patience and to try his acceptance of God's Divine Determining. Gradually, Ayyūb's wealth and possessions were taken away from him and he was no longer able to enjoy the company of his large and loving family. Ayyūb bore these losses patiently at the outset, accepting that he was being tested by his Creator. However, not long after, his health began to deteriorate, to the extent that he feared that it would be difficult for him to continue with his duties of worship. It was for this reason alone that he offered the following supplication, after which the merciful Lord restored him to full health and gave all his possessions back to him:

Verily harm has afflicted me, and You are the Most Merciful of the Merciful.[95]

What gave Ayyūb the strength to accept the loss of his possessions and bear patiently the loss of his family was the fact that he understood and accepted that he did not own what had been given to him, and that the Owner of those gifts could take them back whenever He wished. He understood too that misfortunes are also a sign from God, and must be read and acted upon accordingly. And so he regarded his sickness as an act of mercy from God, for it offered him the opportunity to turn to God in a total state of need. Nursi is of the opinion that everyone is in danger of contracting spiritual sickness, which is far more grievous than Ayyūb's physical illnesses and material losses. It is for this reason that Ayyūb's supplication is also a cure and a means of attracting mercy, for it affords one the opportunity to recognise both one's innate disposition as a servant of God and, as a consequence of this, the need to be a conscious manifester of God's attributes, rather than someone who usurps those attributes for himself and ends up believing that he truly owns them.[96]

The Story of Solomon

According to the Quran, Solomon (*Suleymān*) was not only a prophet but also a very wealthy and powerful king. He succeeded his father David (*Dāwūd*), also a prophet and king. God favoured both David and Solomon with special knowledge whereby they were able to communicate with other creatures as well as humans.⁹⁷ Solomon was a wise ruler who reigned over a large kingdom stretching from Palestine to Yemen.

Solomon's vast army included a bird – a hoopoe – that was charged with delivering messages. It was this bird that brought Solomon the news about a great and powerful queen, Bilqīs, the ruler of Sheba, and the fact that she and her people were not monotheists but sun worshippers.⁹⁸ On hearing this news, Solomon requested that the hoopoe deliver a letter to the Queen. On perusing the letter, which she subsequently read out to her advisers, she was surprised that it was written not in Solomon's name as king but rather "In the name of Allah, Most Compassionate, Most Merciful."⁹⁹ It appears that right at the outset, Solomon was making his position crystal clear to the Queen. Given the size of his kingdom and bearing in mind the gifts of knowledge and wisdom he had been given, including the ability to converse with jinn and insects that were also obedient to his command, it seemed very strange to the Queen of Sheba that Solomon should admit in his letter that he had submitted to One more powerful than any sovereign.

So surprised was she by the contents of Solomon's letter that Bilqīs sought the opinions of her advisor on the best course of action. Although her advisors showed readiness to engage Solomon in battle if their Queen commanded them to do so, she chose to avoid unnecessary violence and destruction and adopted a more diplomatic strategy instead. She decided, as a token of friendship, to send a valuable gift to Solomon. Her intention was to see how he would react, as well as to understand more about his possible military capabilities. However, Solomon did not accept the gift, implying that he was not interested in material wealth for its own sake.

On hearing this news, Bilqīs decided to visit Solomon in person. But before her arrival, Solomon asked those in his vast and subservient army which of them would be able to transport the Queen's grand throne to his palace the quickest. One of his subjects, an *ifrit* from among the jinn, says that he will bring the throne to Solomon before the king is able to rise from his seat, but Solomon rejects the offer. Instead he accepts the offer of another jinn who promises to bring the throne in the space of 'the twinkling of an eye'. Of course, Solomon attributes this power not to the jinn concerned, or to his own command, but to God, and thus offers thanks:

> Said one who had knowledge of the Book: "I will bring it to thee within the twinkling of an eye!" Then when (Solomon) saw it placed firmly before him, he said: "This is by the Grace of my Lord! – to test me whether I am grateful or ungrateful! and if any is grateful, truly his gratitude is (a gain) for his own soul; but if any is ungrateful, truly my Lord is Free of all Needs, Supreme in Honour!"¹⁰⁰

Solomon then asks his army to disguise the queen's throne slightly and to build a palace, specifically with the instructions that the floors must be made of glass. On arrival at Solomon's palace, Bilqīs notices the disguised throne and, seeing her reaction, Solomon asks her if it bears any resemblance to her own, to which she cautiously replies: *"It is as though it was the very same."*[101] Witnessing the miraculous appearance of her throne in Solomon's court, she realises that the power he has been given goes beyond human capability. Conscious of the fact that Bilqīs is an extremely intelligent woman, Solomon continues to show her further signs in order to convince her of the transient nature of this world, and the limited power of even the greatest sovereigns. To this end he invites her to his palace and, thinking that the glass floor is actually water, she lifts up her skirt. This final test leads her to realise that even a powerful monarch like herself is not incapable of misjudgment. Consequently, she concludes that there must be a greater Being whose power and knowledge is not limited, and to Whom the great king Solomon has submitted in total humility.

> *She was told, "Enter the palace." But when she saw it, she thought it was a body of water and uncovered her shins [to wade through]. He said, "Indeed, it is a palace [whose floor is] made smooth with glass." She said, "My Lord, indeed I have wronged myself, and I submit with Solomon to Allah, Lord of the worlds."*[102]

Thus, this story begins with the name of God, and is followed by a sequence of events which clearly indicate the limited and transient nature of created beings and the necessity for a transcendent Being. All these signs become as clear as the glass floor Queen of Sheba stepped on, and thus the story culminates with her submission to the only Sovereign who is not limited and transient.

This story is extremely useful for chaplains as it teaches how 'shepherding' should be carried out. At no stage did Solomon try to force his own beliefs on Bilqīs; rather, his approach was to subtly encourage the queen to read the signs in creation herself and come to her own conclusions.

The Story of Moses

Moses was born at the time when the Israelites were being persecuted by the Pharoah. Having dreamt that a man would arise from among the children of Israel who would disempower him, Pharoah ordered that every new-born boy among the children of Israel be killed:

> *Lo! Pharaoh exalted himself in the earth and made its people castes. A tribe among them he oppressed, killing their sons and sparing their women. Lo! he was of those who work corruption.*[103]

Moses's mother understandably became very anxious about the fate of her son, knowing that soldiers would soon be knocking at her door to take him away and have him slaughtered. However, she did not allow herself to wallow in despair; rather, she put her full trust in God's decree. It was then that God inspired her to take a most unusual action. Not only did God promise to keep her baby boy safe and return him back to her, but He also told her that her son, as messenger of God, would eventually lead the oppressed Israelites to the right path:

> *And We inspired the mother of Moses, saying: Suckle him and, when thou fearest for him, then cast him into the river and fear not nor grieve. Lo! We shall bring him back unto thee and shall make him (one) of Our messengers.*[104]

In Islam, water is a symbol of Divine mercy, as it is a source of life.[105] And the water that we see in the form of rain, rivers, waterfalls, and seas symbolises God's compassion and power.[106] Water also indicates purity, exemplified through the various rituals of ablution before obligatory prayers, as well as being a symbol of glad tidings.[107]

And so Moses, future messenger of God, is cradled gently to the other side of the river where he is spotted by Pharoah's wife, who reasons with her husband that the child would be of material benefit to him in the future, thus convincing him to adopt Moses as their son.[108] God also keeps His promise to Moses's mother that He would bring Moses back to her by ordering the course of events in such a way as to ensure that she became his wetnurse.[109] Thus her trust in God rather than causes or limited, transient beings – even one so apparently powerful as the Pharoah – brought its rewards.

Moses grew up in Pharoah's grand palace and became acquainted with the ruler's distorted views and claim to divinity. It is ironic that, despite having had all of the male infants in the land killed to ensure his own safety, the Pharoah should eventually be brought low by his own adopted son, who had been brought up in his own household. And so Pharoah's plans and his claims to power totally collapsed, for it is ultimately God's plans which unfold in accordance with His will:

> *And when those who disbelieved devised plans against you that they might confine you or slay you or drive you away; and they devised plans and Allah too had arranged a plan; and Allah is the best of planners.*[110]

As an adult, Moses once intervened in a fight between an Egyptian and an Israelite. Unaware of his own strength, he inadvertently killed the Egyptian. Guilt consumed him and he asked God for forgiveness. Realising that he could no longer stay in Egypt, where he would be arrested by the authorities, he fled to Midian.[111] After walking a great distance in the desert, hungry and thirsty, despite his physical strength, Moses felt his impotence and admitted his weakness to his Creator. Eventually he reached a well, which, as mentioned, is a symbol of God's mercy. There he helped two girls to carry water to the home that they shared with their elderly father. Eventually, Midian became a refuge for Moses after he married one of the daughters, but Moses also became the means whereby his ageing father-in-law was able to be helped with his household duties.

After some time, Moses and his family returned to Egypt, and it was on this return journey, near Mount Sinai, that he received his first revelation.[112] Assisted by his brother Aaron (Hārūn), his task as messenger, like the task of all messengers before him, was to guide the people to read the signs in creation correctly. That is, to see everything in creation as a mirror, manifesting God's names in diverse ways and varying degrees. In order to demonstrate to the people that material causes have no real power and are merely the way in which He creates, God manifests His power by way of certain clear signs.[113] However, the signs that God revealed in the form of miracles wrought by Moses failed to convince the Pharoah, who accused Moses of practicing sorcery. In response, the Pharaoh began to wage war against Moses and his followers, who had no option but flee eastwards. When they reached the Red Sea, with no apparent way of crossing in order to escape Pharoah and his army, the waters separated miraculously, enabling them to cross safely. When the Pharoah and his men tried to cross in pursuit, however, the waves returned and consequently they perished:

> *Then We told Moses by inspiration: "Strike the sea with thy rod." So it divided, and each separate part became like the huge, firm mass of a mountain.*
> *And We made the other party approach thither.*
> *We delivered Moses and all who were with him; But We drowned the others. Verily in this is a Sign: but most of them do not believe. And verily thy Lord is He, the Exalted in Might, Most Merciful.*[114]

Chaplains can use the story of Moses to explain that causes have no independent effect and that everything is ultimately under God's control. The story shows that despite Pharoah's immense power and his efforts to rearrange causes in such a way that he would remain unharmed, he was ultimately unable to change his fate. This demonstrates that all that is expected of people is that they have the right intention and that they endeavour not to stray from the right path.

Also in this world, which is a place of trial and tribulation, people are often faced with difficult decisions. The case of Moses's mother shows that despite the pains of parting from her new-born baby, she trusted God's promise and took the right course of action. Similarly, Moses's unintentional act of murder, which, despite his repentance, filled him with guilt and left him no alternative but to run away from his hometown, is another case in point. It shows that despite the difficult journey across the desert, and his feelings of loneliness as a refugee, the outcome of this series of events was in fact a decidedly positive one. For he became the means whereby an elderly man and his family were able to benefit from his assistance, while he himself was rewarded with a family of his own. It becomes clear from this Quranic narrative that human beings often encounter situations which are unpleasant or even painful, but which often turn out to be advantageous, either overtly or in ways that we may not always comprehend. Similarly, there are situations which we may embrace willingly, thinking they are beneficial, but which eventually turn out not to be. As it is stated in the Quran:

> *It is possible that ye dislike a thing which is good for you, and that ye love a thing which is bad for you. But Allah knoweth, and ye know not.*[115]

The task of chaplains as shepherds of transcendence is to help people navigate their way through life in the best possible way, particularly when unfamiliar events present themselves. Thus, chaplains are tasked with supporting and encouraging individuals to trust God's decree and to move forward by reading the Divine signs in accordance with the right criteria.

It is now to Prophet Mohammad that we turn, the Prophet who, it is believed, manifested God's names most comprehensively, and at the very highest possible level.

Mohammad – Seal of the Prophets

God communicates to His servants through His creation, including His prophets, who serve as interpreters of the language of creation. The most perfect of all created beings, and the one who manifested God's names at the highest level, is believed by Muslims to be Mohammad.

In his pre-Prophetic period, Mohammad was accustomed to taking time out of his busy life by staying in caves and other isolated places, where he could devote his full attention to prayer and supplication to his Creator.[116] It was on one of these occasions in Mount Hira that God commanded Mohammad to "Read!". As Mohammad is believed to be 'unlettered', he asked "How should I read?" He was then instructed to "Read, read in the name of your Lord!"[117] It becomes evident that reading is not meant in a literal way here; rather, he was being commanded to read the 'book of creation' and interpret everything, as his predecessors did, in the name of his Lord (*rabb*). This type of reading does not necessarily require functional literacy, as everyone has the innate ability to read and understand the Divine words that comprise the created universe.

What is of significance here is that this 'reading' should be done in the name of the Lord of creation, Who is the Sustainer and Nurturer of all created beings.[118] The ability to read in this way was something that was taught to Adam and consequently to all human beings.[119] Mohammad therefore was already 'literate' in this sense, but was not aware of it until the command jolted his memory. This marked the beginning of Mohamad's 'literacy' or 'true ability to read and interpret' as well as signaling the point at which he himself, as 'seal of the prophets', was confirmed as the best example or 'conscious manifester' (*muẓhir*) of all of God's names.

As a young boy, Mohammad had an innate disposition for kindness and generosity, but as an adult, and an appointed prophet, he became aware that it was going to be his duty to teach others 'literacy' by doing everything in a God-centred way. Thus he would become an exemplar (*uswa*) for others to emulate as the interpreter or instructor on how to 'read' both the creational signs (*āyāt kawnī*) of God and the spoken/written signs (*āyāt ghawlī*), with the aim of enlightening the world:

> Our Lord! send amongst them a Messenger of their own, who shall rehearse Thy Signs to them and instruct them in scripture and wisdom, and sanctify them: For Thou art the Exalted in Might, the Wise.[120]

Making one's life God-centred in every possible way was not easy, even for Mohammad; he was human, after all, and at times had to be reminded of unintentional lapses.[121]

At other times Mohammad, because of his extreme compassion, felt saddened by the rejection of his message by the Meccan aristocrats, by their continued wrong-doings and the oppression and imbalance they caused in Meccan society.[122] Mohammad is referred to as the beloved of Allah (*ḥabībullah*) because of his empathetic compassion for his fellow human beings. He is described in the Quran as being of "great moral character" and as one who is to be emulated.[123] This reminder that one should have an approach which is compassionate without becoming too emotionally involved is one that chaplains can also take on board, not only as a means of ensuring professionalism in their role, but as a way of safeguarding their own personal well-being.

Thus, while the Quran asserts that people are responsible for their own choices, it also warns us that if we wish not to go astray, Mohammad is the best model to follow, for he has the best moral character as well as being the most excellent manifestation of God's mercy.[124]

> Ye have indeed in the Messenger of Allah a beautiful pattern (of conduct) for any one whose hope is in Allah and the Final Day, and who engages much in the Praise of Allah.[125]

Another characteristic of Mohammad for Muslim chaplains to emulate in their pastoral care is his trustworthiness; one of his most well-known epithets, recognised even by his detractors, is 'the trustworthy one' (*al-amīn*). He was also famously tolerant and non-judgmental, as evidenced by the forbearance he showed in the face of those who mocked him and his religion, accusing him of madness.[126] Mohammad was trusted even by those who were openly hostile to him, for he did not allow his own feelings to interfere in situations where just and sound judgments needed to be made.[127] Mohammad therefore possessed all of the suitable qualities of a caregiver, for he manifested Divine names such as *al-Mu'min* (the One who grants security), *al-Raḥīm* (the Merciful), *al-Raḥmān* (the Compassionate), *al-Ḥakīm* (the Wise) and so on at the very highest level.

7

How Can Muslim Theology be Practiced in Pluralistic Settings?

Owing to the increase in international students, universities are keen to meet the faith needs of students with diverse religious needs. One in five universities now has a multifaith centre that reflects the diversity of the student population. However, it is mainly the Christian chaplains and coordinators who tend to lead in these so-called multi-faith settings. While they are keen to be inclusive and encourage interfaith work and dialogue, they are not commissioned by their particular faith body to fulfil the role of a 'multi-faith' chaplain. Thus, the tendency is to recruit volunteers from other faiths – generally from the community – to fulfil this role.[128] Similarly many NHS Trusts have chosen to change the name of their chaplaincy departments to 'Spiritual and Pastoral Care' centres. Some of these institutions have also replaced the title of chaplain with 'spiritual care giver' or 'multi-faith coordinator'.[129]

While the title of 'chaplain' may be problematic, the role of the Muslim chaplain cannot be limited simply to that of 'spiritual care giver', for chaplains are expected to apply a holistic approach to spiritual care, which means that practical, social and educational needs are all provided under the umbrella of their spiritual care giving role. For example, although the main job of Muslim chaplains in the educational settings is pastoral care and spiritual support, many chaplains are also heavily involved in convening religious discussion groups, Quran circles, and interfaith activities such as scriptural reasoning and panel discussions, as well as acting as advisors to their university on issues to do with the faith needs of Muslims, both staff and students alike.[130]

As discussed earlier, one of the roles of the Muslim chaplain is to emulate the prophets through example, explanation and instruction, and by operating generally in the post-prophetic capacity of 'warner' and 'giver of glad tidings'. This means that they are there to support people on their journey with wisdom and compassion and in a non-judgmental way, and without any ulterior motive or expectations. These requirements reflect openly the importance of the Prophet Mohammad's wisdom, an attribute given to all the prophets, but which Mohammad manifested at the very highest level. For just as the Divine oath, 'sworn by the pen', was to be the primary means by which God's names were to be manifested in the book of creation,[131] Mohammad was chosen to be the primary means through which God's names, including those which connote wisdom, such as *al-Ḥakīm*) were to be read and consciously manifested.[132] The concept of *ḥikma* (wisdom) is thus foundational to the approach of the Muslim chaplain. Muslim 'shepherding' or 'pastoral care' is not about proselytising or pressuring people to change.[133] Rather, it is about supporting individuals in a non-judgmental way to find the right path themselves, in accordance with their contexts. It is also about supporting people to the best of one's ability, without worrying too much about the outcome.

As Khosrokhavar has pointed out, there is a tendency for many Muslim chaplains to limit their support to service-users to the externals of the faith alone,[134] despite the fact that humans, as theomorphic beings, partake in all of the Divine attributes, with interests, issues, concerns and problems that are not limited to the exoteric expression of faith. Nor should a Muslim chaplain limit his or her caregiving to self-professed Muslims alone. God communicates with His subjects continuously, and in a language that can be comprehended by all. Therefore, the concept of secular and profane does not exist in Islam, as all beings and events are 'Divine words' communicated from the unseen realm to the world of multiplicity to be read in the correct way. By applying a chaplaincy approach which integrates God's names and attributes in their practice, chaplains can operate effectively in the diverse and pluralistic contexts of their institutions. Examples of case studies of some of the issues Muslim chaplains deal with will be given in Chapter Five to demonstrate how this approach can be applied.

8

What Do Muslim Chaplains Do?

The broad definition of chaplain provided by Ben Ryan as "an individual who provides religious and spiritual care within an organisational setting"[135] implies a distinction between the 'religious' and the 'spiritual', whereas, as discussed, in Islam the concept of the religious must be embedded in the spiritual. It is made clear in the Quran that all created acts occur under God's command and thus every single being in the universe is a divine missive, waiting to be read.[136] Therefore nothing or no-one in the world can be dismissed as pointless or meaningless. Considering that everything and everyone is a message to be read and acted upon in a non-biased and non-judgmental way, and in accordance with the right criteria, there is therefore no clear distinction between the 'religious' and the 'spiritual', whatever people may mean by these terms. Moreover, since all individuals are works of art fashioned by the Creator of the universe, manifesting whether they realise it or not the beautiful names of God, Muslim chaplains are thus in a perfect position to be accessible to all, regardless of faith, beliefs or culture.

There are so many matters that Muslim chaplains attend to that it would be impossible to capture everything. For both students and staff, coming from another town or country to work or study at a new university can be quite overwhelming, as they need to adjust to a new way of life in new surroundings. Chaplains play a vital role in helping such individuals build their own community in accordance with their needs and preferences. By offering moral, spiritual and academic support, they contribute greatly to the well-being of both students and staff.

The unique character of institutions and the diverse needs of every individual that seeks support make it impossible to capture the extent of the multitudinous concerns with which Muslim chaplains engage. Therefore, general headings will be used for some of these issues and in Chapter Eleven, examples of case studies will be given, hopefully to inspire chaplains and help them to support their service-users when similar matters arise. This does not mean that a standard approach must be used for everyone, since every individual and his or her concerns are unique and must be dealt with in context and in accordance with the dictates of the particular situation. However, an overall criterion which encompasses the essence of human need can be applicable to all individuals.

How Does Chaplaincy Differ from Counselling?

Chaplains have been criticised for carrying out a welfare role without the adequate qualifications to do so.[137] However, chaplaincy differs from counselling, mainly because of who chaplains are and whom they are answerable to. As 'shepherds of transcendence' they are not answerable to their institutions alone; they are answerable primarily to God. Contrary to the general understanding that the title of 'shepherds of transcendence' is not an inclusive term, from a Muslim perspective, the concept of transcendence is not fragmented or compartmentalised, but is inclusive of this world and beyond. In fact, chaplains are sought specifically by some service users precisely because they realise that their commitment to their work goes beyond the limits of loyalty to their job. Also, while the rules and ethics of counselling may change over time in accordance with society's expectations, the essential rules and ethics of Muslim chaplaincy, which are timeless and innate, remain unchanged.

Counselling Role	Muslim Chaplaincy Role
Adherence to counselling principles and rules.	Adherence to the Quranic/ontological perspective; articles of faith; pillars of Islam and the Prophetic tradition
Adherence to university regulations	Adherence to university regulations with adjustments when/if necessary to the faith needs of individuals
Based on a materialism	Answerable to God
Non-spiritual framework, e.g. Freudian	Islamic spiritual framework of the self/*nafs* and human nature/*fitra*
Reflective practice	Self-examination, cultivation & spiritual development
Counsellors	'Shepherds of transcendence'
Structured boundaries	Boundaries more flexible

Therefore, although chaplains respect and acknowledge the importance of counselling and other services, and often work closely with them to support the well-being of their service users in their institution, they are aware that the roles of counsellor and chaplain are not the same. The following table gives examples of a few distinctions that can be made between the two roles.

Reading the 'Signs': A Model for Chaplaincy

As discussed, knowledge of existence cannot be separated from knowledge of God, therefore, there is nothing that takes place that cannot be considered to be a 'sign' or a form of Divine communication, and chaplains can empower service-users to read these 'signs' in accordance with their own particular contexts.

This methodology involves the use of God's names in supporting individuals to examine every event in their lives, thus enabling them to make sense of the meaning of the 'signs' being conveyed.

However, to be able to support service-users in their journey of 'reading the signs', chaplains themselves need to have, as Farhad Khosrokhavar expresses, the right kind of 'mindset',[138] and this very much depends on the right kind of training, on experience and on the extent to which chaplains themselves engage in critical reflection.

9

Theological Reflection

As discussed in previous chapters, to be an effective chaplain, a combination of both theological expertise and pastoral experience is required. Another important skill for chaplains in this context is critical self-awareness. Critical reflexivity is and has always been an integral part of human development, and especially spiritual growth, for it allows individuals to step back and examine each situation in the context in which it arises. However, reflective practice did not officially become part of professional training until the 1930s, when the work of the philosopher John Dewey (1859-1952) in this area was integrated into the field of education. Dewey's work emphasized the importance of interaction between the self and the world, which would consequently bring about change or transformation, not only in oneself but also in the environment.[139] His ideas were replicated and developed further, and in the 1980s Daniel Kolb came up with an 'experiential learning cycle' for reflective practice for professionals working in most fields, especially the disciplines of counselling, medicine and social work, as well as education. It comprised the following phases: experience, reflection, theory and action.[140]

Donald Schőn also emphasized the importance of reflective practice for professional practice, adding his own distinctive terms, namely, reflection-in-action, that is, the thoughts and feelings during the practice; and reflection-on-action, which concerns the thoughts and feelings that occur after the action has been carried out.[141]

Judith Thompson et al. suggest a more precise definition for theological reflection, and one which can be applied by chaplains from different faiths. It encapsulates four main characteristics, namely: the progressive, thus enabling transformation; the particular, as it focuses on specific situations; the prophetic, as it is linked to revelation; and the practical, as it linked to the present. In order to distinguish it from other reflective practices, they call it 'Progressing Theological Reflection' (PTR). They describe this two-way process of theological reflection as essential for pastoral practice:

This activity relates insights and resources from a theological tradition, specifically and carefully, to contemporary situations and vice versa, so that a mutually enlightening reappraisal may result. Pointers are sought to action which leads to a response which is more authentically true to the faith tradition on which it is based.

Theological Reflection: A Muslim Perspective

While the Christian concept of 'divine encounter'[142] is similar to the Muslim theological approach of 'reading the signs', the emphasis in the Muslim perspective is to 'read the signs' in an 'Other-Indicative' rather than 'self-referential' way.[143] This means that 'signs' cannot be interpreted in such a way as to fit in with the post-modernist world-view, since it would appear to make God subservient to human needs and would thus be considered reductive and utilitarian, and thus ultimately 'self-referential'.

It is through guidance that human beings can develop – guidance which can be reached through reading and reflecting upon (*taffakur*) the 'signs in creation' (*āyāt kawnī*) as well as those in revealed scripture (*āyāt qawlī*). The triliteral root *f-k-r*, derivatives of which occur eighteen times in the Quran, means 'to think', 'to reflect', 'to ponder upon'. It occurs nine times with the word 'signs' (*āyāt*):

> *The example of [this] worldly life is but like rain which We have sent down from the sky that the plants of the earth absorb – [those] from which men and livestock eat – until, when the earth has taken on its adornment and is beautified and its people suppose that they have capability over it, there comes to it Our command by night or by day, and We make it as a harvest, as if it had not flourished yesterday! Thus do We explain in detail the signs for a people who give thought.*[144]

An unbiased approach requires self-conscious critical thinking and from a Muslim perspective is more than just the ability to examine our own influence and socio-cultural impact on how we evaluate things.[145] A truly unbiased caregiving approach is not limited to the material realm, but involves a paradigm shift that refers to God as the Creator and source of everything. The Quran offers a unique framework for understanding the human condition, one which involves the following main faculties: *'aql* (the rational intellect or *ratio*), *qalb* (the heart, i.e. the intuitive intellect or *intellectus*), *rūḥ* (the spirit) and *nafs* (the soul).

As discussed, the observation of any phenomenon or experience requires reflection (*tafakkur*) and for this the faculty of rational intellect (*aql*) is needed. However, if this rational faculty is limited to the material realm, a true picture of reality cannot be obtained. Reasoning then stands in need of revelation, which appeals to one's innate being (*fitra*) through the faculty of the intuitive intellect, namely the heart. The source of the light of pure knowledge (*ma'rifa*) is channelled through the world of the unseen (*malakūt*) to the inner heart (*qalb*). However, effects of this knowledge first descend to the 'chest' (*ṣadr*), which pertains to the intermediate realm (*barzakh*), and this is where the soul (*nafs*) plays a crucial role.[146] The soul (*nafs*) can be described as the inward spiritual state of the 'self'. While the spirit (*rūḥ*) is the pure state of human beings and does not undergo any change, the soul (*nafs*) is constantly in flux by having to make the choice between 'covering' the spirit and thus tainting the heart (*qalb*); or examining all events in accordance with Divine criteria.

The soul has three possible states or stages: The first is referred to as *nafs al-ammāra bi sū* ('the evil-commanding soul') which is a state in which one follows one's base desires without any kind of critical evaluation; the second is that of the *nafs al-lawwāma* ('the self-reproaching soul'), a state in which one reflects and evaluates one's faults and recognizes the resultant misalignment with the innate predisposition (*fitra*), thus enabling a process of growth and development; the third is the stage of the *nafs al-muṭama'inna* ('the assured soul' or 'the soul at rest'), which is a state in which the heart (*qalb*) is not tainted and is thus able to allow the light of the spirit (*rūḥ*) to shine through.[147] This world is such that the mirror of one's being is constantly being clouded over, making cleansing a continual process.[148] The nature of the soul, its potentiality and duality, as well as the choice to purify or corrupt it, is clearly explained in the following verse in the Quran:

> *And [by] the soul and the One who proportioned it; then He inspired it [to discern between] its iniquity and its righteousness; indeed, he who purifies it has succeeded; and indeed, he who defiles it has failed.*[149]

Thus, human freedom of choice reduces in reality to the choice of one of only two options: to purify the soul or to defile it. The Quran also describes the state of success (*faraḥ*) of those who purify the soul.[150] Without exception all individuals have been endowed with this capacity to discern between right and wrong, for humankind's innate disposition (*fitra*) is in congruity with reality. Therefore, when presented with the right course as directed by revelation, all individuals have the potential to make amendments.[151] There are many verses in the Quran which warn those who stray away from their innate disposition (*fitra*) that they are only harming their own soul. The word 'soul' (*nafs*) often occurs with the word *ẓalama*, which connotes 'wrong-doing' and 'injustice' as well as being in a state of 'darkness'.[152]

As we have seen, prophets are ideal exemplars for chaplains to follow in their shepherding. In fact, following the *sunna* (the way of the Prophet) is a requirement in Islam. But this does not mean following only the external practices of the prophets; it means also emulating them in their striving to purify their souls. There are almost three hundred verses in the Quran where soul (*nafs*) is mentioned, and most of these verses relate to issues concerning self-development. It is made clear that self-reflection is not meant to be a sporadic practice; rather, it is very much tied in with how all events in life are interpreted, and should thus be continuous. After all, the spiritual world (*ālam-i anfus*) and the material realm (*ālam-i āfāq*), are not two competing forces, but very much intertwined. As it is stated in the Quran:

> *We will show them Our signs in the horizons (āfāq) and within themselves (anfus) until it becomes clear to them that it is the truth.*[153]

Reading the Signs in Creation: Divine Unity

If the signs in creation are not read in the name of God (*bismillah*), then they will be read incorrectly. Although God is transcendent, which means that His essence cannot be known, He is also immanent, which means that we can get to know Him through the manifestation of His Names in creation. Spiritual progress or inner striving (*jihād al-nafs*) is about the internal struggle to 'disown' God's attributes and return them to their rightful Owner. It is the lower self (*nafs*) that desires to usurp God's names. According to the Quran, despite the lower self's temporary enjoyment, this usurpation and false ownership militate against one's innate disposition, the outcome of which is a state of wretchedness and loss.[154] Said Nursi, among others, stresses that it is only with the affirmation of God's unity that one can make sense of existence in a meaningful way:

> *Indeed, all man's perfections and his lofty aims are tied to the affirmation of Divine Unity and find existence through its meaning. For if there were no unity, man would be the most unhappy of creatures, the lowest of beings, the most wretched of the animals, the most suffering and sorrowful of intelligent beings.*[155]

Unlike the visible, corporeal world (*mulk*), which can be perceived by the senses, the spiritual realm (*malakūt*) can be perceived only through inner vision, since it is a realm where there is no gradation of Divine attributes: it is the world of the 'preserved tablet' and Divine determining, where God's decrees are recorded. Without revelation, therefore, the unseen realm cannot be fathomed, and although rational intellect has the ability to accept the reality of its existence, owing to its limitations it cannot demonstrate it empirically. The realm of *malakūt* is also a created realm but it is a different kind of creation to that of the realm of *mulk,* and so the same 'laws of God' (*sunnatullāh*) do not apply to it. There is also a correspondence between the two realms, with *mulk* being described as the place of manifestation or the 'mirror' in which the *malakūt* is reflected.[156] Thus just as transient beings are a vital component of existence, and the material world can be neither abandoned nor ignored, one may conclude that one of the wisdoms behind the existence of the corporeal world is that it is the means by which the *malakūt* or inner meaning of creation can be comprehended.

According to the hadith, the reason for the existence of human beings and jinn is to know, love and worship God; this is also implied in many of the verses in the Quran.[157] In other words, the innate disposition of humankind is to be a mirror for the manifestation of God's names. Nursi explains how this responsibility or trust (*amāna*) can be fulfilled in his discourse on the human 'I'.

The 'Trust': The Human 'I'

As discussed earlier, Adam, by virtue of having been taught all the names of God, was given the 'trust' in order to act consciously as God's vicegerent and display these names in creation at the highest possible level:

> *And He taught Adam the names – all of them. Then He showed them to the angels and said, "Inform Me of the names of these, if you are truthful. They said, "Exalted are You; we have no knowledge except what You have taught us. Indeed, it is You who is the Knowing, the Wise."*[158]

Therefore, Adam and, by extension, all human beings as God's representatives on earth, are able potentially to display God's names at the highest level. However, on account of being given freedom of choice (*ikhtiyār*), either one can choose to deceive oneself and lay claim to those names, thus sinking to the level of the 'lowest of the low'; or one can choose to attain the highest level of vicegerency by being the conscious manifester of those names.[159]

According to Nursi, the key to following in the footsteps of Abraham in answering existential questions such as 'Where did I come from?', 'What is my purpose here?' and 'What is my destination?' lies in the enigma of the human 'I' or *ana*. He states that the reason that the riddle of creation can be solved through this immaterial 'I' is because it contains within it 'indications and samples' which hold the key to the knowledge of God's names and attributes:

> *The All-Wise Maker gave to man as a Trust an 'I' which comprises indications and samples that show and cause to recognize the truths of the attributes and functions of His dominicality, so that the 'I' might be a unit of measurement and the attributes of dominicality and functions of Divinity might be known. However, it is not necessary for a unit of measurement to have actual existence; like hypothetical lines in geometry, a unit of measurement may be formed by hypothesis and supposition. It is not necessary for its actual existence to be established by concrete knowledge and proofs.*
>
> *For example, an endless light without darkness may not be known or perceived. But if a line of real or imaginary darkness is drawn, then it becomes known. Thus, since God Almighty's attributes like knowledge and power, and Names like All-Wise and All-Compassionate are all-encompassing, limitless, and without like, they may not be determined, and what they are may not be known or perceived. Therefore, since they do not have limits or an actual end, it is necessary to draw a hypothetical and imaginary limit. The 'I' does this. It imagines in itself a fictitious dominicality, ownership, power, and knowledge: it draws a line. By doing this it places an imaginary limit on the all-encompassing attributes, saying, "Up to here, mine, after that, His;" it makes a division. With the tiny units of measurement in itself, it slowly understands the true nature of the attributes.*[160]

Since the human 'I' has been taught all the Divine names, it can be used as a 'measuring unit' in order to make comparisons. For example, it can say: "Just as I made this house and arranged it, so someone else must have made the universe and arranged it", and so on.[161] And just as Abraham progressed to the level of belief, realising that in fact all created beings are transient and dependent, and that therefore all attributes of perfection such as beauty, power, wisdom and so on must belong to God, so too do all individuals have the potential to abandon their 'imaginary dominicality'. The human 'I' therefore holds the key to reading the signs in creation in the correct way, with of course assistance from the instruction of revelation and the shepherding of messengers.

Since a truly non-judgmental and sincere approach is at the forefront of the shepherding process,[162] the human 'I' which is a component of the soul (*nafs*), can be used as a tool or measuring unit for critical reflection.

How to Read the Signs in Creation

All human beings are able to read the signs in creation, since they have all accepted the 'Trust' (*amāna*) and have been taught all the Names. However, they have also been given the choice to either attribute those Names, such as beauty, order, power and so on, to themselves or to their true Owner. Said Nursi, in his *magnum opus*, the *Risale-i Nur*, uses the term 'self-referential' (*ismī*) to describe the attitude which sees material beings as having meaning only in and of themselves, while the attitude which understands every created being as pointing to other than itself – with 'other' meaning God – he describes as 'Other-indicative'. According to Nursi, evaluating all that one sees, hears or experiences in a self-referential way (*ma'nā-i ismī*) obscures the connection to the Transcendent, thus reducing the value of beings merely to their material being and usage. However, creation seen as Other-indicative (*ma'nā-i ḥarfī*), that is, as signs pointing to God, brings the whole cosmos to life, demonstrating a sense of purpose in existence.[163]

It is only by reading the creation in the Other-indicative way that one is able to recognise one's impotence, acknowledge one's existential poverty, view the cosmos in terms of Divine Compassion, and be engaged in constant reflection and self-examination. In the next chapter, the process for reading the signs in creation in an Other-indicative way will be discussed.

10

Critical Reflection, Self-vigilance (*murāqaba*) and Self-accounting (*muḥāsaba*)

Psychologists today agree that grief is mostly the outcome of how individuals process the events in their lives rather than the actual events themselves; consequently counsellors try to help patients to obtain a more comprehensive view of their situation through a change in thought processes.[164] More recently, the 'growth concept' approach has become popular, which centres the importance of encouraging individuals to learn from, and thrive on, setbacks, rather than having a 'fixed mindset' which shuts down the opportunities to learn from these experiences.[165] However, while these strategies are useful to some extent, they provide no answers for an individual who wants to know why these events have occurred in the first place.

Changing thought processes needs to have a base, a criterion, upon which one is able to examine the events beyond a limited framework. A version of what is widely known and practiced as cognitive behaviour therapy (CBT) is baked into the counselling frameworks stemming from the Quranic concepts of self-vigilance (*murāqaba*) and self-accounting (*muḥāsabah*, and was developed not in the twentieth century but in the ninth century by the Muslim thinker, Abū Zayd al-Balkhī (850-934). In his manuscript *Maṣāliḥ al-abdān wa al-anfus* (*Sustenance for Bodies and Souls*), he discusses the importance of sustaining both the body and the soul, stressing that in order to protect the soul one should aim to control the influence of negative thought patterns.[166] He offers seven thought-changing strategies for combatting psychological symptoms associated with emotionally disturbing influences in order to be able to 'neutralize' and 'desensitize' their symptoms.[167] Both Balkhi's and his predecessor al-Kindi's strategies for changing thought processes to help people come to terms with disturbing events are grounded in the understanding of the nature of this world, which helps to contextualize those events beyond non-rational explanations based on randomness and chance.

The process of self-vigilance requires both the faculties of mind and heart in order to facilitate *tafakkur*, which literally means deep reflection. It also requires *tadabbur*, which means contemplation and remembrance of God. The Quran clarifies the importance of pondering deeply upon all that is in the heavens and the earth at all times, and in accordance with the criteria of revelation:

> *Who remember Allah while standing or sitting or [lying] on their sides and give thought to the creation of the heavens and the earth, [saying], "Our Lord, You did not create this aimlessly; exalted are You [above such a thing]; then protect us from the punishment of the Fire."*[168]

> *Then do they not reflect [tadabbur] upon the Qur'an? If it had been from [any] other than Allah they would have found within it much contradiction.*[169]

Self-vigilance therefore means self-reflection, which requires the avoidance of haste and allowing oneself time to reflect upon all developments, the aim being to see beyond form in the search for meaning and purpose.

Self-accounting or self-assessment is about questioning and becoming involved in all that is happening around us, and deciding whether to choose to act in accordance with our lower, selfish desires or whether to act in accordance with our innate disposition. Thus self-accounting affords us the opportunity to question and reform ourselves.

Based on the processes of *murāqabah* and *muḥāsaba* I have developed the following steps as a method for critical reflection from a Muslim perspective:

1. Observation
2. Introspection
3. Ontological Analysis
4. Correlation to Revelation
5. Interpretation of the 'Signs'
6. Action/Outcome

Since all human beings were taught all of the names of God, everyone without exception has the potential to see beyond the outer form of created beings. This means seeing everything as a sign, pointing to that which is other – i.e. Other – than itself. On this view a flower would not just be viewed as merely a flower, but as a message which is conveying the reason and purpose for its existence. A flower may, therefore, be seen as a manifestation of a Divine name, or a configuration of some or many Divine names. Names such as beauty, wisdom and order, for example, can be seen quite easily in a flower. Also, because of its transient existence, a flower relays the message that its merciful and compassionate Creator is the One who is neither dependent nor transient, but rather everlasting and closer to us than even our jugular vein.[170]

The example of Said Nursi's life experiences may throw further light on how this method can be applied and why this process of critical thinking is deemed to be an appropriate approach.

Said Nursi explains how grief-stricken one can become if events in one's life are viewed superficially, and if the soul is allowed to control the interpretation of events without using the criteria of the Quran. Nursi experienced many calamities during his lifetime, including exile and imprisonment, being poisoned seventeen times, the death of his nephew,[171] and the destruction of his hometown.[172] He describes his grief below; I have shown how the 'critical reflection steps' enumerated above match Nursi's engagement with his grief, thus providing us with an excellent example of the critical reflection process in action.

Observation

The heedlessness arising from my intense grief showed me the world to be terrifying, empty, desolate, and about to collapse over my head.[173]

Introspection

My spirit sought a point of support in the face of innumerable hostile calamities. Its endless desires which stretch to eternity were seeking out something to satisfy them.[174]

Correlation to Revelation

While awaiting consolation in the face of the sorrow and grief arising from those endless separations and deaths, that endless devastation, suddenly the reality was manifested of the All-Wise Quran's verses:

> *Whatever is in the heavens and on earth – let it declare the praises and glory of God; for He is Exalted in Might, the Wise. To Him belongs the dominion of the heavens and the earth: it is He Who gives life and death; and He has power over all things.*[175]

Interpretation of the 'Signs"

It saved me from that pitiful, terrible, sad, separation-stained imagining, and opened my eyes. I saw that the fruits at the tops of the fruit-trees were looking at me as though smiling. "Note us as well," they were saying. "Do not only look at the ruins." The verses' reality brought the following thought to mind: Why does an artificial letter written in the form of a town by the hand of man, who is a guest on the page of Van's plain, being wiped out by a calamitous torrent called the Russian invasion sadden you to this extent? Consider the Pre-Eternal Inscriber, everything's True Owner and Sustainer, for His missives on this page of Van continue to be written in glittering fashion, in the way you used to see. Your weeping over those desolate ruins arises from the error of forgetting their True Owner, not thinking that men are guests, and imagining them to be owner.[176]

Action/Outcome

A door to reality opened up from that error, from that searing sight, and my soul was prepared to accept the reality completely. Like iron is plunged in the fire so that it softens and may be profited from, that grievous sight and terrible state were fire which softened my soul. Through the reality of the above verses, the Qur'an of Miraculous Exposition showed it the effulgence of the truths of belief, causing it to accept it.[177]

Another example of how these six steps of critical reflection can be applied is the experience of Imam Ali, the son-in-law of prophet Mohammad:

Ali was victorious at the 'Battle of the Trench' in 627 AD, but refrained from killing his enemy, Amr b. Abd al-Wudd. and when asked by the Prophet Mohammad about this, it became clear that Abd al-Wudd had reviled Ali's mother and spat on his face. Ali feared that if he had killed him at that moment, it may have been out of personal anger rather than duty.[178]

Let us now apply the six steps above to this situation. In this example it appears that Ali's initial feeling was one in which he realised his own discomfort and anger *[observation of phenomenon]*. He then examined his own feelings about it *[introspection]* and after looking at the bigger picture and realising that his own 'I' (*nafs*) may have been interfering with his duty *[ontological analysis]*, he had recourse to the criteria of revelation *[correlation to revelation]* and subsequently read the event *[interpretation of the signs]* in accordance with what is 'wise' (*ḥikma*), which led him to the decision to let the enemy go *[action/outcome]*.

Chaplains can 'shepherd' insofar as they can facilitate the service-users' nurturing (*rubūbiyya*) of their own embedded theologies so that they can make sense of them and apply them at a practical level. Mastering this process for reflective practice gives Muslim chaplains the skills to help service-users read the events in their life in a meaningful, i.e. Other-indicative, way, as well as limiting bias in their own practice.

11

Matters of Concern for Muslim Students and Staff

A university is more than just a place where one acquires knowledge and qualifications. It is therefore important to have a holistic approach with regards to the needs of both students and staff. This means offering not only academic support, but also spiritual, emotional and social support, as all of these impact on each other. Chaplains play an important role in the development of the whole person by ensuring that these needs are in balance in accordance with individual requirements. They therefore contribute greatly to the well-being of students and staff, and this is often not acknowledged as much as it ought to be.

While Christian chaplaincy in higher education has received some scholarly attention,[179] very little research has been carried out about the work of Muslim chaplains.[180] Thus little is known about Muslim chaplains' contributions to their respective institutions. Muslim chaplaincy differs extensively from Christian chaplaincy owing to many factors, including the different requirements of the faith itself, as well as the social context in which Muslim chaplains carry out their work. Lack of understanding about Islam and the needs of Muslims means that a major part of the role of chaplains is to act as mediators and moderators, and as conduits through which issues can be communicated to different departments and groups. For example, a big part of the role of Muslim chaplains is to build bridges, not only across different religious communities but also between different denominations of the same faith who may differ in their theological beliefs. While it may be argued that other faiths face similar problems, the nature of these issues is not the same. Chaplains play a big role in explaining to their service-users that equality does not necessarily mean the same provision for everyone, as the needs of different faiths are not the same. For example, a designated prayer space is extremely important for practicing Muslims, as it is obligatory for them to pray five times a day, while this may not be an obligatory requirement for certain other faiths.

One of the most important reasons why there appears to be a lack of understanding of what Muslim chaplaincy is about is the absence or inadequacy of direct links between Muslim chaplains and other welfare providers in the same institution. Appointment of Muslim chaplains should never be tokenistic; rather, they should be seen as managers and experts of any issues related to their faith. Relaying important issues concerning Muslims through other mediators, such as non-Muslim chaplaincy coordinators or leads, often loses its efficiency owing to the lack of extensive theological knowledge about Islam on their part. This lack of direct communication and networking, as well as other issues that Muslim chaplains face in their role, will be elaborated upon in this chapter in the form of case studies.

Building Bridges between Students and Staff Needs and University Service-providers: Case Studies

The best way to explain the role of chaplains as mediators, moderators and advocates is to give a number of case studies as examples. These case studies have been shared by Muslim chaplains in various UK universities.

Case Study One

A Muslim chaplain receives an email from the Estates and Facilities department to say that complaints have been raised about students praying in the library in inappropriate spaces, and despite being told several times not to pray there, they continue to do so. The Muslim chaplain talks to the students concerned and discovers that there is very little time for students to go to the university prayer room, as it takes 20-30 minutes to walk there, which would mean that they would not get to their next lecture on time, and thus the only option left open to them is to pray in the library. The chaplain explains the situation to the staff concerned, and emphasizes that for practicing Muslims, the five daily prayers are not optional but rather a necessary outward expression of submission to the faith, which needs to be carried out at specific times. Having understood the situation, the staff suggest that in the short term, they have permission to use the empty rooms in the library rather than praying in front of fire exits. The students concerned accept this offer, but add that they are sometimes unable to find an empty space. The chaplain discusses this situation with a wider group, explaining the need for a prayer room which is more accessible.

Case Study Two

A group of Muslim students at a collegiate university contacts the Muslim chaplain, complaining that *ḥalāl* meat is not provided at their respective colleges. The Muslim chaplain contacts the catering managers and discovers that there is no consistency regarding the provision of *ḥalāl* meat across the different colleges. While some colleges provide one kind of *ḥalāl* meat if pre-ordered, others do not provide any at all. The Muslim chaplain listens to the students' needs regarding *ḥalāl* food provision and relays them to the college catering providers. Some colleges take the needs of students on board and ensure *ḥalāl* meat is provided if pre-ordered. The chaplain convinces the students concerned that pre-ordering is necessary as it ensures against food wastage. A happy medium is reached.

Case Study Three

A student contacts the Muslim chaplain in her institution about problems with accommodation. She says she did not realize that she would be sharing a room with a non-Muslim. Although she admits that she really likes her roommate, the practical requirements of her faith make it very difficult for both parties to share a room. The chaplain explains the situation to the college concerned and the student is given her own room. However, this new room is in a noisy corridor, and it is difficult and impractical for her to use the shared shower facilities. Rather than complaining, she decides to rent an accommodation off-campus and is happy to share a house not too far from the university with three other female students. But this arrangement puts her in an even more uncomfortable situation. Although the house is an all-female share, the non-Muslim girls often invite their boyfriends to stay with them for long periods, and this makes it difficult for the Muslim student to move around freely in the kitchen and shower area. She desperately needs to leave but cannot do so as she needs to pay rent for the full year. Stressed out by the situation to the extent that it begins to interfere with her studies and damage her well-being, she asks advice from the chaplain how she can come out of this difficult situation.

The chaplain mediates between the landlord and the student to explain the exceptionally difficult situation. However, the landlord insists on full payment for the whole year. The chaplain then discusses the possibility of looking for someone else to take her place in the present accommodation and whether the landlord would be happy with this arrangement. On obtaining agreement from the landlord, the chaplain contacts various people and groups and successfully secures a new tenant for the premises. The student goes back to college accommodation. The chaplain takes this further, informing the university accommodation providers of the difficulties Muslims face in shared accommodation and asking them to consider having a Muslim female corridor in some of the colleges. The dearth of separate flats and college accommodation generally has meant that this problem has remained unresolved.

Case Study Four: Religious Commitment versus Educational Commitment

A very stressed student contacts the Muslim chaplain about the difficult predicament in which he finds himself. The student explains that he has received several warnings from his department for missing many lectures and seminars on Friday afternoons. He adds that although he has explained that he must attend Friday prayers at that time, his department has advised him that he needs to prioritize his education. The chaplain contacts his department and explains that Friday prayers are not optional for Muslim men; rather, they are considered obligatory by every school of Islamic law. As a result, male students and staff are bound to prioritize this ritual over all other obligations. The department explains that because there are already so many considerations when devising a timetable, it cannot be changed solely to suit Muslim students. However, considering the genuine need of this student, he will be given permission to listen to recordings of the sessions that he has missed. The student is happy with this arrangement.

Case Study Five: Education, Advocacy and Mediation: Islamophobia

A student complains to the Muslim chaplain about Islamophobic banter in his college as well as on social media. He says that although he is not a practicing Muslim, he is nevertheless extremely upset by the unfounded assumptions and hatred targeted at the faith. As an international student, he did not expect that there would be so little respect for people from diverse faiths and cultures in a British higher education institution. He feels strongly that the university has a responsibility to curb this kind of hatred towards a particular minority. The chaplain listens and asks the individual how he would like this to be taken forward. With support from the chaplain, the incident is reported on the university on-line hate crime tool and the students involved are asked to meet the chaplain, the college administrators and the victim to hear the opinions exchanged first-hand. The students admit that they have negative feelings about Islam and felt they had the right to express these opinions but were sorry that they hurt the feelings of the student concerned. The college managers warn the students robustly that this kind of banter is considered hate crime and thus not to be tolerated; they add that if it continues there will be serious consequences. The students promise not to express these opinions again and they apologize to the victim. The chaplain is concerned that their comments were totally unfounded and reflected the general Islamophobic propaganda in the media. The chaplain points out the importance of rolling out an educational program against racism generally and Islamophobia in particular. The chaplain contacts the Equality and Diversity Team to discuss the possibility of running workshops.

Case Study Six: University Structure: Is the University 'A Muslim Friendly Institution?'

Muslim chaplains spend a lot of time responding to enquires from prospective students and staff who wish to study or work in a university which not only accommodates their academic needs but also serves adequately their religious requirements. Numerous questions regarding practical issues include the provision of *ḥalāl* food in college accommodation, as well as the availability of *ḥalāl* food shops in the community; provision of prayer space; availability of separate accommodation areas for women; accommodation of particular requirements during Ramadan and the Eid celebrations; and numerous other questions pertaining to the practical needs of practicing Muslims. Many also ask about how Muslims are treated in general. The question 'Is the university a friendly place in which to work or study?' often means "Is it inclusive?" Fear of Islamophobia and negative attitudes towards Muslims can often deter an individual from choosing a university which has received negative publicity in this regard. In order to welcome prospective Muslim students and staff to their university, Muslim chaplains assure them that diversity and inclusion are among the main priorities of their institution, as well as offering their personal support with any enquiries in order to ensure that students' experience of study or work will hopefully be both rewarding and enjoyable.

The chaplain's 'prophetic' role,[181] although not formally a requirement, is actually a integral part of their job description. As Schmalzbauer reveals in his survey of American colleges, seventy-seven percent of chaplains identified the commitment to social justice as a very important goal.[182] This prophetic role is particularly essential for Muslim chaplains because of the greater need for their engagement with various university departments as mediators and moderators.

The extent to which different departments and colleges within a university access Muslim chaplains for advice about the needs of their students differs, thus making it incumbent on Muslim chaplains themselves to publicize their role as widely as possible within their own institutions. In some cases, Muslim chaplains tend not to be consulted about issues pertaining to the needs of Muslims on account of the voluntary status of their chaplaincy, despite the fact that they may have adequate knowledge, experience and qualifications to do the job. This situation can be frustrating for some Muslim chaplains as they often feel that they have the potential to play a vital role in the well-being of students and staff, but that they are not being given an adequate enough platform to voice their concerns because of their voluntary status. This lack of recognition adds pressure to the job of chaplains as much of their time is then spent in searching for novel ways of arguing for, and influencing, changes, in an effort to ensure the right kinds of provision are in place, in accordance with the needs of different groups.

Conclusion

In this chapter the important role of Muslim chaplains as advocates, mediators, moderators and champions of social justice has been discussed via a number of case studies, submitted by chaplains from various UK institutions. These case studies are by no means comprehensive; rather, they serve to demonstrate that Muslim chaplaincy is much more than advising on religious ritual.

In the next chapter, case studies of pastoral and spiritual care given by Muslim chaplains will be contextualized against the backdrop of the six principles of faith.

12

Pastoral and Spiritual Care: The Shepherding of Muslim Chaplains

Although pastoral care is grounded in the Islamic faith of a Muslim chaplain, it is possible to create an atmosphere in which diversity is welcomed. Through the application of the concept of '*ḥikma*' (wisdom) in their 'shepherding', chaplains can support all kinds of individuals in a non-judgmental way that takes the individual's context into consideration. There are two concept pairs at play here, namely unity (*wāḥidiyya*) and oneness (*aḥadiyya*) ; and compassion (*raḥmāniyya*) and mercy (*raḥīmīyya*). These are important because understanding and applying them can help Muslim chaplains to extend their pastoral reach to all individuals, whether they follow a particular religion or not.

Unity (*wāḥidiyya*) and Oneness (*aḥadiyya*)

From a Muslim perspective, *wāḥidiyya*, which translates as 'unity' or 'inclusive unity', is a general concept which pertains to all creatures, in the sense that owing to their transient and contingent disposition, all creatures have been created by One who is pre- and post-eternal, permanent and necessarily existent. As such, all creatures owe their nurturing and development purely to that Source. Nursi gives the light of the sun as an example of *wāḥidiyya* from which all creatures benefit.[183]. For example, the sun shines on all of the beings in a garden – the trees, the flowers, the soil, the insects – together, inclusively, at the same time. Rain is another example. When it rains, the rain falls on all of the things in the garden, and not just on one thing. This is an example of 'inclusive unity'. When one talks in the context of the Divine, God's 'inclusive unity' is that which is accessed by all beings equally.

However, in the examples above, although sunlight and rain are given to all of the denizens of the garden equally, each of the different beings uses sunlight, or rain, in its own unique way. The plant uses sunlight for photosynthesis, for example, while the soil and the worms in it process sunlight in other ways unique to them. This aspect of uniqueness is referred to as *aḥadiyya*, which also translates as 'oneness', 'unicity' or 'exclusive unity'. This '*aḥadiyya*' aspect of Divine unity is very much related to the concept of Divine determining (*qadar*), according to which the needs of all species are accommodated for in accordance with their particular and unique needs.

Compassion (*raḥmānīyya*) and Mercy (*raḥīmmiyya*)

The concepts of *wāḥidiyya* and *aḥadiyya* can also be applied to the dual concepts of compassion *raḥmāniyya* and mercy *raḥīmmiyya*. While the Creator of the universe is compassionate (*raḥmān*) to all His creatures, that compassion is particularised in accordance with the unique and specific needs of every individual and every species. While general compassion may include things such as sustenance being given to all creatures in general, particularised compassion, or mercy, inheres in the fact that every creature will receive sustenance in a manner that accords with its unique and particular needs. Chaplains therefore must also acknowledge the difference between the terms *wāḥidiyya and aḥadiyya*, while manifesting the Divine names *Raḥmān* and *Raḥīm* in their pastoral care. This means adopting an approach that is not only compassionate to all, but which also adapts that compassion to suit the unique needs of every individual.

Therefore, since all individuals as theomorphic beings partake in all of the Divine attributes, this human commonality enables Muslim chaplains to reach out and support the diverse needs of their community, regardless of religious, spiritual or any other affiliations. In this chapter a few examples in the form of case studies will be given in order to shed more light on the pastoral role of Muslim chaplains. Although all cases are real events experienced by students and staff at university, some of the issues from other cases studies may have been included in order to protect confidentiality. All names are in any case pseudonymous.

Case Study One

Background

Merve is a member of staff at her institution. She came from Turkey with her husband and four children and settled in well in their new surroundings. Her husband was able to manage his business from his home in United Kingdom without having to travel too often to his home country. However, without the extended family around, the pressure of work and caring responsibilities for four young children became too much for Merve. Her husband did not share any responsibility for cooking and caring for the children, apart from occasional help with their schoolwork. Merve also felt that deep down her husband resented the fact that she had an important academic role while he was a businessman, and that he was thus pressurising her to be more attentive to her role as wife and mother, rather than to her work. Merve was an only child and her parents had sadly died in a car crash a few years before, so she did not have any immediate family to support her. Extra pressure was put on Merve by her husband's family, who took every opportunity to remind her of her 'Islamic' duties to her husband, children and home life. The pressure of settling in a new job, as well as all the demands which were put on her, affected Merve's physical and mental health. She sought the help of health professionals, as well as the well-being team in her institution. She also sought the help of the Muslim chaplain, as she was filled with feelings of guilt over what her partner described as 'failing to satisfy her husband in her home duties'.

First Meeting

Main points discussed with Muslim chaplain:

As a practicing Muslim, Merve wanted to clarify what her duties were as a wife. She also understood her husband's feelings with regard to her position in university and wanted advice on how to reassure him about the important role that he played as both husband and father.

I asked Merve what she considered would be the best outcome. She stated that she loved her husband and hated the fact that he felt this way, and how his family used religion to convince him that she should give up her professional role. Ideally, she wanted to have a happy home life where both partners supported each other. She stated that with that acceptance, they could then work things out together in a harmonious way, sharing tasks to make time for family social activities as well.

As both partners were practicing Muslims, I used the Quran and the hadith as resources for Merve and her husband to study together. Topics included the concept of the ideal home in Islam, as well as the roles of men and women. From a Quranic perspective, ideally the home should be a place of peace and tranquility (see Quran 16:80). The word *maskan*, which means 'dwelling place', is derived from the triliteral root *s-k-n*, derivatives of which have meanings which include 'to calm down', 'to rest,' 'to attain peace of mind and tranquility', and 'to feel at ease with'. Therefore, in Islam, the home is posited as a place of sanctuary, a place where one can retreat from the pressures of the outside world: a space, potentially, for physical, mental and spiritual rest and recuperation. It seemed that ultimately this was the kind of home environment that Merve was also seeking. Therefore, the starting point would be to ensure that this was the aim of both parties. And if this were the case, then the next step would be to tackle the obstacles which obstruct their mutual aim.

Second Meeting

At the second meeting, Merve confirmed that ultimately her husband also wanted an ideal home environment – one of tranquility, compassion and mutual understanding. After studying the Quranic literature, they both agreed that this could be achieved only if rules were based not on cultural or personal, egoistic expectations, but on precepts which allow for an environment that is conducive to a balanced and harmonious life. They felt that this was important, not only for themselves but also for their children. They both asked for support on how to apply Islamic principles in their life to achieve this.

Third Meeting

A meeting was arranged to see both parties together, to discuss how Islamic principles can be implemented in their home life. Both parties were informed that from the jurisprudential aspect of the faith, there is a consensus among the majority of Muslim scholars that it is not compulsory for a woman to serve her husband and that he cannot withhold financial support if she refuses to carry out tasks such as cooking, cleaning, washing, sewing and other such functions. In fact when Aisha, the wife of Prophet Mohammad, was asked what the Prophet used to do in his house, she replied: "He used to keep himself busy serving his family and when it was time for the prayer, he would get up for prayer."[184] In another report Aisha is reported to have said: "He did what any one of you would do in his house. He mended sandals and patched garments and sewed."[185]

Once the juristic-legalistic aspect of responsibilities was clarified, the question of how tranquility could be brought back to the home was discussed. As both parties were firm believers, the concept of Divine determining (*qadar*), one of the principles of faith, was broached. They agreed that everything in creation has been created for a specific reason, purpose and function, and that the form, shape and duties of all created beings had been bestowed on them in accordance and proportion with the roles they played as threads in the vast tapestry of creation. Thus, from the perspective of duty, there is no hierarchy of importance. No two things are the same, hence each being has an important function to play. The duty of all beings, including humans, is not to make unfair comparisons but to carry out their responsibilities to the best of their ability and with the optimal use of the bounties and blessings bestowed on them. I then asked the two parties how their unique knowledge, experience and expertise within their own particular fields could be used to facilitate harmony and to bring a sense of peace to the family.

Fourth Meeting

In this final meeting Merve and her husband shared their private deliberations with me. They felt that they also needed to listen to their children in order to hear their expectations and contributions. All parties agreed that they need to work together and help each other with housework and other duties, so that weekends could be mostly allocated to social activities and home life.

Fifth Meeting

Merve reported back that her husband no longer opposed her working at the university. Also, with everyone making an effort to share tasks, they all now had time for a social life as a family. More importantly, they were beginning to regain the tranquil space of home for which they all so ardently yearned.

Case Study Two

Background

Carol requested a visit to speak specifically to the Muslim chaplain. She was a practicing Christian, while her boyfriend was a firm believer in an ancient Egyptian religion. Both parties wished to get married, but Carol was concerned that her religion's being monotheistic and her boyfriend's being polytheistic would cause a problem, particularly since both were thinking of having children in the future. Carol wanted to discuss this with someone from a totally different faith to obtain as unbiased an opinion as possible.

Before seeing Carol, I had to self-reflect (*murāqaba*) on my own biases in order to ensure the best course of action for Carol. This self-questioning (*muḥāsaba*) led me to the principle of Divine determining and the importance of supporting Carol within the framework of her own context.

First Meeting

At the first meeting, Carol clarified that she was a practicing Christian and that her faith meant a lot to her. She had already talked to her boyfriend about this, who insisted that they would allow their children to follow the religion they chose, rather than impose their religion on them. I asked Carol if she was happy with this suggestion and how she thought it would be possible on a practical level. Carol poured out her own thoughts, which I summarized back to her. She seemed to suggest that there could never be a neutral space, and that conflict would be inevitable. I then asked Carol to write down her priorities and the things that she would be willing and unwilling to sacrifice. I also asked her to ask her husband to do the same and to bring back what they had written to the next meeting.

Second Meeting

After writing down her priorities, it seemed that Carol had already made up her mind about the best course of action. Although she loved her boyfriend very much, she was not ready to sacrifice her faith and she knew that since ultimately her boyfriend was also committed to his faith, this could create conflict and disharmony within her home. Carol thanked me for giving her the space to think things through in her own mind so that she could take the right course of action.

Case Study Three

Background

Noor was from India. She explained that she was given an award from her government to do a degree, an opportunity that she was happy to take. Doing a degree abroad would not only pave the way for her to achieve her aim and become a teacher in her village back home, but it would also provide her with a way out, a route of escape from family plans to have her married off. She was not yet ready for this commitment, she felt, and certainly did not want a suitor to be chosen for her. Apart from all these pressures, she also had physical disabilities which added further stress, causing her to have panic attacks. She had already visited her doctor, who prescribed anti-depressant tablets and other medications for her. She had also sought support from the university counselling service. She now felt that she needed moral support and had specifically asked to see the female Muslim chaplain at the university.

First Meeting

Noor explained that she was well behind in submitting her assignments and that her department had refused to give her any more extensions. She said that this situation made her panic even more, preventing her from focusing on her assignment. She said that she had given up all social life and had made great timetable plans to ensure that she did not get behind, but when she sat down to work, the panic attacks started. She said that she felt that she was being punished from all sides; she felt trapped. As a practicing Muslim she prayed to God but, in her own words, she felt no release from her present situation. She was reaching out to the Muslim chaplain for moral support and the best course of action.

As Noor was looking for advice on changing her situation in the context of her faith, I gave her a few verses from the Quran to reflect upon. I also gave her references to a few exegetical interpretations of those verses as well as a few hadith. Although Noor believed in God as the most merciful and compassionate sustainer (*Rabb*) of all creatures, she felt that she needed to strengthen her connection with Him. Therefore, the verses recommended were mainly about humankind's relationship with God, and the role that believers are expected to play in their short journey in this realm. Noor was happy to read the material given to her and to come back and discuss whether they applied to her situation and, if so, how.

Second Meeting

At our second meeting, Noor appeared to be less anxious. She said that the spiritual material given to her helped her a great deal, but that she needed to unpack the verses more by discussing further on how she should aim to change her frame of thought. She stated that the following verse from the Quran was particularly helpful, but that she wished to discuss it further:

> *Verily those who say, "Our Lord is God," and remain firm (on that path), – on them shall be no fear, nor shall they grieve [yaḥzanūna].*[186]

From the exegetical material that Noor had access to, she understood that the fear mentioned in the above verse related to fear about the future, while grief was linked to the events in the past. I asked Noor within the context of her readings of the Quran and the sayings of the Prophet how she might come to be less fearful of what the future holds for her. Her response was that she was "stuck, almost trapped in a kind of bog'" where she found any movement difficult, while realising that she needed to make small changes in her life. Firstly, she said that she needed to have more trust in God, as ultimately everything was under His control: whatever would happen in the future would be part of His plan, which meant that she should turn to Him whenever she felt helpless. We agreed that no one can know what is going to happen in the future, and so to worry about something that 'might' happen is irrational, since there is no certainty that what we may be fearing will ever happen; indeed, events may unfold in a manner totally differently to how we imagined. She also agreed that negative thoughts about the past are also pointless, since they erode time and energy which could be better focused on the present.

Noor stated that now that she understood the Muslim perspective a lot more clearly, she felt less desperate; she felt that there was an open door which she could strive to move towards.

Support was also given to Noor to ask for an extension for the submission of assignments so that she could now begin to tackle them with a renewed frame of mind. Noor also asked for on-going spiritual support via email, which was duly afforded to her.

Case Study Four

Background

Murni was a PhD student from Indonesia, married with two small children. Her husband took time off work to be with her and support her with her studies. However, she said that very little support was forthcoming from her husband, and this led to her being way behind her submission deadlines. She feared that if she was not able to complete her research, not only would she have to give all the money back to her funders, but she would also be at risk of losing her job. She contacted the Muslim chaplain for advice.

First Meeting

At the first meeting, Murni found it difficult to talk as she was in a very emotional state. She apologised for crying, saying that there was no one she could talk to, and nowhere she could let her emotions out. She was offered a tissue and assured that in confidential space of the chaplain's office she was welcome to be herself and express her feelings in any way she wished. After a cup of tea and a biscuit, Murni felt comforted somewhat and was able to tell her story. She complained that she had no life, just constant anxiety, because she had cut herself off from her fellow students, as well as her Indonesian circle of friends, in order to be able to prioritize her children and her studies. However, this sacrifice was not enough as she was receiving very little support from her husband. She said that her husband did not cook or clean, and was not available to help at the weekends because he socialised and took part in sports activities. In the week he did not look after the children properly; often she came back from university to find the children's needs had not been adequately taken care of. Feeding the children, taking care of their personal hygiene, cooking for her husband, as well as cleaning the house, left her exhausted and sometimes unable to satisfy the sexual demands of her partner, which further impacted on their relationship. She felt that she could not talk to anyone from the same culture as they appeared to have the same mindset as her husband. Moreover, Murni explained that her husband had no interest in listening to anyone or taking advice.

It seemed that Murni was socially isolated, and that this was impacting on her mental health. The chaplain suggested that Murni might like to attend the weekly women's Quran circle and bring her children along with her. She said that she really needed that social and spiritual support and would make time to attend. She said that she had accessed the university counselling support, but that it hadn't really helped because she needed practical support more than anything else. The chaplain also suggested talking to her husband about a compromise and a plan of action whereby he could incorporate some home duties into his free time, thus enabling Murni to have at least some periods of extended study time without being anxious about her family.

Second Meeting

Murni reported back that her husband was not ready to make any changes. However, she did say that she really enjoyed the Quran circle. She felt that she was with like-minded people and that it was comforting to have the children with her while getting both spiritual and social support. Murni became very friendly with some of the students in the Quran circle, some of whom offered to babysit for her at the weekends. This would enable her to progress a little faster with her research.

Third Meeting

Murni explained that she really felt much better after attending the Quran circles, as this gave her the spiritual strength which she so needed. She also enjoyed the company of like-minded people and was very grateful for their occasional help. However, she could not make a fixed childcare arrangement with them as they were also students with busy lives. She explained that although her supervisor understood and was compassionate towards her predicament, she could not delay sending her chapters any longer.

Murni also explained that she did not want to place her children at the university nursery for two reasons: firstly, there was the financial burden; and secondly, she was not happy about leaving her children with strangers. She added that if she was allowed to go back home to Indonesia, her parents would look after her children, and she would be able to study with more peace of mind.

Fourth Meeting

After many months there was no improvement in Murni's situation. She decided to go back to Indonesia in the hope that they would allow her to finish her studies there. The chaplain also provided her with a letter explaining the situation Murni found herself in, just in case this would help to show that the only barrier to finishing her studies was indeed childcare, something which would not be an obstacle back home.

The next time Murni contacted the chaplain from Indonesia was to say that she had finished writing her chapters and now wanted information and support concerning printing and binding. The chaplain informed Murni that she (i.e. the chaplain) had contacted the Graduate Office, who had said that since Murni was abroad, she would be able to submit her dissertation online.

Months later, Murni got in touch with the chaplain to say that she had passed her doctoral exam and had been accepted for promotion at her place of work.

Case Study Five

Background

Ali is a first-year undergraduate student. He identifies as being British but explains that although his parents migrated from Iran to the United Kingdom many years ago, they still identify as Iranian Shia Muslims. Although his parents have brought him up in the same tradition, Ali does not want to follow them blindly, but rather to make his own investigation. Moreover, he feels a similar kind of pressure from fellow students since he started university. He wishes to visit the Muslim chaplain to learn about Islam himself without influence or pressure to make the kind of changes in his life which he may not be ready to make.

First Meeting

Ali said that when he left his hometown to start his undergraduate studies, he thought it would be much easier to have some control over his own spiritual and social journey. However, this was not to be the case. He said that while some Muslim students pressured him to come to Friday prayer, others did not even consider him to be Muslim, simply because his parents are Shi'ites. He explained that he wanted to be around Muslims because he wished to learn about Islam. But they seemed to mainly talk about practice and very little about the faith itself. He came to the Muslim chaplain for advice on the right course to search for meaning and conviction in the Islamic faith.

Ali said that he believed that there must be a Creator because this world cannot possibly be the outcome of an accident. However, he needed to know this Creator better in order to be able to build a closer relationship with Him. The chaplain pointed out to him that most of the verses in the Quran are about matters of belief. The emphasis in the Quran is on belief in one God and in the connection between the self, this world and the next. We agreed to pick out some verses together and go through them. Ali said that he was really happy to go through this spiritual journey to find purpose and meaning for his existence. I promised Ali to send him more verses together with comments from diverse exegetes, Muslim thinkers and other commentators, together with supporting hadith so that he could study all of them and come back for another meeting with any questions that might arise.

Second Meeting

Our second meeting was taken up by a discussion about all the material Ali had read. He said that he was "buzzing with excitement" and had "many questions to ask". He was particularly excited about the story of Abraham and his journey of conviction concerning the temporality and transient nature of this world and the evident need for permanence. He also stated that his questions about the injustice in this world were also answered by the verses in the Quran which explain this world as a place of test and trial; as a temporary abode and a place where one can strive to plant the seeds for a place of permanence in the next world.

Ali asked if he could continue to see the chaplain every fortnight to discuss his readings. The chaplain accepted.

Third Meeting

After another study session, Ali reported that he now understood the importance of prayer and made sure that he prioritized that over anything else, even his studies. He also attended Friday prayers. I asked if his fellow Muslim students were supportive. He stated that some were very kind while a few still assumed that he must be Shi'ite because his parents were Iranian. He stated that in fact he had no affiliation to Shiism, for at this stage he just wished to follow the criteria of the Quran and the way (*sunna*) of the Prophet. He stated that he was a lot happier now and could concentrate fully on his studies as he had found a purpose in life.

Ali asked the chaplain if he could keep in contact via email for continued support and the chaplain stated that her door for support would always be open to him. The chaplain also gave him links to a few reliable and friendly on-line study groups which he could join to further increase his knowledge in the faith.

Case Study Six

Background

Martina was a devout Catholic from Venezuela. She was very unhappy about the Islamophobic headlines in the media as well as the attitude of some students about Islam and Muslims in her university. She contacted the Muslim chaplain to find out how she could help to combat prejudice and Islamophobia.

First Meeting

Martina explained that her religion was one of kindness and mercy and she was not comfortable when any faith community was targeted with such hate and lack of compassion. She wanted to discuss how she could help dispel myths in the outside world as well as among the closer community.

The chaplain explained that she had organised with a team of volunteers to receive visits from schools as well as community programs such as scouts and cubs, and that Martina would be welcomed as one of the volunteers. Martina accepted this invitation as the aim was to show kindness and friendship and to dispel myths about Islam.

Martina also joined the Inspirational Women's Group organised by the Muslim chaplain. The Group offers female students from all faiths and none the opportunity to talk and discuss about inspiring women.

Martina enjoyed supporting school visits and being part of the Inspirational Women's Group for the whole year of her master's program. She was sad to leave, but she kept in touch as an alumni student.

Once back home, she contacted the Muslim chaplain to inform her that she was happily in a full-time job but wanted to do more. She stated that she had encountered much ignorance about Islam in her hometown and even in her place of work. She asked the advice of the Muslim chaplain on how to approach the mosque in her local community to help with their Islamic education and other programs. Support was given, along with a reference, and she was happy to be part of their volunteering programs.

Case Study Seven

Background

Imran was an international undergraduate student from the United Arab Emirates. He contacted the Muslim chaplain for support via the counselling service. Imran's Muslim girlfriend, whom he had planned to marry by mutual consent after their studies, had split up with him and formed a relationship with another Muslim student, whom she married shortly afterwards. Imran was absolutely devastated and experienced severe depression, resulting in his being prescribed anti-depressants. He informed the chaplain that because he had stated to the counselling service that "life was not worth living any more", social services had been contacted for assessment and he had been sectioned. He said that being in hospital had been a terrible experience for him and that they had "no right to imprison me like an animal" or "pump me full of tablets". He stated that his health had been adversely affected by the tablets, and that this had prevented him from going to the gym and keeping up with his sport programs.

First Meeting

Imran informed the chaplain that with his doctor's consent, he had happily come off his medication as it adversely affected his health and his figure. He stated that he had also stopped going to the counselling service as he was very angry with them for referring him to the social services. He had discovered that the university had a Muslim chaplaincy service and had contacted the Muslim chaplain for support. At the first meeting he stated that he was a practicing Muslim and that the reason for contacting the chaplaincy was that he "desperately wished to know how to cope with relationship separation from a Muslim perspective."

At the first meeting the chaplain listened to Imran's experience and allowed him to release his exasperation, which was mainly about his being sectioned without substantial reason. He said that his statement "life was not worth living anymore" was just a figure of speech, since as a Muslim he was well aware that he could not take his own life. After allowing Imran to share his experience, the Muslim chaplain explained that the people in the counselling service were just doing their duty as they have to take expressions of suicidal ideation seriously since they can never know what is in people's hearts and minds. The chaplain then asked Imran how he would like to move forward. He stated that he needed help with:

1. Understanding the Muslim position on separation and coping strategies.
2. Getting back to his studies.
3. Getting back to his sports and fitness programs.

The Muslim chaplain stated that help would be given to enable him to understand the Muslim perspective on separation through verses in the Quran and other Muslim literature. His college would be contacted to follow up on how he was to resume his studies. And he could join his college gym again and follow a gradual fitness programme. The Muslim chaplain also gave Imran some verses from the Quran to ponder and to discuss at the next meeting.

Second Meeting

At the second meeting Imran reported that he had started his gradual fitness programme, which was helping him to manage his depression. His college also arranged with his department to defer his assignments owing to the time lost during his mental illness and hospitalization. He said that he now needed to be able to cope with separation and that wished to discuss the following verse with the chaplain in particular:

> *But perhaps you hate a thing, and it is good for you; and perhaps you love a thing and it is bad for you. And Allah Knows, while you know not.*[187]

The chaplain asked Imran what he understood from that verse. He said that because ultimately what had happened to him was part of God's plan, then his experience must have been necessary, although at present it was difficult for him to accept that. He also said that the verses from the Quran suggested to him by the Muslim chaplain concerning the quality and character of the 'friends of God' were very helpful, since if one claims to be close to God, then one must believe in Him and trust His decree.

The Muslim chaplain elaborated on Imran's understanding, explaining that this is why belief in God is the main principle of faith in Islam, and why Divine decree is also one of the principles of faith. She explained that trusting in God means accepting God's judgment on how He decrees that everything in the realm of creation should be created and proportioned. This means that things that happen should not be attributed to causes or to other people, but that we should view everything as being part of God's decree, which consequently must be the best decree, even though from our limited view point it may be very difficult to grasp and internalise. The Muslim chaplain agreed that it is not always easy to understand the events that happen in our lives. However, knowing and trusting that ultimately God is in control provides us with a rope that we can hold onto at times of hardship. The chaplain related the story of Jalāl ad-Dīn Rūmī (1207-1273), the famous 13th century Muslim scholar and mystic poet, who gives a good example of how distorted the view of limited creatures can be. He tells of an ant that is crawling across the carpet in a mosque and becomes very angry because it cannot make sense of all the lumps and bumps which it has to climb over. The ant remarks:

"What is this, these bumps and strange colours and patterns; this must just be some meaningless obstacle course that someone has put here. What a useless thing to have made!"

The Muslim chaplain explains that from the point of view of the carpet maker, seen from above those 'bumps' are part and parcel of the carpet's beautiful patterns. Similarly, human beings are not always able to understand the reasons for unwelcome events because of their limited view, but as long as there is trust in God and resigned acceptance (*riḍā*) in God's will, the weight of calamities will eventually become much lighter to bear.

The Muslim chaplain asked Imran if he turns to God at difficult times. He said that he did and that would not have been able to cope if he had not been a believer. He said that since his experience of loss, he had turned much more to God for solace and comfort. The Muslim chaplain then asked him whether, since his experience had led him to a closer relationship with God, he still saw his situation in a totally negative light. Imran said that he now understood that something good had come out of this experience.

Third Meeting

Imran expressed a desire to read and discuss more chapters from the Quran as this had been very helpful for him to adjust to a life without the woman he thought would one day be his partner in life.

He also explained that he had come out of that state of wishing to withdraw from life and was now pushing himself to accept a new pattern of life, which he was adjusting to gradually.

The chaplain continued to read and discuss chapters from the Quran with Imran at further meetings. He also joined the Islamic Society and took part in their activities.

Imran continued to keep in touch via email and later informed the chaplain that he had passed his degree and was back in the United Arab Emirates.

Months later Imran contacted the chaplain to say that he had now totally put the past behind him and that he had met a wonderful girl to whom he would soon have the pleasure of getting married. He added that he just wished that he had contacted the chaplaincy service sooner rather than later, as what he really needed desperately at that time was guidance on how to approach his difficult situation within the framework of his faith.

Notes

1. Ryan 2015, p. 10.
2. Such as *ḥakīm*, *shaykh* and *ālim*.
3. Gilliat-Ray, Ali, and Pattison 2013.
4. Ibid.
5. Long and Ansari 2018.
6. Kwofie 2022.
7. Caperon, Todd, and Walters 2017, p. 16.
8. Encyclopaedia Britannica, "Chaplain".
9. Ibid.
10. For more information on pastoral theology, see: Richardson and Bowden 1983, pp. 428-430.
11. For more information on William James's lectures, see: Cooper 2002.
12. For more information about Boisen's theological belief, see: Asquith Jr. 1982.
13. For a critique of Hiltner's theology, see: Campbell 2000.
14. Pattison and Woodward 2000.
15. Atkinson and Field 1995, p. 42.
16. Ballard 2000.
17. Richardson and Bowden 1983, p. 455.
18. Ibid., p. 88.
19. Ibid., p. 49.
20. Gilliat-Ray, Ali, Pattison 2013, p. 25.
21. For example, see: Adamson 2007.
22. For more information on Avicenna see: Afnan 1958.
23. For example, see: Jayyusi-Lehn 2002.
24. Adamson 2007, p. 5.
25. Al-Ghazālī 1997.
26. For more information on al-Ghazālī, see: Griffel 2009.
27. See: Gilliat-Ray 2006, p. 45.
28. Ibid.
29. Ibid., p. 51.
30. Ibid., p. 58.
31. See for example, Peters and Bearman 2014.

32   The chaplain wishes to remain anonymous.
33   Newitt 2011, p. 106.
34   See: Gilliat-Ray 2006, pp. 71-72.
35   For example, Masters course in Muslim Chaplaincy at Markfield Institute.
36   See: Khosrokhavar 2015, pp. 67-82.
37   For a discussion on the mis-use of the term *ulamā* (Muslim scholars) instead of the term *fuqahā* (Muslim jurists), see: Murata and Chittick 1994, p. 44.
38   See for example, Jayyusi-Lehn, 2002.
39   See: Glassé 2001, p. 248.
40   Ngyuen 2019, p. 17.
41   Quranic Arabic Corpus, on-line tool, accessed 11 August 2022. <https://corpus.quran.com/qurandictionary.jsp?q=slm>
42   See: Rescorla 2020 and Rosenbur 2012.
43   Quran, 7:172.
44   Quran, 2:151.
45   Quran, 2:120.
46   Quran, 2:272.
47   Quran, 3:101.
48   Ṣaḥīḥ al-Bukhārī, 2262. Qīrāts literally means the reciters of the Quran.
49   Ibid., 7138 and 1829. Qīrāts literally means the reciters of the Quran.
50   Quran, 2:213.
51   Quran, 2:272.
52   For a discussion on this Prophetic tradition see: Schimmel 2011, p. 99.
53   Nasafi 2012, p. 46.
54   Quran, 9:128.
55   Muḥammad Ḥusayn Ṭabātabā'ī, was a Shi'ite scholar, born in Tabriz, in north-western Iran.
56   Ṭabātabā'ī 1974, V1, p. 178.
57   Quran, 2:30.
58   Quran, 2:31.
59   Quran, 2:32.
60   Abū-l-Qāsim al-Qushayrī, the Persian Sufi's work includes his mystical commentary on the Quran, as well as his treastise on the doctrine of Sufism, called the Risālah.
61   Al-Qushayrī 2017, V8, p. 86.
62   See: Quran, 7:11-25.
63   Iqbal 2013, p. 85.
64   See: Quran, 20:115.
65   See: Quran, 95:4.
66   See: Quran, 95:5.

67 Quran, 7:16.
68 See: Quran, 7:20.
69 There are many verses in the Quran which are about God's forgiveness, such as: 42:30, 42:34, 4:99, 22:60, 53:26 and 66:8.
70 See: *Hadith Qudsi* in *Jāmī At-Tirmidhī* and *Musnad Ahmad Ibn Hanbal*, 34, accessed 7 July 2020. <https://sunnah.com/search?q=forgiveness>
71 Al-Ghazālī 2015, p. 15.
72 Quran, 16:120 and 4:125.
73 Ṭabātabā'ī 1974, V1, p. 178.
74 Quran, 6:75.
75 Al-Qushayrī, V8, p. 228.
76 Quran, 6:74-79.
77 For further discussion about Abraham's journey concerning monotheism rather than proof of existence of God, see: Beheshti 1973, Chapter 3.
78 Quran, 2:164. See also other verses such as: 26:28, 24:61, 57:17, 13:4, 16:12, 16:67 and 30:24.
79 Al-Attas 1955, p.133.
80 See: Quran, 22:46.
81 See: Gianotti 2001, p. 130.
82 Ṣaḥīḥ al-Bukhārī, 4777 (Book 65, Hadith 299).
83 See: Nursi 1994, p. 446.
84 Quran, 103:1-3.
85 See: Quran, 12.
86 Kathīr 2014, p. 80.
87 See: Quran, 12:21, where the word *mathwā* is used for home, indicating a "place of comfort and safety".
88 Jāmī 2013.
89 See: Quran, 12.
90 See: Quran, 12:39-40.
91 Quran, 21:87.
92 Said Nursi is a twentieth century Muslim scholar and the author of the Rīsale-i Nur.
93 Nursi 1995.
94 Ibid., p. 19.
95 Quran, 22:83.
96 See: Nursi 1995, pp. 21-28.
97 For example, see: Quran, 27:16, 27:17, 27:18, 27:19 and 21:81.
98 See: Quran, 27:22-26.
99 Quran, 27:30.
100 Quran, 27:40.

101 Quran, 27:42.
102 Quran, 27:44.
103 Quran, 28:4.
104 Quran, 28:7.
105 See: Quran, 25:54.
106 See: Quran, 25:48.
107 See: Quran, 25:48-49.
108 See: Quran, 28:9.
109 See: Quran, 28:13.
110 Quran, 8:30.
111 Quran, 28:14-28.
112 Quran, 28:30.
113 See: Quran, 28:31-32.
114 Quran, 26:63-68.
115 Quran, 2:216.
116 Cook 1996.
117 See: Quran, 96:1.
118 Ṭabāṭabā'ī, V20, pp. 546-9.
119 See: Quran, 96:5.
120 Quran, 2:129.
121 Quran, 80:1-15.
122 Ramadan 2007, pp. 84-85.
123 Quran, 68:4.
124 See: Quran, 21:107, where prophet Mohammad is described by God as "mercy/ *raḥma* to the worlds".
125 Ibid., 33:21.
126 See: Quran, 37:36, 15:6 and 68:51.
127 See: Al-Sheha 2006, p. 46.
128 See: Aune, Guest, Law 2019, pp. 18-19.
129 See: Gilliat-Ray, Ali, Pattison 2013, p. 48.
130 See: Aune, Guest, Law 2019, pp. 11-12.
131 Quran, 68:1.
132 Quran, 96:1.
133 The Quran clarifies that there is no compulsion in religion. See: Quran, 2:256.
134 Khosrokhavar 2015, pp. 67-82.
135 Ryan 2015, p. 10.
136 For example, see: Quran, 97:4 and 7:37.
137 See: Evans 2015.
138 Khosrokhavar 2015, pp. 67-82.
139 For more information on John Dewey's ideas on reflective practice, see: Rodgers 2002.

140 See: Thompson, Pattison, Thompson 2008, p. 21.
141 For a discussion on Schön's distinction between "reflection-in-action" and "reflection-on-action" see: Thompson, Thompson 2008, p. 16.
142 See: Oliver 2006, pp. 123-7.
143 See: Nursi 2008, p. 757. Further discussion of these two terms will follow on in this chapter.
144 Quran, 10:24.
145 For more information on Theological Reflection, see: Thompson 2008.
146 See: Nakamura 1994, p. 32.
147 See: Quran, 22:46: *So, have they not travelled through the earth and have hearts by which to reason and ears by which to hear? For indeed, it is not eyes that are blinded, but blinded are the hearts which are within the breasts.*
148 For the different stages of the soul (*nafs*) see: Quran, 12:53, 75:2, and 89:27.
149 Quran, 91:7-10.
150 Ibid.
151 See discussion about the primordial covenant. Also, Quran, 27:14, which clarifies that the inner soul is capable of discerning between right and wrong.
152 For example, see: Quran, 2:54, 2:9, 2:48, 2:57, 4:97 and 65:1.
153 Quran, 41:53.
154 For example, see: Quran, 4:110, 4:111, 5:30, 17:15, and 9:118.
155 Nursi 1998, p. 23.
156 See Nakamura 1994.
157 See: Nursi 2007, pp. 23-24.
158 See: Quran, 2:31-2.
159 Ibid.
160 Nursi 2008, p. 558.
161 Ibid.
162 See: Quran, 2:44.
163 Nursi 2008, p. 466.
164 See: for example: Beck 1976 and Ellis 1970, 88-102.
165 Dweck 2015.
166 Leaman 2006, 30-33.
167 Ibid.
168 Quran, 3:191.
169 Quran, 4:82.
170 Quran, 50:16.
171 Vahide 2005, 266.
172 Nursi 1995, 315.
173 Ibid., 317.
174 Ibid.

175 Ibid.
176 Ibid.
177 Ibid.
178 See: Rayshahri 2000, pp. 218-19.
179 For example, see: Craft 2009 and Davis, Dunn, Davis, 2004.
180 Apart from Sophie Gilliat-Ray, Mansur Ali and Stephen Pattison's book, *Understanding Muslim Chaplaincy* there is very little literature on Muslim chaplaincy generally and Muslim chaplaincy in Higher Education in UK specifically.
181 Prophetic role is used in the sense of promoting spiritual care at organisational as well as individual levels, and challenging practices which obstruct human flourishing.
182 Schmalzbauer 2021.
183 Nursi 1994, pp. 271-272.
184 Saḥīḥ al-Bukhārī, 6039 (Book 78, Hadith 69).
185 Tirmidhi: Hadith 2489.
186 Quran, 46:13.
187 Quran, 2:216.

Bibliography

Adamson, P., *Al-Kindi: Great Medieval Thinkers* (Oxford: Oxford University Press, 2007).

Afnan, S. M., *Avicenna, His Life and Works* (London: George Allen & Unwin Ltd., 1958).

Asquith Jr., G. H., "Anton T. Boisen and the Study of 'Living Human Documents'", *Journal of Presbyterian Historical Society*, 60,3 (1982), pp. 244-265.

Al-Attas, S. M. N., *Prolegomena to the Metaphysics of Islam* (Kuala Lumpur: International Institute of Islamic Thought & Civilisation, 1955).

Atkinson, D. J. and Field, D. H. (eds.), *A New Dictionary of Christian Ethics and Pastoral Theology* (Leicester: Inter-Varsity Press, 1995).

Aune, K., Guest, M., and Law, J., *Chaplains on Campus: Understanding Chaplaincy in UK Universities* (Coventry, Canterbury, and Durham: Coventry University, Canterbury Christ Church University, and Durham University, 2019).

Ballard, P., "The Emergence of Pastoral and Practical Theology in Britain", in: Woodward, J. and Pattison, S. (eds.), *The Blackwell Reader in Pastoral and Practical Theology* (Malden, Oxford, and Carlton: Blackwell, 2000), pp. 59-67.

Beck, A. T., *Cognitive Therapy and the Emotional Disorders* (New York: International Universities Press, 1976).

Beheshti, S. M. H., *God in the Quran: A Metaphysical Study*, trans. by A. N. Baqirshahi (Tehran: International Publishing Company, 1973).

Campbell, A., "The Nature of Practical Theology", in: Woodward, J. and Pattison, S. (eds.), *The Blackwell Reader in Pastoral and Practical Theology* (Malden, Oxford, and Carlton: Blackwell, 2000), pp. 77-86.

Caperon, J., Todd, A., and Walters, J. (eds.), *A Christian Theology of Chaplaincy* (London and Philadelphia: Jessica Kingsley Publishers, 2017).

Cook, M., *Mohammad* (Oxford: Oxford University Press, 1996).

Cooper, W., *The Unity of William James's Thought* (Nashville: Vanderbilt University Press, 2002).

Craft, C. D. M., Weber, W. M., and Menke, D. J., "Campus Ministers in Public Higher Education: Facilitators of Student Development", *College Student Affairs Journal*, 28,1 (2009), pp. 61-80.

Davis, J. K., Dunn, M. S. and Davis, J. S., "In Their Own Words: Campus Ministers' Perceptions of Their Work and Their Worlds", *The College of Student Affairs Journal*, 23,2 (2004), pp. 173–184.

Dweck, C., "Carol Dweck Revisits the 'Growth Mindset'", *Education Week* (2015). <https://www.edweek.org/leadership/opinion-carol-dweck-revisits-the-growth-mindset/2015/09>

Ellis, A., *The Essence of Rational Psychotherapy: A Approach to Treatment* (New York: Institute for Rational Living, 1970).

Encyclopaedia Britannica, "Chaplain", accessed 22 June 2020. <https://www.britannica.com/topic/chaplain>

Evans, S., "NHS Pastoral Care Should Be A Non-discriminatory Service for All", *National Secular Society, Opinion*, (2015). <https://www.secularism.org.uk/opinion/2015/07/nhs-pastoral-care-should-be-a-non-discriminatory-service-for-all>

Al-Ghazālī, A. H., *Al-Ghazalī on Disciplining the Soul and on Breaking the Two Desires (The Revival of the Religious Sciences)* Books 22 and 23, trans. by A. H. Murad, (Cambridge: Islamic Texts Society, 1997).

Al-Ghazālī, A. H., *The Alchemy of Happiness* (NY: Routledge 2015).

Gianotti, T. J., *Al-Ghazzālī's Unspeakable Doctrine of the Soul: Unveiling the Esoteric Psychology and Eschatology of the Ihyā* (Leiden: Brill, 2001).

Gilliat-Ray, S., "Educating Ulama: Centres of Islamic Religious Training in Britain", *Islam and Christian-Muslim Relations*, 17,1 (2006), pp. 55–76.

Gilliat-Ray, S., Ali, M., and Pattison, S., *Understanding Muslim Chaplaincy* (London and New York: Routledge, 2013).

Glassé, C., *The New Encyclopedia of Islam: Revised Edition of the Concise Encyclopedia of Islam* (London: Stacey International, 2001).

Griffel, F., *Al-Ghazali's Philosophical Theology*, (Oxford: Oxford University Press, 2009).

Iqbal, M., *The Reconstruction of Religious Thought in Islam* (New Delhi: Kitab Bhavan, 2013).

Jāmī, N., *Yusuf and Zulaikha*, trans. by D. Pendlebury (Iran: Katchaloo, 2013).

Jayyusi-Lehn, G., "The Epistle of Ya'qūb ībn Isha'q al-Kīndī: On The Device for Dispelling Sorrows", *British Journal of Middle Eastern Studies*, 29,2 (2002), pp. 121-135.

Kathīr, I., *Stories of the Prophets* (UK: Create Space Independent Publishing Platform, 2014).

Khosrokhavar, F., "The Constrained Role of the Muslim Chaplain in French Prisons", *International Journal of Politics, Culture, and Society*, 28,1 (2015), pp. 67-82.

Kwofie, D. B., *The Relationship Between Pastoral Care and Shepherding* (Legon: Trinity Theological Seminary, 2022).

Leaman, O., "Al-Balkhi, Abu Zayd", in: *The Biographical Encyclopedia of Islamic Philosophy* (London: Bloomsbury Publishing, 2006).

Long, I. J. and Ansari, B., "Islamic Pastoral Care and the Development of Muslim Chaplaincy", *Journal of Muslim Mental Health*, 12,1 (2018).

Murata, S. and W. C. Chittick, *The Vision of Islam* (New York: Paragon House, 1994).

Nakamura, K., "Imām Ghazālī's Cosmology Reconsidered with Special Reference to the Concept of 'Jabarūt'", *Studia Islamica*, 80 (1994), pp. 29-46.

Nasafi, A., *Persian Metaphysics and Mysticism, Selected Treatises of 'Azīz Nasafī*, introd. and trans. by L. Ridgeon (London and New York: Routledge, 2012).

Newitt, M., *Being a Chaplain* (London: SPCK, 2011).

Nguyen, M., *Modern Muslim Theology: Engaging God and the World with Faith and Imagination* (London: Rowan & Littlefield, 2019).

Nursi, B. S., *Signs of Miraculousness*, trans. by Ş. Vahide (Istanbul: Sözler Publications, 2007).

Nursi, B. S., *The Flashes Collection*, trans. by Ş. Vahide (Istanbul: Sözler Neşriyat, 1995).

Nursi, B. S., *The Letters*, trans. by Ş. Vahide (Istanbul: Sözler Neşriyat, 1994).

Nursi, B. S., *The Rays Collection*, trans. by Ş. Vahide (Istanbul: Sözler Neşriyat, 1998).

Nursi, B. S., *The Words*, trans. by Ş. Vahide (Istanbul: Sözler Neşriyat, 2008).

Oliver, G., *Holy Bible, Human Bible: Questions Pastoral Practice Must Ask* (UK: Darton, Longman & Todd Ltd., 2006)

Pattison, S. and Woodward, J., "An Introduction to Pastoral and Practical Theology", in: Woodward, J. and Pattison, S. (eds.), *The Blackwell Reader in Pastoral and Practical Theology* (Malden, Oxford, and Carlton: Blackwell, 2000), p. 3.

Peters, R. and Bearman, P., *The Ashgate Research Companion to Islamic Law* (Farnham: Ashgate, 2014).

Quran, Chapters 2-10, 12-13, 15-17, 20-22, 24-28, 30, 33, 37, 41-42, 46, 50, 53, 57, 65-66, 68, 75, 80, 89, 91, 95-97, 103.

Quranic Arabic Corpus, on-line tool, accessed 11 August 2022. <https://corpus.quran.com/qurandictionary.jsp?q=slm>

Al-Qushayrī, A., *Laṭā'if al-Ishārāt (Subtle Allusions): Great Commentaries on the Holy Qur'ān*, trans. By K. Z. Sands (Amman and Louisville: Royal Aal al-Bayt Institute for Islamic Thought and Fons Vitae: 2017).

Ramadan, T., *In the Footsteps of the Prophet: Lessons from the Life of Muhammad*, (Oxford: Oxford University Press, 2007).

Rayshahri. M. (ed.), *Mawsu'at al-Imam Ali b. Abi Talib*, V1 (Bayrūt: Dar al-Hadith, 2000).

Rescorla, M., "The Computational Theory of Mind", *Stanford Encyclopedia of Philosophy* (2020) accessed 23 February 2023. <https://plato.stanford.edu/entries/computational-mind/>

Richardson, A. and Bowden, J., *A New Dictionary of Christian Theology* (London: SCM Press Ltd., 1983).

Rodgers, C., "Defining Reflection: Another Look at John Dewey and Reflective Thinking", *Teachers College Record*, 104,4 (2002), pp. 842-866.

Rosenbur, A., *The Atheist's Guide to Reality: Enjoying Life without Illusions* (London: W.W. Norton & Co., 2012).

Ryan, B., *A Very Modern Ministry: Chaplaincy in the UK* (London: Theos, 2015).

Ṣaḥīḥ al-Bukhārī 1829, 2262, 4777, 6039, 7138.

Schimmel, A., *Mystical Dimensions of Islam* (Chapel Hill: University of North Carolina Press, 2011).

Schmalzbauer, J., "Campus Prophets, Spiritual Guides, or Interfaith Traffic Directors? The Many Lives of College and University Chaplains", *Journal of College and Character*, 22,2 (2021), pp. 156-162.

Al-Sheha, A., *Muhammad the Messenger of Allah*, trans. by A. Murad (Rabwah: The Islamic Propagation Office, 2006).

Tabātabā'ī, M. H., *al-Mizān fī l-tafsīr al-Quran*, V1 and V20 (Beirut: Mu'assasatal-A'lamī lil-Maṭbū'āt, 1974).

Thompson, J., Pattison, S., and Thompson, R., *Theological Reflection* (London: SCM Press, 2008).

Thompson, S. and Thompson, N., *The Critically Reflective Practitioner* (Hampshire & New York: Palgrave Macmillan, 2008).

Tirmidhi: Hadith 2489.

Vahide, Ş., *Islam in Modern Turkey: An Intellectual Biography of Bediuzzaman Said Nursi* (Albany: State University of New York Press, 2005).

Part 2

Voices of

Muslim Women Chaplains in

Higher Education

Introduction

Part Two of this book is devoted to the voices of Muslim women chaplains in Higher Education in the United Kingdom. While most people tend to be familiar with the term 'imam', not many people know about the work of Muslim chaplains. Male chaplains tend to either be more acceptable or are deemed to have a higher rank, purely because their role tends not to be distinguished from the role of imams. The aim of Part Two of this book is, therefore, to make heard the voices of six Muslim women chaplains currently working in different universities in the United Kingdom, through chapters they themselves have written, detailing their roles in their host institutions. Three further women chaplains, whose time constraints prevented them from contributing chapters, agreed to take part in interviews. It is our fervent hope that the voices of the nine Muslim women chaplains showcased in this book will serve to raise awareness of the existence and significance of Muslim chaplaincy in general, and the crucial role played by Muslim women chaplains in particular.

1

Ameena Blake
University of Sheffield

What is a Chaplain?

In 2022, I began working in higher education in the University of Sheffield (TUOS) as a Muslim chaplain. I was elated. My father had been a professor in the university and it felt like I was coming home. At the same time, not really knowing what the role would bring, I felt slightly apprehensive. I had what I later grew to realise was a slightly stereotypical, presumptuous view of what chaplaincy was. I expected I'd be attending lots of one-to-one pastoral support meetings with students and staff, and organising and attending polite faith and/or interfaith events whilst drinking cups of tea and biting into slices of homemade Victoria sponge. I expected to be approached to advise others on Muslim matters, relying on my background in Islamic scholarship.

Previously, my professional life had felt distinctly separate from my community and pastoral work. I had been teaching English in secular secondary schools. Having completed an MA in Educational Leadership, I moved into a school leadership and consultancy role before taking an Islamic Studies MA and accepting a lecturing role at Markfield Institute of Higher Education, which is arguably an Islamic university. I had also been tending to the spiritual, pastoral needs of the Muslim community as a sideline for nearly three decades.

In most faith communities, there are those who dedicate themselves to the well-being of others, providing emotional and practical support from a faith perspective. Within Islam, the notion of a supportive and unified community is idealised as the *umma*, or community of believers, and is an integral part of Muslim life. It could be that my ideas of what to expect from my role stemmed from this, from the cultural connotations around the definition of chaplaincy, or even from my roots as someone who was brought up as a Christian in the

Anglican church, where the chaplain was an individual serving community pastoral needs. Caperon (Todd, Caperon, & Walters, 2017) aptly explains that in the twenty-first century, although there is currently a wide provision of chaplaincy, the role is not only ambiguous, but also seems not to have an agreed definition, and so although the idea of chaplaincy carries Christian pastoral connotations, within current chaplaincy there are many models and methods developing which may offer the role of chaplain great opportunities to be embedded through secular organisations, but which may simultaneously muddy the waters.

This chapter will map my own chaplaincy journey over a few months and chronicle how it has moved into areas of the university that are not directly chaplaincy related including EDI (equality, diversity and inclusion), which has raised a number of questions which need to be examined within the chaplaincy context. Firstly, there is the issue of whether and how chaplaincy can run effectively within a higher education sector that is avowedly secular; and secondly, there is the issue of how Muslim chaplaincy could adapt to change through strategic leadership.

Chaplaincy and Societal Change

It is important to consider the current position of chaplaincy alongside the issue of the position of the Muslim woman and where she sits within the chaplaincy context. It is also important to explore some factors that strengthen as well as threaten chaplaincy in times of societal and organisational change.

Although historically chaplaincy was an integral part of higher education (HE), Gilliat Ray explains that 'there has been a clear secularisation of higher education from the era when Christianity had a foundational place in the life of early universities' (Gilliat Ray, 2000). In its more recent history, it has been regarded as a stand-alone Christian-centric pastoral service that runs alongside university well-being services as opposed to being diffused through them. Chaplains are often approached where there is a specific faith-related question posed by an individual, or at times of grief and tragedy, to address spiritual needs; or in order to officiate at religious events such as memorial services.

In the current social climate, we see society becoming less inclined towards formal religiosity. Schuhmann (2018) explains that particularly in the West, we exist in a society that is not only pluralistic but also increasingly secular. Secular society is experiencing a reversal of the previously clear division between religion and state, albeit in a new form, with religion and spirituality slowly being de-privatised and returning to public life under the umbrella of EDI and identity.

Schmidt (Schmidt & Askeland, 2016) explores the process of change occurring in the public sector which is having a negative impact on church attendance. This, along with the changing landscape of the religious demographic, inevitably brings the identity and direction of chaplaincy into question.

Moreover, it is interesting to note that with a clear lack of organisational data regarding religious identity, the latest UK Office of National Statistics (ONS) census data is perhaps the best indicator that we have. It shows a thirteen per-cent decline in people identifying as Christian and a twelve per-cent increase in those identifying as non-religious between 2011 and 2021 (ONS, 2022). This does not necessarily indicate a decrease in belief or spirituality; rather, it suggests a change in religious identity, along with the acknowledgement that there is an increase in the number of people who recognise and embrace minority faiths – something which is very evident in the case of Islam (Cobb et al. 2015) And this translates directly to the demographic makeup of HE.

On the other hand, census data regarding religion and belief can be regarded as ambiguous. The ONS survey section on religious belief is not mandatory on participants and although many could presume the term 'non-religious' to mean atheist, it can also refer to a whole range of beliefs, or to those with no belief, from atheists or agnostics to those who are spiritual in some way or pagan, even, but not following a world religion. These sit in a group that identifies as non-religious in some way, and thus placing them in one homogenous section is at the very least unhelpful, be it in terms of data analysis or, indeed, in terms of serving these groups from a chaplaincy perspective. Nevertheless, the recognition that there is a need in organisations for a variety of chaplains and advisors remains.

A few studies have been conducted to look at the benefits of chaplaincy, in particular how it benefits spiritual well-being. Not only has it been shown to enhance well-being, but when used strategically, it has been shown to strengthen the link between individual and organisational values (Wolf & Durstmüller, 2022). Spirituality looks different for different people and chaplaincy could be argued to be a facilitator of spiritual connections through multifaith work as well as one-to-one support. The space created for Muslim chaplains over the past decade or so could be a direct result of the secular narrative giving way to more pluralistic narratives, together with an increase in demand for alternative spiritualities in the context of a less Christian-dominated multifaith provision. The result for chaplaincies is the realisation that there is a need for change, but together with uncertainty about where change should be or how it should look like.

Organisational Change and Chaplaincy

In HE, organisational change or, as it is often termed, restructure, is commonplace, and so when an organisation such as a university changes strategic direction, it can be a complex process. Lewin (2011) focuses on the concept of centralisation (the control that central leadership has) and decentralisation (the autonomy given to other areas of the organisation). If an organisation is too centralised, it risks becoming static and failing to move forward; if it is excessively decentralised, it risks becoming disorganised, with no clear path forward. With varying abilities and timelines for introducing and embedding change into different areas or departments, it is clear that achieving a good balance of change is challenging. Some departments, especially those used to more independent work practices, may resist change and wish to continue with the longstanding culture they are comfortable with. Chaplaincies often fall into this category as there tends to be low staff turnover and high autonomy of work practice. Resistance to change is also a psychological part of any change process, and when culture becomes static, as it has among many chaplaincy teams, resistance is often strong. Lewin (2011) explains that the reason for organisations to exist is to achieve overall strategic goals; this often overrides embedded culture in departments and makes balancing these concepts a tough task for lead chaplains.

As we have seen, a contributory factor to the static nature of chaplaincy is its bolt-on position within HE in relation to the main university. In the University of Sheffield this can be evidenced in a statement produced by the university senate in 2002. The document refers to chaplains as 'Individuals appointed by external bodies' (The University of Sheffield), reflecting the external nature of chaplaincy appointments at the time. For the following decade, not being employed directly by the university created a semi-separate identity and accountability for the chaplaincy, which was essentially an outside organisation, engaged and operating within the university. This negated any need for internal management and fostered a presumed independence. Although structures have changed in recent years because, 'sociocultural trends reflect changes in a society's attitudes, behaviours, and cultural values,' (May, 2010, P21) echoes of this system remain. An integrated chaplaincy offers scope for both wider and more integrated work and impact for chaplaincy teams. Sometimes this depends on internal factors, but it can depend on outside factors or influences such as the organisation that appoints and funds either the chaplaincy or individual chaplains within it. Although there are advantages to an autonomous system, as it allows for a neutral stance, there are also drawbacks, such as the potential for disruption of management requirements and objectives that are at odds with one another between the outside organisation and the university leadership. To resolve this, contractual agreements, clear hierarchical structures and clarity of decision-making processes are important.

At the University of Sheffield, there has been a shift within EDI from multi-faith within a secular structure towards the adoption of an inclusive identity-based practice. The chaplaincy has for many decades adopted a multifaith model of chaplaincy, consisting of a team of chaplains and advisors from different faiths to serve the HE community. They operate in the university but tend to retain significant autonomy. The team is managed by a lead or co-ordinating chaplain, currently an Anglican. The autonomous, almost bolt-on nature of chaplaincy is due historically to the secular presumption that faith or religious identity should remain private, yet the growing recognition in HE that identity, including faith and religion, are a key part of the individual, has been a driver of change. Policies, including the Equality Act of 2010 (UK GOV, 2010) are being examined in a bid to move towards greater accountability and transparency with regards to how EDI equality can be better embedded in the sector. The equality act mentions a number of 'protected characteristics.' (UK GOV, 2010) which include the right to religion or belief. These characteristics are a subsection of EDI; however, the question remains how to embed the rights of those with protected characteristics into organisational culture and change. Protected characteristics such as race or gender usually have some existing policy and procedure which can be built on. When this is the case, change can be easier to plan and embed since the organisation is better equipped to move forward within existing procedural structures. In the case of religion and belief, since decades of secularism have caused it to become pigeonholed and privatised, the result is that across HE, organisational confidence around religious literacy is minimal to the point of being taboo, and people often feel uncomfortable discussing their own and other people's religious beliefs, especially in a professional environment. As a result, even though there are usually significant numbers of religious or spiritual people in HE, there is a lack of existing infrastructure or expertise to facilitate a religiously inclusive working practice. An added complication is that most HE organisations do not collect baseline data to identify a religious demographic. These factors present a need for the building of new foundations of data, internal strategy, guidance and policy in order to embed protection of religion and belief within HE communities. One obvious key department in this process would be the chaplaincy department, but the question is: how can chaplaincies contribute; and do they currently have the structure and capacity to do so?

The model of chaplaincy and leadership adopted may be key to success here. Positive spiritual chaplaincy, a model that moves organically with and through the structures, is more suited to a secular organisation as it will be able to adapt according to organisation objectives and serve a wider range of people (Wolf & Durstmüller, 2022). Unlike the widely adopted Christian or multifaith structures, models such as this may be a more effective fit for HE when looking at chaplaincy as a service that is run through equality, diversity and inclusion (EDI).

A further challenge to chaplaincy is leadership style, which, within chaplaincy, has remained relatively static, and consequently has not necessarily developed in line with wider university leadership styles. There is also the question of management, and who manages and salaries chaplains, since many Christian chaplains are still recruited and paid by the church. Moreover, leadership has often been white and male-dominated, conducted in a style that centres an individual, shepherd-like leader tending to the religious and pastoral needs of the HE community, without necessarily considering secular issues. Training of religious leaders in most organised religions remains an in-house affair, with specific theologically based approaches being adopted which do not change much over time. For instance, to become ordained, the Anglican clergy member will need to complete education and training through long established church processes. Similarly, for Muslims, most imams will qualify by attending a seminary course and attaining an *ijāza* (permission) to teach certain Islamic disciplines or schools of law and legal theory that they have studied. Although pastoral, one-to-one work is a part of theological training, bespoke training in non-religious-based leadership models are not usually included. Religious communities do not generally see significant cultural change over time and, as such, there has been no need for leadership styles to change. As a result, there has been no move towards strategic planning or development of modern leadership skills in chaplaincy teams. An embedded culture of "this is the way we have always done things" is often seen, no doubt because it makes the culture feel more stable, and so, 'Many organisations have policies and procedures that were established decades ago and that may or may not have relevance to today's business reality.' (Cran; 2015, p. 5)

In the case of religious leadership, it could be argued that these models have been present not just for decades but for centuries. This can mean that when HE makes a strategic shift such as with EDI, chaplaincy can be left behind, placing it in a potentially difficult position, thus presenting a need for training and change management.

Regarding chaplaincy team culture, departmental, bubble-like micro-cultures form according to the makeup of individual teams. Factors can include personality, job rank, pay grade or even ethnicity, language or age, or religion. Most people have experienced 'them and us' type attitudes in teams. Formation of a group culture is inevitable and can enhance team performance, but it can also become destructive if it is not directed by an effective leadership. In some cases, if one team member is perceived as being different from the rest of the team, isolation or bullying can occur. In chaplaincy teams, cases have been seen of Muslim chaplains feeling isolated by Chrisitan colleagues, while female chaplains see their opinions being ignored or overruled by male chaplains. This is less likely when leadership hierarchy and chaplaincy departments are embedded in non-chaplaincy departments such as student services, with a non-chaplain manager as well as a lead chaplain who work together to manage the lead chaplain and chaplaincy team.

Muslim Women in Chaplaincy

The work of women – Muslim women in particular – is relatively recent in the changing dynamics and make-up of chaplaincy teams. Religious female leadership in modern times has been a contentious issue with many, including some Christian denominations, who remain divided around the question of female religious leaders. Likewise, debates remain within Muslim scholarship around what female leadership looks like. Contrary to stereotypes and unlike many other world faiths, women have been at the core of Islamic society since the revelation of the Qur'an nearly fifteen hundred years ago. Participation of women and their good treatment was emphasised by the Prophet Muhammad (PBWH) and within Quranic verses.

Although there is a majority scholarly consensus on some minor matters relating to women, such as the impermissibility of females leading males in prayer (i.e. taking the role of imam), this has been politicised and hyperbolised in some societies in an attempt to present Islam as oppressive of women. Avenues of female Muslim leadership are open and, as such, the criterion for leadership in Islam should not be gender but skill. Since the early Muslim generations, leadership positions have included numerous women as judges, politicians and scholars, with particularly famous examples such as the granddaughter of the Prophet Muhammad (PBWH), Nafisa bint al-Hasan, who was a great scholar of Islam. In modern times we see women managing mosques and Islamic centres, as well as participating in political life and teaching students of both sexes. As a result, for a Muslim female to act as chaplain is undoubtedly permissible from a jurisprudential perspective and women have unique qualities that they can bring to a pastoral role such as this.

Within most religions, there are varying interpretations of the foundational texts and Islam is no different. Challenges for Muslim women moving into leadership stem from two main areas. Firstly, some scholarly interpretations which can feel contrary to what is seen in the Qur'an and the understanding of early Muslim generations suggest a historical shift in exegesis. Secondly, cultural values can be problematic. For example, gender mixing for Muslims looks different in different countries and cultures, and its history differs along similar lines. In culturally conservative countries such as Saudi Arabia or Afghanistan, women may rarely be seen in public owing to strict cultural precepts and a particularly conservative interpretation of text, whereas in Malaysia women are seen in public as well as in positions of leadership. When moving to countries such as the UK to live or study, Muslims will often bring these values with them and so a wide variety of Islamic and cultural practices can be seen.

As a chaplain, it is important to respect differences, remain non-judgmental and understand that people hold different opinions, stereotypes and sets of values from both within and outside Islam.

Accordingly, female chaplains can face challenges to their roles that male chaplains do not face. Muslim women, including myself, often get asked about why we cover.

When I first joined the chaplaincy team, a Christian female chaplain approached me specifically to ask why I had been oppressed into wearing a hijab by the Muslim faith and the males within it. I responded by asking her if she considered nuns who also adopt a form of hijab in Christianity as being oppressed by Christian males or the Christian faith. She of course answered in the negative, understanding immediately the inappropriate nature of her question. It is important to recognise that questions are often loaded with preconceptions and presumptions that the Muslim woman is uneducated, unable to choose for herself and is wearing hijab to submit to a barbaric, oppressive, male-dominated society. Stereotypes like these are so embedded in the implicit biases of Western society on account of centuries of media bias that they can be difficult to get past for all involved. Questions are, in my experience, almost always asked innocently and as such should be answered with tact and sensitivity. On a personal level, though, it can often feel as though the Muslim female narrative has been stolen from Muslim women and politicised. Moreover, Muslim women can face cultural biases from within Muslim communities themselves. There are those who dislike women working, promoting strict segregation, and there are those who abhor even the idea of a woman engaging in public speaking. Then there are those secular Muslims who are opposed to women covering, sometimes to the point of actively discouraging it. As a result, the female chaplain has the added responsibility to be a beacon of Islamic women's values to Muslim and non-Muslim communities alike. Her leadership and voice can facilitate the vocality of many women whose narratives and wishes have been drowned. The key is to be able to verbalise this and bring about gentle change and re-education where necessary in an intelligent, respectful and inclusive way. Nevertheless, cultural resistance and the stereotypification of Muslim women remain as constants, which create a barrier to their achieving leadership positions in chaplaincy.

Leading Chaplaincy and Volunteers

The University of Sheffield has shifted towards a more strategic model of operating which has developed in an organic way. Incoming leaders with specifically related skills have replaced outgoing ones, thus bringing about change. Change has also meant realignment of management structures. Chaplaincy has not been brought along in this sense as it remains fairly autonomous, and yet it needs to be placed within university structures. Chaplaincy in the university sits in student services (SSS) with a manager from SSS who is tasked to oversee the chaplaincy work. The core team is made up of four salaried posts; one full-time salaried Anglican chaplain, who is also the coordinating chaplain; myself as part time Muslim chaplain; a full-time business administrator (non-religious); and an Anglican support worker. In addition to the salaried core team, the chaplaincy has a number of voluntary chaplains and advisors representing nine other faiths and beliefs. The majority of these are engaged in advisory roles; owing to commitments, they are not usually actively involved in the running of the chaplaincy. Studies show that volunteer organizational commitment can be inferred from an individual's degree of association with an organisation.' (Bang et al. 2013) but achieving volunteer commitment in the voluntary sector is notoriously difficult and chaplaincy relies heavily on volunteer teams. Owing to the nature of the role, relying on volunteers at leadership level creates a level of instability; yet they are needed to support the work since chaplaincy is almost always under-resourced financially and human resource-wise. As a result, although volunteers are essential, they cannot – and I would argue should not – be relied upon at the strategic planning level as they are not able to provide the long-term stability needed. Research suggests that volunteers need both emotional attachment as well as clear objectives and a stable organisational structure if they are to remain committed (Bang et al. 2013). This means that it is important for core chaplaincy teams to offer a structure providing shared strategic direction, emotional motivation and clear, achievable goals, as well as the development tools, training and flexibility that volunteers need to complete their work.

Chaplaincy team success requires effective leadership and management within the top layers of the chaplaincy team for volunteer engagement. If we place this in the context of the capacity of chaplaincy to become a central cog in strategizing and embedding EDI across the organisation, it is evident that either the core team needs to be expanded in terms of human resources and training, or, alternatively, it needs to act as facilitator and trainer for others. In a study conducted by Kim, it was found that when chaplaincy operates in large organisations, there are 'many constraints that need to be addressed' (Kim et al., 2020). He found that regardless of challenges, when managing chaplains also worked across other departments, they identified 'collaboration and team leadership' as key areas that led to success, regardless of departmental 'differing goals and competing priorities.' (Kim et al., 2020) These chaplains had been developed to manage across different departments, receiving training to enable them to complete the role, which had the added effect of changing the nature of their leadership in chaplaincy. This makes embedding chaplaincy across the organisation easier, although it is important to note that building strategy on paper takes far less time than organisational change. Nevertheless, 'organisations cannot afford to "stand still", and thus the "no change" approach is not an option' (Marshall, 2019).

As studies show that it is possible to integrate chaplaincy into other departments with the correct input, this is the piece of work I initiated in my role as Muslim chaplain.

The fact that the University of Sheffield chaplaincy is funded by the university makes it accountable to a non-faith management structure, presenting less opportunity for outside faith-based organisational biases to intrude since organisations do not have the same level of financial influence as in the past. Nevertheless, most chaplains are linked in some way to a faith-based organisation, and this can at times present complications with relation to governance. Volunteer Anglican chaplains within the Sheffield system, for example, are appointed and must be endorsed by an Anglican committee, which is an echo of the aforementioned historical church funded/university-based model. Similarly, the Muslim chaplain is accountable to a steering group from the local community which was formed two decades ago as a body initially advocating the appointment of a Muslim chaplain within the university and subsequently ensuring that the role remained in place. Neither role is currently funded by either group; one is a voluntary role and the other is funded and managed by the University of Sheffield. Moreover, both groups have individuals who are not part of the university structure or chaplaincy.

This is important when building links with outside religious communities but needs to be managed carefully so that chaplains are not faced with sets of expectations and objectives from external stakeholder organisations that conflict with internal objectives and strategies. If such a situation is allowed to develop, it could threaten the teamwork of chaplains as well as creating negative microcultures, for instance a Muslim club or a Catholic club. As chaplains are loyal to their faith, questions regarding bias and neutrality could be present and therefore it is preferable for organisations to assess stakeholder positions when looking at their multifaith chaplaincy team structure so that this can be avoided from the outset.

Muslim Chaplaincy in the University of Sheffield

Muslim chaplains are a relatively new addition to chaplaincy, a fact which can be viewed through different lenses, and as 'the role of a Muslim chaplain in higher education (HE) is not clearly defined due to its recent history and the lack of an infrastructure' (Rajput, 2016), it can be seen as either a weakness or an opportunity in terms of chaplaincy development. Muslim chaplaincy is also vulnerable owing to a lack of representation, the absence of training and a dearth of funded roles. And yet there is a growing Muslim need for chaplaincy in the HE sectors. Consequently, Muslim chaplains are often expected to work in a voluntary capacity, which makes it difficult to offer a stable service. I have been contacted on numerous occasions by organisations searching for a chaplain to support Muslims in crisis. Often the chaplain arrives too late, or the organisation is unable to find one and an urgent need either goes unattended or is dealt with by a non-Muslim chaplain who lacks the relevant knowledge and experience to be able to support Muslims.

One possible factor behind the dearth of Muslim chaplain positions could be societal negativity towards Islam and Muslims, which strays into organisations in the form of implicit bias and islamophobia. There is significant demand to have provision of religious and spiritual support for Muslims which, if ignored, could be seen as negligence. This includes provision of prayer spaces, halal food and access to advice, support and guidance. Some HE organisations have embraced this and have employed Muslim chaplains to serve their communities; others have failed; relying instead on existing Christian teams to serve Muslim needs without the requisite tools to do so. From a strategic development and EDI perspective, this presents a problem in organisations that have a large Muslim demographic without a paid – and thus stable – Muslim chaplain in the team to lead in this area.

The Muslim Chaplain, Islam and Chaplaincy Practice

The external expressions of Islam in the form of ritualised practice are specific in nature, for rite and ritual permeate Muslim life at all levels. Prayers run across the working day and there is the obligatory nature of the Friday prayer which often clashes with timetable and working hours. Muslim modest dress in the form of the obligatory hijab, loose clothing and, in some cases, the niqab, is worn by many Muslim women and can become a challenge in areas such as dentistry, where uniform and certain hygiene standards are required. There is a demand for the provision of halal food and Muslim-compatible accommodation within the HE sectors. Enquiries are made regularly by departments and students concerning these areas and others, such as sharia-compliant student finance and pensions for staff. In addition, staff meetings and pastoral one-to-one sessions are regular and take up a large chunk of working hours.

One-to-one support offered by the Muslim chaplain is unique. It must offer a safe space away from complications such as family, friends and the mosque. Muslims are just beginning to understand the nature of chaplaincy and what it entails, yet there is still a perception that chaplaincy is a Christian phenomenon, together with echoes of a lack of trust in organisational support systems. This could stem from the heavy governmental monitoring of Muslim communities adopted post 9:11 through strategies such as Prevent, which alienated many Muslim communities. It also placed organisations such as universities and schools in the position of being both a support system and a monitoring system with regard to Muslims simultaneously; as a result, mistrust was fostered and continues to exist to some extent. And the chaplaincy is often seen as part of the institution. Building good relationships with students and staff, as well as with Islamic societies, can help to alleviate this lingering sense of mistrust. Transparency is paramount, as is the willingness to provide others with information regarding the purpose of chaplaincy. With the implementation of these aims in mind and taking into consideration the fact that Muslim chaplains often sit within local communities as well as in their universities, progress can be made towards bridging the trust gap. Over time, the number of Muslims accessing the one-to-one sessions has increased and overtaken other faith groups with, on average, five-one to-one sessions for Muslims taking place each week in the University of Sheffield.

As a female chaplain, I was initially concerned that male Muslims might require a male chaplain to speak to. To this end, I ensured that my male counterpart chaplains and advisors were available. However it became clear that male Muslims seemed to feel comfortable speaking to a female chaplain.

I regularly speak to both male and female students regarding a whole range of topics, some of them very sensitive. Listening skills and the ability to remain neutral and non-judgmental are essential tools of the chaplain since many of the problems discussed concern the struggle that Muslims have to stay away from matters that are considered sinful in Islam. Providing one-to-one services is just one of the duties of the chaplain and I found the basic infrastructure in place for Muslims in the University of Sheffield to be good. There are eight prayer spaces on the main campus, a few food outlets with halal provision and an active Islamic student society, as well as bi-annual cultural awareness sessions for staff. This was built up over the previous decade by my colleague, mentor and predecessor, Muslim chaplain Imam Qari Mohammed Ismail, and it provided me with an excellent foundation on which to build through leadership and strategy construction.

Vision and Strategy for Muslim Chaplaincy

My vision for Muslim chaplaincy is for it to run through the University of Sheffield both directly and indirectly in different ways. But strategy, vision and time are needed for this to happen. Being Muslim often fits into different boxes of protected characteristics which regularly include religion and belief and race, which means the need for effective services is increased owing to Muslims being targeted for racial or religiously motivated hate crime, since the majority of Muslims are from racial minorities. Islamophobic hate crimes are often recorded by reporting agencies as racially rather than religiously motivated since there is a lack of understanding of the difference between the two, and often even victims are unclear of the perpetrator's motive. This presents a need for the Muslim chaplaincy to straddle several areas of EDI strategically. My initial goal was to observe and informally speak to people from different areas, including staff and students, regarding their experiences.

Following the period of observation, I came up with two main points:

- Muslim chaplaincy should have a significant part to play in the religion and belief strategy.
- Strategy should be built to support staff and students across the university and also to help the university to enable it to offer Muslims the best possible experience in their lives on campus.

Each area requires formulation into actions, so I created a Muslim chaplaincy strategic plan – one which could also feed into the religion and belief plan as well as into the chaplaincy plan. When planning, statistics and data are important, particularly if planning is to be presented at leadership level as a business case or for funding purposes. Although there is no comprehensive data, it is estimated that the University of Sheffield Muslim demographic is around fifteen percent, distributed across different areas.

Information Gathering Involved Looking at Three Areas

Resources (Financial and Human)

In my case there was myself and the rest of the core team, as well as a steering group for the Muslim chaplaincy. Steering group members are all working full-time or are not present except for attending meetings and large events in chaplaincy. They do not provide much support for the day-to-day running so although they are a potential human resource, they are not current. Financial resources consist of two areas: a shared pot of university supplied budget; and a pot of ring-fenced funds raised by the steering group which has barely been used over previous years.

Performance

Initial stages of strategic planning involve organisations looking at themselves internally to assess what the current position is. Performance is always a powerful indicator of how an organisation is performing, particularly when organisations are examined by external bodies (Reuss & Burkhart, 1993). In my case it was difficult on account of several factors. Firstly, although regular Muslim chaplaincy reports had been produced in the past which gave a good overview of activities, I was putting together the first strategic plan for the Muslim chaplaincy, and thus I needed qualitative data which was not available. Owing to the sensitive work done by chaplaincy and its pastoral remit, gathering performance data could be viewed as too invasive and clinical.

In Muslim chaplaincy, for example, one-to-one meetings could be measured quantitatively, but data on how many individuals use the prayer spaces on campus each day would be more difficult to collect and would impact on the experience of the worshippers. In a large structure there is definitely a need to measure and demonstrate performance, as teams should be able to demonstrate impact. Nevertheless, how it is measured in chaplaincy needs to be carefully considered to retain a safe space. In this case, the action is to look at reports as well as setting up a sensitive way to collect data to measure future impact.

What Services are Being Provided and How

Services have been developed by the Muslim chaplaincy over the past decade and this is easier to measure: eight prayer spaces across the campus; some provision of halal food; Islamic awareness training twice a year for staff who wish to attend; availability of one-to-one sessions; consultation services; availability of chaplain for grief and/or bereavement sessions; and participation in multifaith activities.

Having a Chaplaincy Vision, Objectives and Considering KPIs

At the point when an overview is as clear as possible, a vision and objectives can be created. The vision and mission for the Muslim chaplaincy is:

> To build a motivated team of chaplains, advisors and volunteers who provide excellent pastoral, consultative services and support to Muslims and non-Muslims across the university community, working for long term positive impact.

Having a long-term vision and mission is an important part of teams and it should act like a foundation for work. It enables team members to visualise the long-term goals together in a simple way, whilst providing context to the work along the way that may otherwise lack contextualisation. Without this, and without returning to the vision regularly, direction can inadvertently change, leading to demotivation and confusion, especially in our case where volunteers are central to the work. There is the added benefit of vision and mission as it 'attracts talented people' (May, 2010) and on a macro level, 'Vision provides the long-term perspective and your reason for being' (May, 2010). For smaller teams working within a larger organisation such as chaplaincy in HE, vision should be compatible with the wider organisational vision or mission statement to avoid contradiction; conversely, the team should be given a clear and transparent idea of where their work fits into the larger organisational vision. As chaplaincy is work that straddles different areas, the vision should help keep it stable and focused in line with the objectives. For the purpose of the University of Sheffield, I combine the vision and mission statement together as the work is stable, unlike other organisations that may have a separate mission statement which changes over time as their speciality changes.

The next stage is to form objectives that will feed into action plans. This is where consideration of the aforementioned findings in the areas of resources, performance and services help to map out how these areas can be developed to build objectives.

Current Resources

Current Resource	Opportunity to build
Muslim Chaplain working 17.5 hours per week – time and capacity limitations.	Muslim chaplain to act as facilitator to build a larger team from other resources across the university, including student ambassadors and Muslim staff.
Muslim chaplaincy steering group – largely inactive except at meetings	Share vision and mission to engage the steering group as well as agree their engagement expectation to support.
Business admin and support worker working with chaplains	Share vision and mission and ensure that their time resource is being utilised efficiently.
Finances. There is a shared pot of funding for chaplaincy activities as well as some existing funds ringfenced for the Muslim chaplaincy.	Funding can be applied for from within and outside the university.

Performance

Current	Opportunity
Comprehensive reports from the past several years.	Use the reports to summarise historical qualitative impact and activity
Rough guesstimates on how many people use prayer spaces and attend events.	Form a system that can anonymously collect data on event attendance and prayer space use.
Emails and appointment records.	Look at email streams over the past six months to measure the number of one-to-one meeting requests.
Speaking to people: students, USIC, steering group members.	Develop a survey system that can collect performance data using qualitative and quantitative methods.
Listening project data is available from 2021.	Use listening project data to feed into new systems as a foundation of data analysis.

Building an effective and dedicated team must be one of the key objectives. Although elaborate strategic action plans look impressive, especially when showing managers, the plans and the objectives that lead into them must be realistic and smart. Resources, be they human, time or financial, all have limitations and need to be developed over time. Development should also be effected with consideration for balance and cohesion across resources. For example, there is little point having a motivated team of twenty along with a great plan if there is not enough money to finance the work. When funds are scarce, it has a domino effect on human resources and, by extension, on the capacity of the chaplaincy work. Realistic goals enable the team to remain focused and motivated as well as feeling fulfilled.

The method of collecting performance data needs to be developed so it is in line with wider university structures which include having KPIs (key performance indicators) to measure longer term impact. Performance indicators should be not only linked with the strategy and vision but shared with the whole team. This ensures that there is a shared understanding of where the team is going and what its goals are, and also that the team members feel included. (Parmenter, 2010). For a Muslim chaplaincy which is at a disjointed stage, having shared KPIs could engage the team. To be really effective, for our purpose the KPI should cover different areas.

KPI Table for the Muslim Chaplaincy

KPI	Detail
Staff and team	1. Volunteer numbers and retention as well as staff and team satisfaction including salaried staff and others in the chaplaincy team.
Finances	How are finances utilised and have we raised funds for activities in the next period?
User statistics	Numbers using services and if they increase or decrease. This will also include looking at marketing of the Muslim chaplaincy and considering whether we are attracting the service users we want to attract.
User satisfaction KPI	2. Discerning what service users feel about the services and measuring whether their experience is improving over time.

As the current system is largely not measured, KPIs will be set using the data available for one-to-one meetings and guesstimates. New data can then be analysed towards the end of the initial semester to create a new foundation of data which will be continued. The KPI cycles will be in December and June. The first set of data will form a foundation on account of the lack of existing data and incorporation of a new system; once an academic year has passed, progress will be seen more clearly and data will be accurate.

Services

Services sit at the centre of a chaplaincy and although we do not often consider them in business terms, the principles are similar. As in business, chaplaincy markets a product to consumers – in this case the university community. The table below gives the current services offered and the relevant opportunities.

Current	Opportunity
Eight prayer spaces across the campus	Market prayer spaces and look at providing further spaces if needed
Some provision of halal food	Use survey data, networking and student voice to build better provision of halal food.
Optional Islamic awareness training twice a year for staff	Use the religion and belief strategy to create better awareness and literacy of Islam and Muslim needs on campus.
One-to-one sessions	Create a more effective marketing and comms network to build awareness of the one-to-one services.
Multifaith activities	Nurture working relationships with student societies and outside religious groups to ensure that better inter- and intra-faith activities are built.
Consultation services	Build a pilot with the medical school in line with the religion and belief strategy to disseminate services for Muslim staff and students.

Understanding the relationship between resources, performance and services is important to visualise when considering how Muslim chaplaincy can be built, as well as thinking about where it is positioned within the university structures in terms of work.

Adopting shared working documents plays an integral part of any strategic plan. In the case of the Muslim chaplaincy, the working document can become complicated as it must straddle several different areas of the university as well as sit comfortably in the wider chaplaincy. Moreover, it must demonstrate strategic links to other relevant plans and actions such as the religion and belief strategy, chiefly in order to avoid working against or duplicating other areas of relevant work. It helps that the chaplaincy team is already a part of other areas but in such a large organisation it is inevitable that there will be some duplication of work; a contingency for this can easily be built into the action plan in the form of conversations that happen as and when needed whenever duplicated work becomes apparent.

As the full action plan is too comprehensive for this chapter, only two examples of the process will be outlined: one of a pilot scheme taking place between the Muslim Chaplaincy and Medical Faculty; and the other, an action taken for islamophobia awareness month in November, 2022.

The Medicine and Dentistry Faculty Pilot

This faculty has a high number of Muslim staff and students. The faculty director is keen to ensure that EDI is being embedded in the school so students and staff get good services. I had developed an action plan based on the information I had, along with looking at objectives of the religion and belief strategy, in order to, 'create an environment to maximise access, experience and learning for students for whom religion, belief and no belief is an important aspect of their identity.' (The University of Sheffield, 2022) The benefit of having a pilot is that since data are limited and the strategy is new, the pilot will enable data collection, planning and actions in a smaller arena as the Muslim chaplaincy team is in development stages. It is thus an achievable goal.

The action plan example is based on one action area. The medical school is attached to the hospital which houses Muslim prayer spaces and a further prayer space in the chapel. The hospital is large and students struggle to get to the space and back during lecture breaks and laboratory time, thus making it difficult. Some students were praying in available lecture rooms or other spaces. When listening to the opinions leads to strategic planning and change, it can have a wide impact. There is a clear importance for effective action plans, explaining that the format of action plans can differ but should include whichever columns may be needed to ensure that the plan fits with the objective and method of working. (May, 2010)

- EDI Impact: Students feel more included and are able to attend lectures without the embarrassment of coming in late.

- Religion and Belief Strategy Impact: Strands of the strategy are being achieved through Muslim chaplaincy.
- Business Impact: Whether by word of mouth or through good marketing, having good facilities can often determine which university students choose.

One Part of the Action

Action	Links to	Timeline/ who?	Notes
Conduct a survey	Religion and belief strategy. EDI, Chaplaincy.	Three months. Chaplain/ Comms team/ Islamic Society	Survey will be across Muslims in the faculty. Data gathered will measure need and satisfaction.
Analyse Survey Results and form action plan	Religion and belief strategy. EDI, Chaplaincy.	Two months Chaplain/ faculty director	Analyse data results using qualitative and quantitative methods. Form an action plan. Feed back into the religion and belief strategy.
Provide larger prayer spaces within the faculty to support students and staff on this site	Religion and belief strategy. EDI, Chaplaincy.	One year Facilities team/ Faculty director/ Muslim chaplain consultant	Demand is significant in this area with current facilities small and involving a long walk which affects morale and lecture/ work times
Measure impact with follow-up survey and use of facility data.	Faculty/ Religion and belief strategy.	Three months. Chaplain/ Comms team/ Islamic Society	The exact same survey is used along with data showing how many students are using the improved facilities. This data then feeds into the religion and belief impact data

Once the action and evaluation cycle has been completed and the impact measured, to complete the process, evaluate how things have gone and use this to adjust the plan where needed. Action plans with this regard will remain fairly generic and can be adjusted where needed depending on which area of the university they are piloting.

The Future of Muslim Chaplaincy in Higher Education

Statistics suggest that the number of Muslims in HE is increasing. A report by the Aziz Foundation into the religious make-up of UK students in HE found that between 2012 and 2016, 2.2% of students identified as Muslim and although they point out that the data are not completely accurate, they discovered that more than 50% of them are Muslim females. (Aziz Foundation et al., 2018) These statistics, when put in the context of the rising Muslim population seen in the census data 2021, suggests that Muslim chaplaincy is a field that has future demand. The question of whether Muslim chaplaincy is sustainable is up to us.

It has been shown in this chapter that HE is moving towards an inclusive model of working and one of the key objectives is the inclusion of people with a religion and belief identity. Muslims are arguably the largest faith group who have faith specific needs, and as such, development of excellent Muslim chaplaincy provision is essential. For years those needs have been not just ignored but often avoided. The fact that chaplaincy has remained Christian dominated, culturally static and has failed to adopt progressive leadership models has been a significant barrier to progress in the field of chaplaincy in EDI. There is the added barrier for Muslims chaplains – but for Muslim women chaplains in particular – of stereotyping and glass ceilings, as well as Islamophobic and cultural bias. Nevertheless, I have found that by combining planning skills with pastoral know how and taking the lead in facilitating a culture of religious inclusive practice and literacy, there exists significant opportunity for Muslim chaplains to secure future faith provision for generations of Muslim staff and students to come.

But a word of warning: As with all large organisations, the focus on inclusion and protected characteristics will, at some point, move out of the spotlight to another priority, with the result that chaplaincy may get left behind if it fails to develop.

Glossary

EDI – Equality, diversity and inclusion
HE – Higher education
KPI – Key performance indicators
Ummah – Unified community (Muslim)

2

Syeda Midhat Batool
Loughborough University

My Journey as a Female Muslim Chaplain in Higher Education

> *A chaplain is a faith-based individual who provides spiritual care and support in secular environments such as prisons, hospitals, universities, and the armed forces. The word 'Chaplain' itself comes from the Latin word for a cloak, and part of the metaphor of chaplaincy is the imagery of "cloaking" someone in the care and support they need to work through the various challenges they may be going through.*[1]

Although the words 'chaplaincy', 'chaplain' and 'service' are Christian terms, the concept is deeply ingrained in the essence of the Islamic ethos of care and service to humanity, for service to the Creator lies in service to the creation.

> *We know from our tradition that our beloved Messenger served many different roles in his life. He was a teacher, an advisor, a caregiver, and a shepherd to his people. This is essentially what the role of chaplaincy is about. The Chaplain may serve as an educator, a friend, and a mentor, but throughout it all, he is a constant and regular source of spiritual upliftment and nourishment for those they serve.*[2]

In the foreword of Sophie Gilliat Ray's book *Understanding Muslim Chaplaincy*, Dr Siddique mentions the subtle connection between the Christian term 'service' and the Islamic understanding of the term *khidma*.[3]

There is also an implicit theology in the Islamic tradition that supports and encourages what might be called 'pastoral care'.

> *Though, pastoral care and pastoral roles are central to Christian Ministry, the Islamic aspect of pastoral care lies in 'helping people individually and corporately to grow and to flourish, and to resist and overcome diminishment and debilitation as they try to love God and humanity.*"[4]

In the light of the above definitions, a deeper connection between the practices of our faith and the institution of chaplaincy can be seen. This may even suggest that practicing Muslims are chaplains at heart and by default owing to their basic inclinations towards helping, supporting and uplifting those in need. For these are traits ingrained in the very fibre of our Islamic faith. Yet while the above-mentioned qualities constitute the core requirements for performing the duties of a Muslim chaplain, this in no way undermines the need for professional qualifications and training for this role.

Undoubtedly, the presence of a Muslim chaplain in HE is essential. In his report entitled *Islam in the Universities of England*, Dr Siddique has stated the outcomes of student surveys highlighting the care needs of Muslim students.

> *Having a Muslim chaplain/advisor was seen as important for all universities, regardless of the size of the Muslim population, because of the specific needs of Muslims and the discrimination that Muslim young people and students encounter.*[5]

Although the Arabic word 'imam' is at times assumed to be a synonym for the word 'chaplain' in English, this is not the case. The iman in Islam is always a male member of the congregation whose main duties are to lead the five daily prayers in the mosque; to deliver the Friday sermon; and to provide religious/juristic guidance to members of the community. A chaplain, on the other hand, can be a female, and while leading the prayers is not her responsibility, the facilitation of this process most certainly is.

I have been serving as a female Muslim chaplain at Loughborough for the past twelve years, and our chaplaincy team, together with whole institution of chaplaincy in the university, has evolved to a great extent in the last decade. Initially I was the only Muslim chaplain, with no male counterparts until a male Muslim chaplain was taken on five years after I began my job. Today, we are a sizeable group of multifaith chaplains who work well on their own in their respective faith groups, yet also work together as a team in our collaborative chaplaincy events.

In this chapter, I will discuss the tradition of chaplaincy in Islam, its various dimensions, and the varied roles and responsibilities of a Muslim chaplain. I will discuss the different attributes and areas of expertise required of a Muslim chaplain, including my own experiences and shortcomings in all these areas. I will expound on my role within my chaplaincy team at the university; my recollections and insights regarding my position as a female chaplain; the events that led me from pedagogy to chaplaincy; my learning journey; the challenges and rewards, the disappointments and the inspirations; and the ultimate motivation that has kept me going through the past twelve years as a voluntary, part-time chaplain, without any salary or monetary reward. I will also discuss how the role of a female Muslim chaplain is different from that of a male Muslim chaplain, and how both roles are perceived within the university community and the wider Muslim community.

In short, I will try to relive my journey as a female Muslim chaplain as concisely and precisely as I am able.

The Roles and Responsibilities of a Muslim Chaplain

> *I do love what I do, I love the responsibilities that I have, the role that I play, the awareness that I bring, the guidance that I give, the care that I provide, the shoulder, the ear that I give.*[6]

These words of a Muslim chaplain resonate with my own feelings. To me, chaplaincy is an extension of the Prophetic tradition of selflessness and mercy towards humanity. A common perception about the role of a Muslim chaplain is that it is basically all about ensuring the provision of halal food and prayer facilities, or providing pastoral care for Muslims on campus. These undoubtedly are some of the responsibilities a Muslim chaplain must shoulder, but the chaplain's role is far more complex and comprehensive than common perception suggests. Although there is theoretically no limit to the various roles and responsibilities a Muslim chaplain may shoulder, the nature of Muslim chaplaincy varies from institution to institution. Nevertheless, these roles pertain to the four broad areas of chaplaincy mentioned in the Siddique Report. They are: spiritual needs; counselling and emotional needs; educational (i.e. religion-specific) needs; and continuity and point of contact.[7]

In my capacity as Muslim chaplain I have also catered for the spiritual, educational, pastoral and emotional needs of the staff and students at the university. It is hard to compartmentalize these roles precisely as there is almost always overlap between them. However, I have tried to group my various services or duties under these four headings and would add to this list another very valuable service that I have been providing, namely trying to eliminate differences and clarify misunderstandings.

Spiritual Needs

- Providing one-to-one pastoral sessions.
- Representing Muslims on campus at various multifaith events.

Counselling and Emotional Needs

- Advocacy for Muslim students on various issues including islamophobia and other forms of discrimination.
- Availability and accessibility: always being available online for any pastoral support or general enquiries.
- Listening, signposting and referring students to the relevant departments at times of need.

Educational (Religion-specific) Needs

- Delivering weekly/fortnightly talks for staff and students during term time.
- Being a point of contact for all university staff and students with regard to any information required concerning Islamic rituals or events.
- Assisting and supporting research students with any faith-related issues or queries.
- Helping university students to find participants for surveys and other research components in their faith-related research.
- Supervising the training of trainee chaplains from Markfield Institute of Higher Education.
- Assisting the alumni and students at other universities in the region if they ask for help.
- Providing written information about various aspects of Islam in the form of handouts and flyers.
- Dispelling myths about Islam and tackling Islamophobia by delivering speeches at Islam awareness events at the university; writing informative articles about Islamic beliefs.

Continuity and Point of Contact

- Being a point of contact for all Muslim staff and students.
- Being a point of contact for consultation and policy making.
- Assisting the ISOC (Islamic society) in their various activities.
- Being the link and connection between the university administration and the Muslim student body.
- Dealing with complaints from/against Muslims on campus.

Giving information, support and guidance to the new Muslim student committee which is elected annually.

- Eliminating differences and clarifying misunderstandings.
- Clarifying misunderstandings between students and the administration, or among various student groups.
- Dispelling misconceptions and providing information to the university administration concerning certain Islamic traditions, practices or rituals.
- Being mindful of, and attending to, the needs of minority student groups.

If I were to try to write a summary of all the occasions on which I have provided my services to the staff and students at the university over the past twelve years, I would end up writing a book. Nevertheless, I will still try to capture a few 'snapshots' as examples of my work under the five subheadings outlined above. For easier reading I have combined spiritual and emotional needs under the heading 'Pastoral Sessions'.

Pastoral Sessions

Before proceeding, I would like to mention briefly the required code of conduct for chaplains when dealing with sensitive and emotional situations. This will go some way to explaining just how 'easy' the job of a chaplain can be when dealing with certain pastoral cases.

Chaplains need to be good listeners. They need to provide a safe, confidential and comfortable environment during all pastoral sessions. They must show care while remaining aloof; keep emotionally distant while remaining friendly; be culturally sensitive and aware; and be ready and able to wipe away the tears of others without shedding their own. Chaplains must always remain balanced and, at the most crucial times, be prepared to use the head rather than the heart. Chaplains must also be well-read and informed with regard to all current social issues.

> *The Muslim chaplain or advisor is seen as a person with the skills and knowledge to give guidance which need not rest solely on religious doctrine and will also include the ability to listen and support with moral attentiveness and yet do so non judgmentally.*[8]

In some cases, being a good listener solves a lot of the problems, since students in general – and not necessarily Muslim – tend to get depressed during exam times, for example, or fall out over small issues with roommates or colleagues.

At times, just having somewhere to go simply to vent their frustration is enough to take the weight off their shoulders, and they often walk out of the pastoral session relieved and much lighter in mood. Such students often come back just to say a quick hello or have a chat, because according to these students, chaplaincy is like an oasis, a safe haven, or a home away from home where they can relax and unwind.

Occasionally, Muslim students come to the chaplain's office in a somewhat depressed state, bringing with them a confession concerning a sin they have, or might have, committed. Here I would like to stress that confession of sins to a religious figure of authority is not an Islamic tradition.[9] Muslims tend to profess repentance to, and ask forgiveness from, Allah directly. Nevertheless, as Muslim chaplain my source of guidance is the Holy Quran and the *sunna* of the Holy Prophet Muhammad (PBWH). He was both *bashīr* and *nadhīr*, i.e. the one who gives glad tidings (about salvation) and who warns (about sin and wrongdoing).

> *We have sent you with the Truth as a bearer of good news and a warning...*[10]

I always seek guidance from the above two sources and try to implement them in my life and my role as chaplain. I try to listen to those in distress calmly and then give them the reassurance that Allah is most forgiving and merciful. I also relate the following verses from the Holy Quran to remind them of the mercy of their Lord.

> Except those who repent and amend and make manifest (the truth), these it is to whom I turn (mercifully); and I am the Oft returning (to mercy), the Merciful.[11]

> Except those who repent after that and amend, then surely Allah is Forgiving, Merciful.[12]

> And those who when they commit an indecency or do injustice to their souls remember Allah and ask forgiveness for their faults, and who forgives the faults but Allah, and (who) do not knowingly persist in what they have done. [3:136] (As for) these, their reward is forgiveness from their Lord, and gardens beneath which rivers flow, to abide in them, and excellent is the reward of the laborers.[13]

To me, Alexander Pope's famous saying, 'To err is human, to forgive divine' seems an embodiment of the above verses of the Holy Quran.

The word of Allah has a deeply healing effect, and it often helps service-users deal with peer pressure and negative cultural influences connected with prohibited acts such as the consumption of alcohol. In such cases, students feel the burden taken off their shoulders and walk away happy and relaxed. Many come back for more guidance and frequently come to the prayer room. Owing to my accessibility, students and even staff members contact me regarding different spiritual, religious and personal issues in these pastoral sessions. The female Muslim international students are the ones who rely the most on me, calling me for help and guidance on various matters related to campus life any time they need. Although my role is part time, I am always available via phone, text or email. Consequently I receive all sorts of queries and questions from students, such as: appointments for pastoral sessions; requests for help in finding participants from the Muslim community for their research surveys; requests by some students to interview me personally regarding Islamic aspects of their research; and calls from new students asking about accommodation or transport routes to the university. Quite often, students call me in the evenings without a prior appointment. They call about various issues: exam stress; accommodation problems; an urgent need for religious guidance; disagreement with other committee members; discrimination; racism; Islamophobia and a hundred and one other issues. Some of these calls turn into lengthy conversations and we speak until they feel at ease. If I am unable to resolve an issue on my own, I refer them to the relevant person/department within the university.

Referral or signposting seems to be a trivial task, but it can have a profound impact on service users, especially if they are new international students, for example, finding their way around their new lives and situations. Signposting or showing the way to a traveller who is lost or helping them in any way is also a part of our prophetic tradition. In the university context, the international student, or the student from a different city or village, is in many ways a good example of a traveller who may not be sure of his or her route or bearings.

Educational (Religion-specific) Needs and Tackling Islamophobia

Throughout my tenure as chaplain, I continued my weekly/ fortnightly talks for the students and staff at the university on diverse topics related to Islamic education. During Covid we held hybrid sessions, meeting online when I was physically away from the university.

In my effort to counter the misinformation about Islam, I write informative articles about various aspects of Islam and put copies on display for staff and students outside our chaplain's office and in the open spaces within our chaplaincy, where they do get picked up.

In November 2019, during 'Islam Awareness Week', I prepared an educational display in the CFS with laminated printouts of the Hadith and *sīra* (biography of the Prophet) under the title 'Celebrating the Prophet of Mercy'. This was in order to enlighten the university community about the life and personality of the Prophet Muhammad (PBWH). In 2020, after the Islamophobic event in France, the Muslim students were quite disturbed, I conducted a hybrid session on the topic of Islamophobia and blasphemy, and so which was well attended, and we had a lengthy discussion around this topic, with students asking many questions. I later authored a detailed paper about the 'Status of Prophet Muhammad' (PBWH) to reflect the Muslim stance and to express the deep reverence and devotion that Muslims have for their beloved Prophet. The ISOC were on the same page as me on this issue and they circulated it widely among the university community. A year later, a member of the Quaker group asked my permission to read it in their congregation, which I gladly granted.

In 2016, during Islam Awareness Week, my speech on the topic of love and war in Islam gained some attention. I talked about the rules of war in Islam and the fact that war was supposed to be waged between two armies at some distance from the city in order to avoid 'collateral damage'. I explained that it is not allowed to harm innocent citizens or destroy infrastructure or agricultural plantations: even plucking a leaf from a tree was prohibited for the Islamic armies, and the conquest of Mecca at the time of the Prophet Muhammad (PBWH) was a clear manifestation of this rule.

After my speech, our coordinating chaplain, Deacon Jan Sutton, and some fellow chaplains came to me, some of them in amazement, and admitted that they were not aware of this peaceful aspect of Islam, adding that 'Islam is quite similar to Christianity'.

Unfortunately, the real face of Islam has been marred by the negative media representation. The following facts in this regard are appalling:[14]

CfMM Report: State of Media Reporting on Islam and Muslims

> A detailed study of print and broadcast media revealed a serious problem in the way British media reports about Islam and Muslims. The study examined over 10,000 articles and broadcast clips referring to Muslims and Islam over the period of 2018-2020, revealing that:
>
> - 59% of all articles associated Muslims with negative behaviour.
> - 37% of articles in right-leaning and religious publications were categorised with the most negative rating of "very biased".

- Over a third of all articles misrepresented or generalised about Muslims
- Terrorism was the most common theme.
- 43% of all broadcast clips associated Muslims with negative behaviour.
- Platforming of the far-right on a number of debate programmes has allowed the propagation of false stereotypes about Islam and Muslims.

Although no task of a Muslim chaplain is less important than another, tackling Islamophobia and dispelling myths about Islam always takes precedence, as it works towards the benefit of the wider community and helps educate the university community about Islam.

In cases related to Islamophobia or racism, I inform my coordinator, who is quite supportive and approachable, and who deals with such issues head-on. One late evening during the February half-term break in 2018, I received a phone call from a PhD student who sounded quite alarmed. He told me that a student at the university had received a threatening letter regarding the notorious 'Punish a Muslim Day'[15] and he forwarded me a picture of the letter and envelope as well. I immediately called our coordinator, who in turn contacted the chief operating officer at the university. Within ten minutes, police arrived on campus to check this letter. Our coordinator then called me back to asked about the whereabouts of the student who had received the letter. I duly got back to the student who had called me and we realized that the photograph he had sent me was a forwarded message from an incident in another city, not Loughborough. Nevertheless, the university proceeded to issue a statement, showing solidarity with the Muslim students in this regard. In this respect, I would give credit to Loughborough University for its clear stance against Islamophobia.

Continuity and Point of Contact

> *University students are non-permanent: they come and go. What is needed is a point of contact for newcomers and continuity for those who have yet to finish their education in the university.*[16]

Since the ISOC office holders have only a one-year tenure, a Muslim chaplain remains the point of contact and continuity on campus. I also conduct a welcome session with the new students at the beginning of the term; on many occasions the ISOC itself arranges it. We do an icebreaking session with the international students to make them feel comfortable, introducing them to life in Britain and how to familiarize themselves with the cultural, linguistic and, above all, the climatical differences. This session is highly appreciated by incoming students, who later frequent the CFS and regularly attend our weekly sessions.

Other than my allocated days, I would always make myself available for the ISOC events in the evenings to support the students and I would drive down to the university even after my regular teaching hours were over. At times, thanks to my contacts within the Loughborough community, I was able help the female international students with accommodation issues. Two years ago, a PhD student, who was returning for a few weeks to the UK from her home country for an exam re-sit, called me in panic as she was let down by the accommodation services at the very last minute. I was also out of country at that point, but I contacted my acquaintances in Loughborough and within a day, two offers of accommodation had been made to her in Loughborough town by two different Muslim ladies.

At times, students from other universities in the region contact me for religious guidance for their research or to help them find participants for their surveys. One such recent example is of a PhD student from a university in Leicester who asked for guidance about the Islamic stance on limb amputation on medical grounds. We had a detailed conversation online which lasted two hours. She told me that she found my contact details on her university website. This reminded me that in the past, someone from that university had approached me for occasional support for female Muslim students and I had given my consent. I feel happy if I can help anyone, and maybe that is the reason I chose to be a chaplain.

Eliminating Differences and Clarifying Misunderstandings

A significant role of a Muslim chaplain is to help ease or erase differences or misunderstandings by becoming a bridge or link between the university administration and the students. In my very first year at Loughborough, a situation of mistrust occurred between the Muslim students and the Director of Student Services, occasioned by the decision to demolish a hall that was used by the Muslims for Friday prayer. Muslims students were not happy with the decision and saw it as an unjust move to deprive them of their praying space. I went to meet the Director of Student Services to convey the concerns of the Muslim students, and he explained to me that the hall in question had been considered unsafe by the engineers and needed to be demolished for their own safety. He even proposed the option of using another sports hall for the same purpose, offering to arrange a tour of the hall for the ISOC office holders. I conveyed this message to the ISOC and the issue was resolved.

The same happens conversely as well. Occasionally, the chaplaincy would have some doubts or misunderstanding regarding certain students, and they would contact me for clarification. On one such occasion, our coordinator came to me with an A4 poster in Arabic that was displayed on the door of the male prayer room. She looked quite concerned, as though she thought it might be some kind of threat or insulting message. In actual fact, it was a well-known Arabic supplication that Muslims recite when entering a mosque or a prayer area. When I explained it to her, she heaved a sigh of relief but requested that English translations be written next to any such texts in the future. I then printed out and laminated the same supplication along with the English translation to replace the original poster.

On another occasion, I received an email from the library regarding an allocated prayer facility for the students within the library in response to the Muslim students' request. The library is not within appropriate walking distance from the CFS. I welcomed this initiative as it would benefit a huge number of Muslim students who use the library. However, our coordinator did not like the idea. She thought that it would give the impression that the prayer room in the CFS was inadequate, adding that if the university had already provided a prayer facility for the students in the CFS, it was not a good idea to ask for more in other departments. She even highlighted other issues related to the granting of a prayer space to one religion and not the other. She was not happy that I had responded without consulting her. Since I was not on campus, I called her and had a lengthy conversation with her about the issue. I explained that unlike the members of any other faith on campus, Muslims must pray five times a day and the provision of a small, quiet room could be an ideal solution for them. I related to her my earlier conversation with a PhD student who used to pray behind her desk in her office. I informed her that the provision of a separate quiet room in any department would in no way reduce or diminish the value or status of our prayer room in the CFS, and that the congregational prayers could only be held in the CFS and would carry on as usual. I assured her that the allocated prayer areas could only benefit the students, who otherwise would either pray in small corners or behind tables in their respective departments or would delay or miss their prayers altogether. I even gave her an example from my own student life when I would do my mid-day prayer, during my hour-long lunch break, in the university prayer room which was a fifteen-minute walk from my Education Department. However, I would have no option but to do my afternoon and early evening prayers in any available empty room within my department in the ten-minute break we had in between classes. This helped her understand the Muslim perspective, and she even asked further questions for clarification regarding ablution and the absence of washing facilities in the library. I explained that Muslims do not necessarily need to make an ablution before each prayer as long as their previous ablution has not been voided in the interim. is intact. Many Muslims tend to remain in a state of ritual purity throughout the day, often performing two, sometimes three prayers, with the same ablution.

Loughborough is the second largest town in Leicestershire, with a sizeable community of resident PhD students and alumni who live off campus, but who always help the ISOC in events on campus, especially when it comes to providing, or arranging for the funding for, the iftar food on each of the thirty days of Ramadan. They also offer their support for other events and ventures, such as the provision of imams to lead the congregational prayers. Although the overall atmosphere on campus is one of harmony and brotherhood, on one occasion a PhD student called me and informed me about a disagreement in the prayer room which involved some raised voices that she could hear from the female side of the prayer room; her husband, himself an alumnus, was also present on the occasion. This disagreement started on account of a suspected discrepancy in the collected funds for the Ramadan meals. I immediately sent a request for a meeting with the ISOC committee, the concerned alumni and senior students, who met with me and our male Muslim chaplain the very next day and the matters were resolved without further escalation. I explained to the imam that keeping the records of the funds open to the public was their moral and religious obligation, and I cited example of the second Muslim Caliph, Hazrat Umar (r.a.), who was once called out during his Friday sermon to explain how he managed to make the shirt he was wearing from the piece of cloth that had been given to all Muslim soldiers, implying that he must have taken two pieces of cloth as one piece was not enough for the shirt of a man of his height. He did not get offended or raise his voice; rather, he very calmly asked his eldest son to respond on his behalf. His son had combined his own piece of cloth with that of his father in order to make a shirt that would fit, and he explained this in full to the congregation. This was an example for all Muslims to keep themselves open for accountability.[17]

I was also a point of contact for the chaplaincy administrator and the coordinating chaplain for minor maintenance issues involving the prayer room, the ablution areas and the chaplaincy kitchen used by the Muslim students. After a few years, the students took on this role themselves in my absence.

Since we always have Muslim international students from all over the world, including the Middle East, the role of Muslim chaplain becomes vital in educating the university administration about the cultural idiosyncrasies which could cause misunderstandings on both sides. Once a Saudi student offered to change the carpets in the prayer room with better and thicker carpets marked conspicuously with the direction of Mecca. He insisted that during Ramadan students spend much time worshipping in the prayer room and that thicker carpets would bring ease for all the users of the prayer spaces during and after the holy month of Ramadan. In my view, it was a very generous offer for a free upgrade of the carpets in the prayer room. The university, on the other hand, had reservations about this proposal, interpreting it as an indication of a desire for ownership over the prayer room by a particular community of students.

I then explained this concept of *ṣadaqa jāriyya* or 'ongoing charity' to my coordinator, who was liaising with the administration. I emphasised that Muslims tend to use their charitable donations on community projects which benefit the public at large, such as digging wells in areas with little water, or installing a water cooler, an air conditioner or fans in mosques, or, indeed, buying new carpets on which to pray. The main idea of this charity is that the reward of the good continues to accrue to the giver as long as the charity remains effective and in use.

I even assured her that the student in question was simply doing that as an act of charity to benefit all the users of that space, and thankfully she understood this stance. However, the university still refused the offer, but agreed to replace the carpets themselves. The student then provided the details of a supplier who could do the job at a decent price. The university declined that as well, and consequently a hefty sum of money was paid to a particular supplier chosen by the university, and the carpets in the prayer room were replaced. This made me wonder about the financial priorities of a university which claimed to have budgeting issues when it came to paying a salary to its Muslim chaplain!

According to a survey in the Siddique report, '… the university should pay for chaplaincy because it is a service provided 24/7 for the university [and] which benefits the university…'. They argue that this gives the chaplains/advisors legitimacy and a recognised role on campus. Muslim chaplains/advisors will be able to play a proactive role in generating activities and helping both students and staff at the university.[18]

Catering for the Needs of Minorities and Averting any Possible Sectarian Disagreements

I have also been quite mindful of the needs of Muslim minority groups such as the Shi'ites, and I have facilitated them their use of the CFS premises for holding their own religious gatherings. Once I even held a talk about the events of Muharram; I even wrote a detailed article about the love that Muslims have for the Ahl al-Bayt and presented it especially for the Shi'ite brothers and sisters.

Once, a Shi'ite international student was offended by a speech made by a Sunni imam during the Friday sermon. She looked quite upset. I was sitting next to her during the prayers and she later confided in me concerning her feelings. I consoled her and reassured her that no derogatory language against any group would be acceptable on campus. I then called a meeting of the ISOC committee and the imam who had led the prayers and reminded them that the CFS facilities – and Muslim prayer room in particular – had been provided by the university for all of the Muslims on campus, irrespective of their denomination, race or colour, and that such discriminatory behaviour against anyone would not be tolerated. The imam was an alumnus who always volunteered to lead congregational prayers. They all agreed with me and assured me that they would be more careful in future.

Perceptions about the Role of a Female Muslim Chaplain

When I started as the first ever non-Christian and the only Muslim chaplain at the university, my role was quite unique and central, and I had to deal with all the problems and issues of the Muslim students on campus, irrespective of their sex. In one such instance, during my regular weekly meeting with the ISOC committee, the need for an imam for the second Friday congregation was brought up. During summer, the Friday congregation was held at two different times to accommodate students and staff with varied timetables. The ISOC committee did not have a student who could lead the second congregation for Friday. Ideally a male Muslim chaplain could have easily done this job. Although I could not personally lead the congregation, I arranged a two hour 'Friday sermon' training session in the same week with a Muslim scholar for a group of ISOC boys to resolve this problem. I have never felt any restraint or limitation imposed on me in my role as a female Muslim chaplain, for there have always been ways to work around the problems.

During my time teaching on the chaplaincy training course, I would come across trainee male chaplains interested in HE chaplaincy but who tended to choose salaried roles in the NHS or the Prison Services rather than a voluntary role in HE. Some young Muslim trainee chaplains also joined us briefly at different times but never stayed for long. Fortunately, a few years ago, our chaplaincy team was honoured with the addition of a very senior Islamic Scholar, brother Daud Matthew. He is like a father figure to me and I also look up to him for his knowledge and wisdom. His presence also took away massive responsibilities from my shoulders, as I counted on him to deal with all the issues concerning the male prayer areas and the male Muslims on campus. He also attends all the staff meetings on Thursday mornings – something which was not possible for me owing to my other teaching roles. There is no competition between us, no tension over whether one role is primary and the other secondary, for we both facilitate each other in our roles as Muslim chaplains. Besides, our motivation for work is not the salary, promotion or other incentives, but rather a sense of duty, and so our jobs are more about collaboration rather than competition.

I used to hold weekly circles for sisters in the CFS during term time; I later changed the name of these weekly circles to 'Timeless Transmissions' and made them all-inclusive for both brothers and sisters and included our male Muslim chaplain and students in these sessions.

Challenges of Working in a Pluralistic and Interfaith Context

I thoroughly enjoy working in a pluralistic and interfaith context. Ours is a diverse group of chaplains from different religious and cultural backgrounds, yet we all have mutual respect and harmony and always support each other in our work. We do have meaningful and insightful conversations on various religious and pastoral issues, as well as light-hearted banter. Though we all adhere to different belief systems, we practice mutual respect and tolerance.

In 2019, just a week after the dreadful mosque shooting incident in New Zealand, I coordinated an Islamophobia Awareness event in Leicester in collaboration with MEND entitled 'Stand Together in Faith'. Our lovely team of chaplains not only supported me but participated fully in the event, taking part in the panel discussion and showing their solidarity with the Muslim community. We all stood together in faith as we always do at university as a matter of course.

Qualities and Code of Practice for a Muslim Chaplain in Higher Education

The need for a well-defined code of practice covering the roles and responsibilities of a Muslim chaplain cannot be understated.

> *All students in the study agreed that the Muslim chaplain/advisor should have an understanding of student issues and university life, be approachable and have a certain level of training in counselling, and a good knowledge base about Islam. More*

> *particularly, a key factor emphasised by students is that the chaplain should be independent of the wider Muslim community and accountable to university administration.*[19]

With consensus among the academic staff, community leaders and Muslim chaplains/advisors themselves, the salient qualities of a Muslim chaplain/advisor were agreed upon based on the outcomes of this survey as follows: [20]

- A good knowledge of Islam, with preferably some kind of formal Islamic qualification.
- Understanding of British society and university culture.
- Understanding of other faiths and a willingness to engage with them positively.
- Communication and counselling skills and willingness to listen and be approachable.
- Being open to all denominations within Islam.

I fully agree that all these five qualities should be present in a Muslim chaplain. Moreover, a chaplain needs to have a broader vision and perspective that is only possible with a true understanding of the religion, reflecting his/her love and tolerance for all human beings, irrespective of religion, race or colour. Good communication and counselling skills, the ability to listen and to be there for everyone are undoubtedly the qualities most sought after in a chaplain. To sum up, a Muslim chaplain, who is the representative of the Muslim society, needs to follow the *sunna* of the Holy Prophet (PBWH) not just in appearance and attire but in its true essence, namely by being a blessing and a mercy for all humanity.

Additionally, a particular need that I have felt in the HE context is for chaplains to understanding the academic culture and preferably be educated to degree level. In an interview with one of the Christian chaplains during my chaplaincy training placement, he emphasised the fact that having an academic qualification is not a mandatory requirement for the job of a chaplain, but that universities value and prefer those chaplains who have good qualifications. He also added jokingly that this gives them a reason to boast about their high standards.

Though this fact in no way proves that academic qualifications per se can make one a good chaplain, actually having a qualification at the level of degree or above may serve to boost confidence, enhance understanding of the academic culture and campus life, and enable the chaplain to better relate to the students and understand their problems. Moreover, Islam also lays a lot of stress on acquiring knowledge for both men and women as it gives confidence, refinement and assertiveness to an individual.

According to the teachings of the Prophet (PBWH):

The angels will lower their wings with great pleasure before one who seeks knowledge, and the inhabitants of the heavens and the earth and the fish in the deep waters will ask forgiveness for the learned man.[21]

Where do I Stand According to this Criterion, and What are my Shortcomings?

Though I had stepped into this field from a career in academe, with a completely different qualification and skills set, I embarked on the training and educational journey required for my new role as a chaplain. I will try to assess my own strengths and weaknesses in the light of the five qualities and code of practice for a Muslim chaplain mentioned above, one by one:

- In terms of my formal Islamic education, I have a BA in Islamic Studies. I have studied Quranic exegesis and have completed a three-year part-time Diploma in Islamic Studies which included instruction in most of the classical Islamic disciplines such as Quranic interpretation, hadith, Prophetic biography, Islamic law and legal theory, Sufi thought and Arabic. I am also an avid reader of religious and spiritual texts which I study to enrich my religious acumen. I aim to further enhance my qualifications in this field and intend to enrol in an MA in Islamic Studies this year, followed by a PhD, God willing. In terms of professional qualifications, I have a Certificate in Muslim Chaplaincy Training from Markfield Institute of Higher Education, passed with distinction; I have also been teaching certificated courses in 'Muslim Chaplaincy at Markfield Institute of Higher Education since 2012 and have supervised the placements of trainee Muslim chaplains from Markfield Institute at the university.

- My higher education qualifications are proof to some extent of my understanding of academic culture and campus life in Britain I have two MA degrees in English Literature and in Applied Linguistics and TESOL respectively, and a CELTA and a CertEd. I had been a secondary school English teacher before commencing my role as chaplain, but later moved on to more flexible teaching positions in FE, universities and Higher Education institutions as an EAP Teaching Fellow to find more time for my chaplaincy responsibilities.

- I was also quite active on the interfaith front even before commencing my role at the university, I had a leading position in ICWA (Islamic Centre Women's Association) where I organized community events for ladies and children and delivered fortnightly religious education sessions. I would also attend the meetings of the Christian-Muslim Dialogue group, the Hindu-Muslim Forum and the Leicester Council of Faith. Thus, I had a reasonable understanding of other faiths and the experience of engaging with them positively.

- Owing to my leadership role, I had been open to engagement with all denominations within Islam. I had been a public speaker and an orator during my student life, which enhanced my communication skills. The willingness to listen and be approachable is a trait I learned during my teacher training and chaplaincy courses.

- As far as counselling skills are concerned, I do not have any formal training in counselling, but we have a counselling department in the student services to which we refer any students in need of counselling. Back in 2014/15 I was quite keen to enrol on a part time Islamic Counselling course and I asked my university whether they would finance it, but my request was declined due to lack of funds. Prior to this, all my qualifications had been self-funded. Later in 2019, our coordinator did manage to find a small amount of funding, but other commitments meant that I could not embark on the course that year. And then, of course, everything changed the following year because of Covid. Nevertheless, a counselling course remains on my wish list for the future.

My Chaplaincy Training Experience

My chaplaincy experience would be incomplete without mentioning my chaplaincy training and placement at Loughborough University in 2008. At that time, Loughborough University chaplaincy had no representation of any faith other than the various denominations of Christianity. The Muslim prayer space was also an isolated room in a separate building next to the chaplaincy. I received a very warm welcome from both the university and the chaplaincy. The then Coordinating Chaplain, Rev. Simon Richardson, supervised my placement, making it a very holistic, informative and insightful experience for me. This placement comprised meetings and deeper conversations about religion, spirituality and the future of Muslim chaplaincy at Loughborough with the Vice-Chancellor, the Pro-Vice Chancellor, the International Director and various other high office holders at the university. I also had the opportunity of interviewing all members of the Chaplaincy team, the members of seven different student faith groups, and the representatives of Loughborough Students Union. I had some insightful conversations with the chaplains about the role of an HE chaplain that helped me understand my own role better in the same context and later helped me define in detail my own perspective of the role of a Muslim chaplain. This placement also included a guided tour of the university, the faith room in Loughborough College, the Loughborough Council of Faith office in town, the student union building and other important office buildings at the university, together with my chaplaincy supervisor.

During my conversation with the International Director, the prospect of allocating an isolated prayer room for the Muslims on campus was brought up, According to his observation, the Muslim community in Loughborough was quite reserved and he had formed his impression about all Muslims based on this observation. He wanted to hear my views on the topic, and I explained that international students come to Britain to experience university life, to have human contact and to forge meaningful interaction, as well as working towards their academic qualifications. I explained that a sizeable number of students from educated and professional families from the urban areas of Pakistan tend to come to Britain for higher education. They either return to pursue their careers or they move on to professional roles here. They enjoy and celebrate being an active part of our multicultural community and have no desire to live in isolation. I made this statement based on my own personal experience as an international student from Pakistan, and my observation of a large number of highly educated Pakistanis settled in Britain from my own circle of friends, their friends, my own friends and family, university and school fellows, our siblings, cousins, and the wider community of Pakistani professionals – all forming a substantial number of people who had come to the UK for higher education.

On the other hand, during my engagement with the BAME communities, I had come across a set of Muslim ladies from Pakistan, Bangladesh, and India who came to Britain in the Sixties with their parents or spouses for unskilled jobs in deprived rural area. The problem is that although their second generations have blended well into British culture, the first generation is still reserved and isolated owing to language and cultural barriers. This turned out to be a moment of realization for the International Director and he agreed that this situation was quite relatable for him as well. He added that he also knew of a similar scenario in the German population in Nottingham. On the one hand there were highly educated German families in his own circle, while on the other hand there was a population of Germans in the same city who came as coal miners back in the Sixties, and he had never seen them both as one entity. This conversation had taken quite an interesting turn as we were engaging in a very meaningful discussion about the topics of stereotyping and labelling of one community but not the other, though in a very subtle manner.

Eventually, we agreed on the possibility of a multifaith centre with a separate prayer area for Muslim students, a space where students from all religious and cultural backgrounds could meet and greet each other and share a common space. He also mentioned the prospect of my joining the university as a Muslim chaplain in return for a free PhD enrolment. This topic was also discussed in a subsequent meeting with the VC. All these meetings were very pleasant and enlightening, and I felt valued and welcomed in their institution and was deeply impressed by the VC and her managerial team.

In short, all my meetings and interviews not only helped broaden my insight into chaplaincy but also gave me the opportunity of meeting amazing people. I also had a detailed meeting with the ISOC office holders and met Muslim sisters individually in the prayer room on various occasions.

On the final day of my placement, my supervisor told me something which I'd like to quote here:

> *Midhat, you have done a great service to your faith.*

I was astonished by this statement, as I could not think of any significant religious accomplishment during the whole placement, given that I had neither propagated my religion nor had I converted anyone to Islam. Although I upheld my basic religious identity, preserving decorum and adhering to my dress code, I had just been my easy-going and chatty self, full of smiles and light-hearted conversations, and so I was keen to hear what service he thought I had done for my religion. His next words were even more surprising. For he said that just by being my normal self, open and articulate in all my interactions, yet upholding Islamic values, I had helped dispel certain misconceptions that people have of Muslims, thus helping to change the mindset of people against Islam. He added that this was one of the reasons all the officers and the VC were interested in meeting me.

After this conversation I was not sure if I needed to laugh or cry or to feel proud or sad. I did feel honoured at the fact that I was able to transform the tarnished image of Muslims at least in one institution, but at the same time I was even more saddened and bewildered at the way Muslims in general are seen. I held that thought with me and throughout my later career as a Muslim chaplain, dispelling myths about Islam became a priority through my talks, informal conversations, written articles, speeches, and my conduct, as I have already mentioned above.

Eventually I passed my Certificate in Chaplaincy with distinction, and I received amazing feedback from the university. On the final assessment day at Markfield, when all the students were asked to talk about their placement experience, it dawned on me that my experience at Loughborough had been quite unique and possibly more enriching than it had been for any of my fellow students on the course. For most students, the chaplaincy placement experience consisted of visiting the prayer room, meeting Muslim students, meeting the other chaplains and so on, while I had a very holistic experience that helped me explore chaplaincy in its breath and depth and all its broader aspects within the university.

Furthermore, our external examiner, the director of St Philips Centre, invited me to be a part of Leicester Council of Faith and thereafter invited me to join various other interfaith forums and events at the St Philips Centre and beyond. I did partake wholeheartedly owing to my newly found passion of dispelling myths about Islam and Muslims. He even invited me to represent the Muslim women of Britain at a multifaith conference in Belgium.

My Chaplaincy Experience Prior to my Job Offer

Although I did not get the job offer by the university immediately after my placement, the chaplain in me was quite active even during my teaching roles. However, I was aware that things are quite different in a professional context where legal and organizational procedures, including referrals, documentation, approval from the line manager and so on, take precedence before I would be able to take any immediate decisions on my own.

On a lighter note, in one such instance, when I was teaching in a language school in Oxford to teenagers from Europe, one of my colleagues told me that a Muslim student in her class had told her that he would not be able to attend lessons on Friday morning as he had to attend his congregational prayers. I immediately realized that the student was trying to use religion as an excuse to skip lessons. I knew that the time for the commencement of Friday prayer was more than an hour later than the class and that there was no need for him to miss that class. I called for the student and he told me that he was new in the city so it would be hard for him to find out about a nearby mosque. Since it was lunch break and we all were sitting in the university restaurant, I looked around and spotted a male Muslim staff member, I sent the student to him and he agreed to take him along after the lesson, the next day, so there was no need to miss the class. We had a good laugh about this and my colleague thanked me for clarifying the confusion about Friday prayers and Muslims created by the young student.

After completing my training as Muslim chaplain, I started feeling 'directly responsible for all the problems of humanity', which was how my husband described my demeanour. This remark was made after a significant number of similar instances, where I even started loaning out money to complete strangers in the name of care.

I should also relate here a more serious example of an encounter I had with a revert sister in the Islamic Centre who wanted to talk to a female faith advisor and was sent to me. We met after one of my fortnightly lectures at the centre. She felt lonely among her own friends and family and had had bitter experiences in life that had overwhelmed her with sorrow and grief. As a newly trained chaplain I knew that chaplaincy is about being there for a person in need, providing them with a quiet, comfortable and confidential space and an empathetic listening ear so they may pour out their bottled-up emotions and troubles. I sat with that sister in a quiet room for over two hours and she poured her heart out to me. She seemed quite confused and out of place and wept most of the time. My heart went out to her but I had no means of healing her wounds. She told me her life story between sobs and even after venting for over two hours her heart didn't seem to have gained any ease: the more she dredged up out of her past, the more her wounds bled.

To me she seemed like a small trailing plant tossed about in the storm, trying in vain to cling onto the stem of a nearby tree for support and protection. At that time, I was that tree and moving away from her was like leaving her to the mercy of the storm. This urge to help her despite all odds was not just due to my training as a chaplain; this was the essence of my being as a Muslim which told me that I could not just walk away, and that I had to relieve her from her distress in some way. In normal circumstances I would have been quite reluctant to invite a total stranger to my home but my sense of duty as a chaplain took precedence, and after a few moments of deliberation I invited her to my home, introduced her to my family and invited her to eat with us. This change of scene made her feel good and she enjoyed the company of my children as well. It was getting quite late, so I even offered her a bed for the night, which she readily accepted. I realized that she needed that sense of belonging she had lost after leaving her old religion and that some bitter experiences in her past had left her totally isolated and lonely. It was the long weekend and she ended up staying with me for three days, after which she was smiling again, joking and playing with my children, who had also formed a good bond with her. When she left, she was quite at peace and had made lasting bonds with me and my family. As she was leaving, I gave her some gifts. Her eyes welled up, but these tears were of joy, gratitude and love; she knew she would always be welcome in my home again and that was quite comforting for her.

When I reflect on this event, I can clearly see that doing what I did was my natural response to that situation and that any true Muslim would have done the same as it tied in well with my own religious beliefs. This trait of helping others at times of need lies at the core of our religious ethics and has been stressed upon repeatedly in our religious texts. The following hadith explains the same concept.

> *It was narrated that Abu Hurairah said:*

> "The Messenger of Allah said: 'Whoever relieves a Muslim of some worldly distress, Allah will relieve him of some of the distress of the Day of Resurrection, and whoever conceals (the faults of) a Muslim, Allah will conceal him (his faults) in this world and the Day of Resurrection. And whoever relives the burden from a destitute person, Allah will relieve him in this world and the next. Allah will help His slave so long as His slave helps his brother..."[22]

The Unexpected Offer

One fine morning, almost three years after the completion of my Muslim chaplaincy training, I received an email from my Chaplaincy Supervisor with an offer for the position of full-time resident Muslim chaplain at Loughborough University.

Although my circumstances had changed, and I had moved on in my life to a full-time teaching job in a secondary school and had even moved to a new house in a different town about thirty miles away from Loughborough, I was still pleasantly amazed by this unexpected offer. I wanted to politely turn it down, but instead of doing so via an email I agreed to meet the Chaplain supervisor in person and explain my new circumstances to him.

He advised me to reconsider my decision and not to rush the refusal. When I asked him if they had advertised the job, he said, "Loughborough is very particular about whom they appoint", indicating that the post had been created for me based on my placement experience.

He then took me on a tour of the newly built Multifaith Centre, now the CFS – Centre for Faith and Spirituality. This seemed like an accurate image of the multifaith centre discussed in the meeting with the International Director during my placement. I was amazed to see the massive transformation of the old chaplaincy into a purpose built multifaith centre with large prayer rooms, separate ablution facilities and praying spaces for males and females, and a spacious conference room just opposite the prayer room to accommodate the overspill of big congregations of worshippers on Fridays, There were also quiet rooms, a chapel, a number of chaplains' offices, and open areas for sitting and relaxation.

He even showed me the office of the Muslim chaplain referring it to as "your office."

Loughborough University was ready to offer me a four-bedroom house with all bills paid in return for my services as Muslim chaplain; during my meeting with the Director of Student Services, he asked me to see the house as well. I explained that I had quite recently bought a new house in a different town and was in a full-time paid job. However, I felt truly obliged by the recognition given to me by the university, so I agreed to give it some more thought. I was further moved by the fact that the university had taken my placement recommendations very seriously, and that the reason for the delay in sending me the offer was the time taken on this wonderful transformation.

I finally agreed to take on the role initially as a part-time voluntary chaplain, visiting the university one day a week. I said that at the start of the following academic year I would then take the full-time role that the university was offering me. In this way I was giving up one day a week from my paid job in order to fulfil this voluntary role. This turned out to be a big mistake, at least from a worldly point of view, as will become obvious a little further on in the chapter.

The university gratefully accepted my offer and eventually I began my journey as an HE Chaplain in December 2011. The Coordinating Chaplain of the CFS, who had also been my placement supervisor, hailed it as a truly momentous day in the history of Loughborough University, as I was the university's first ever non-Christian chaplain. He even claimed that I was the first ever female Muslim chaplain in HE in the country.

The initial days of my appointment were quite hectic and exciting, which included setting up my office, having meetings with the chaplaincy team and the ISOC office holders, and navigating my way between the chaplains' office and the prayer room and other quiet areas. My learning journey was facilitated through advice, support and guidance at every step and I was also full of zeal to perform my responsibility with sincerity, dedication and commitment.

The Support and Encouragement for the Role of a Female Muslim Chaplain

I felt quite fortunate in the respect that I received a very warm welcome both by the Chaplaincy team and the Muslims on campus, and by the fact that my being the first ever Muslim chaplain at the university was celebrated. Right from the outset I developed a good rapport with the Islamic Society and all of the brothers and sisters at the ISOC were quite excited at the prospect of a Muslim chaplain at the university. I used to have weekly meetings with the ISOC Chair and office holders, and they would update me about any issues pertaining to the Muslim students, prayer or ablution facilities or room bookings and arrangements for any upcoming events. They would even invite me to their annual committee meetings on various occasions. They were quite keen and excited at the prospect of my joining the university as a full-time chaplain in the near future and would discuss various other activities and events that could be conducted daily in the prayer room and the university.

Within a month of my appointment, the ISOC started a weekly sisters' circle in collaboration with the CFS, where free tea was served to the attendees by the CFS. This weekly event was advertised by the ISOC and the CFS as 'Tea with Sister Midhat' and was well attended by the female Muslim faculty members and students. ISOC office holders would help with the set-up and advertisement of the event each week and even provided snacks for the attendees. These sessions remain ongoing even after a decade with slight modifications and changes in format, title and venues, transforming into hybrid and online sessions during Covid. The 'Tea with...' event is no longer running.

In the early days of my appointment, it was decided that we would turn this into a daily event once my full-time chaplaincy role commenced, as it would allow a larger number of sisters to attend these sessions. ISOC sisters also planned that on alternate days we would have a change in topic or format in order to reach out to all levels and interests of students. We were also aiming to develop lasting ties with the wider university community in the town, especially the families of international students and alumni, as well as creating more opportunities for showcasing Islam and organizing events for integration and the dispelling of myths about Islam. I also had one-on-one and group meetings with Muslim PhD students and staff who were not a part of the ISOC; I conducted pastoral sessions; I had a catchup meeting with my supervisor; I visited the prayer room and the ablution facilities and so on. On most occasions my day would be packed so fully with back-to-back meetings and jobs in between that I would have to delay my lunch break till I got home, which was after 5pm. At that time, I used to think that I would be able to manage such a workload better once I'd started my full-time position.

A Tough Decision

By the spring of 2012, the management of the university had changed, with a new VC in office along with a new team. It also dawned upon me that the university's offer for a house on campus was no longer available and they were happy for me to continue as a part-time volunteer as they could not find the funds to pay the rent for the chaplain's house which had been initially offered to me the year before.

I realised that since I had offered my services free of charge out of good will and sincerity, and was completing a weeks' work in one day, fulfilling all my responsibilities diligently, the university did not feel the need to create a full-time job for a Muslim chaplain. This came as a big disappointment for me, my coordinator, and the ISOC as well. They even wrote a letter to the Chief Operating Officer at the university, asking that my part-time role be converted to full-time, but to no avail.

This also taught me how a change in management can change the whole outlook of a higher education institution: a position that was treated as an important addition to the university's ethos overnight turned into just an extra add-on, there simply to tick a certain box on a list of services offered by the university. Changes continued apace. The CFS moved to a new building, the number of chaplains kept increasing and a new coordinator was appointed to the centre. Originally the chaplains were officers directly under the VC, but according to the administrative structure I came across during my placement, which later moved way down as a subsidiary of the student services, our CFS was also moved to another building opposite the student services building. In the years to come more and more line managers were inserted between the position of our coordinator and the director of student services. Most of my colleague chaplains are volunteers and work with dedication with their respective student groups. Recently there has been a lot of emphasis on completing timesheets for the work done by the chaplains. This could be a means of authenticating the presence of the additional line managers, but I find this expectation illogical and unrealistic, firstly because we normally fill timesheets in paid jobs where we get paid for the hours we put in, so I do not see the point of filling in the meticulous details of the hours put in when there is no salary paid. The chaplains give their precious time to serve staff and students, not for filling in lengthy paperwork. I would rather spend my time listening to the students than pen-pushing. Secondly, the chaplains were meant to bring that 'otherness' to the secular university atmosphere and their services cannot be weighed in terms of hours they put in. Chaplaincy is not a nine to five job; it is basically a round-the-clock dedicated service. According to John Milton,

> *They also serve who only stand and wait.*[23]

Hence being available even in the evenings for the frantic calls of the students in distress, when the salaried staff have already finished their day's work and totally switched off from their responsibilities, a chaplain is still there, and mentally and emotionally available for the students just a phone call away. This aspect of the role of a chaplain cannot be transmitted on the time sheets but secular mindsets cannot fathom the depths of spiritual realms.

Coming back to my story, after the university totally changed its stance about the full-time job offer given to me the year before, my coordinator and I had a meeting with Dr Ataullah Siddique, my late noble teacher and mentor, and the then director of the Markfield Institute of Higher Education. He was the one who had arranged my placement at the university and later offered me the job of teaching on the chaplaincy training course, where he would proudly introduce me to the new students in each chaplaincy session. He was quite astounded at this change of stance by the university. He clearly advised me that since the university had not stood by their offer, I was no longer obliged to provide my services to them. He also added that even if I chose to stay, it would be on my own terms and at my own convenience, and whatever services I provided to the university would basically be my favour to them.

I felt quite empowered by his words of wisdom, which showed me a clearer way forward. Volunteering for a day at university for me meant giving up a full day of my paid teaching job. My coordinator also agreed with Dr Siddique. He believed that I had no reason to stay, but added that I must consider the feelings of the Muslim students, especially the sisters who really looked up to me. This thought melted my heart, and I made the decision to stay, again my inspiration from the prophetic tradition of the concept of *ihsān* or selfless giving.

Before proceeding further, I would like to state my own understanding of this beautiful concept:

When we let go of our ego and blend in the wider scheme of the universe, that is *ihsān* When we lose ourselves in service to the Lord and just become a silent object, tool, or a means of service just like a blade of grass, or a dew drop, or a worm in the soil, or a tree, a cloud, or the wind – they all perform their most significant roles in the universe by remaining insignificant. That is *ihsān*.

Thus, it does not matter who or what or where I am, my purpose is to serve selflessly, and when this concept of self-projection, recognition, appreciation and gratification melts into the heat of the intense love of the Lord, this 'I' and 'Me' transforms into 'Thy' and 'Thee' and I would be one with the Lord.

And here I am, over a decade later, providing my services to the university with a special focus on the Muslim students, particularly the sisters.

Nonetheless, I believe I had an immense passion and capacity for dedicated 'service' which could not be utilized in a part-time voluntary role at the university, so I have diverted some of my passion for service to more rewarding deeds of charity for the past two years by setting up a charity that works for the betterment of destitute widows and orphans in a far-flung village in Pakistan. We raise funds for regular monthly food rations, building collapsed walls and roofs, creating empowerment opportunities by providing sewing machines, hand carts and setting up small corner shops, providing bereavement funds and medical aid and so on. Even the ISOC raised some funds for the orphanage by conducting a bake sale on campus last year. I now frequently travel to Pakistan to work on the ground and keep the donors updated with all the progress of the work. I have found this to be the most satisfying experience of my job, and I have written about it in my online blog as well. Al-Ma'un is named after the sura Al-Ma'un in the Holy Quran, which means small acts of kindness. Our motto is 'Service to the Creator by Serving the Creation'.

Conclusion

In this chapter I have related the experiences of my chaplaincy journey as briefly as I could by showing glimpses of my various roles and responsibilities and outlining the nature of my job. I have also discussed the research findings concerning the requirements and prerequisites of the role of a Muslim chaplain; my own strengths and shortcomings; my contributions to the university; my limitations and the reasons behind them and the story of my chaplaincy journey right from its outset.

Due to the restraints I have stated above, together with time constraints. I was only able to channel a small percentage of my abilities into this voluntary part time role. I also feel guilty at times for not doing more like my other colleagues in full-time paid positions. Though I am not present on campus full-time, I am always available online 24/7 for students for pastoral sessions via phone, and even online weekly Islamic educational sessions. In fact, I conducted these sessions remotely last year, even when I was out of the country.

If I look back and analyse my role as chaplain, I see it as a God-given opportunity to serve. Despite my limitations and restraints, I still think that I could have done better.

3

Amra Bone
University of Portsmouth

Sowing the Seeds of a Career in Chaplaincy

One frosty morning I trudged along the corridor to my school's Common Room feeling rather anxious as if every one's gaze would be upon me when I opened the door. Lo and behold there came along one of my fellow students seeking my guidance on a personal issue. I was intrigued if not bewildered, because why me? Many thoughts rushed through my head, and after a few moments of silence, I came to and was able to respond. How can I help? This very early experience was, unbeknownst to myself, setting me on a path of serving my fellow human beings. I have treasured many memories since then, while others are perhaps best left behind.

In this paper I aim to present some of my personal experiences, reflections and aspirations. In order to show the breadth of my work I will be discussing certain examples of my work and a number of case studies; the names of institutions will not be given for particular cases and pseudonyms will be used to preserve the confidentiality of individuals.

Whenever I do give the names of institutions, it is intended for the purpose of showcasing different models of chaplaincy. In the main section, I will take you along my memory lane, exploring from the earliest to the latest encounters and adventures, along with my own perspectives on the world of chaplaincy. Why did I become a chaplain? What is Muslim chaplaincy? And I shall list the kind of jobs I do and illustrate them with case examples in order to highlight the importance of Muslim chaplaincy. As a Muslim woman I will also be reflecting on the particular qualities and abilities that Muslim women can contribute to this field.

The first opportunity I had to engage with this kind of work was very early on in my life as a youth club leader, prior to studying at university. I had been approached by a local community leader who had asked me if I would be interested in leading a youth club. This club was being led by his daughter. It came as a surprise as I had never thought about it. I did begin to think that perhaps my social demeanour was such that others found it helpful, kind and compassionate, and that this made me in some way more approachable than some others. It was not long after that I found myself leading a Muslim Girls Youth Club, guiding and coaching them in sports activities as well as holding discussions with them on their personal and Islamic issues, at times even speaking to parents. This enabled me to interact with young women, listen to their issues and concerns, and hopefully give them a sense of self-confidence. This was a wonderful preamble to the work of chaplaincy which I thoroughly enjoyed. However, at the time I was totally ignorant about chaplaincy. But this part-time job was more than just a job: somehow it gave me a sense of inner satisfaction and a kind of spiritual upliftment.

At school I loved mathematics, particularly algebra, and when I got home from school, the first thing I'd do would be my maths homework. Looking back on this, I believe it was because I found my maths teacher to be a wonderful person; his personality inspired me to work hard in his class. Thanks to him I went on to study mathematics with Arabic studies at university. In my second year we were based in Egypt, and I was able to combine the two subjects, learning Arabic whilst teaching English and mathematics, and living with a number of different families, thanks to whom I was able to discover their unique and different culture. Although I did not appreciate it at the time, this was to become extremely useful in my later work in chaplaincy. In retrospect one can say I was being prepared to walk the path towards chaplaincy.

During my Master's course at the University of Birmingham, I was the student council representative, tasked with taking their concerns to the staff body. I had developed listening skills and had won the confidence of students to represent their cases. Later I joined the university as a Lecturer in Islamic Studies. As a lecturer and a tutor there I supported students both academically and pastorally. I enjoyed my time at Birmingham and remained there to complete my PhD.

My First Chaplaincy Appointment

My first formal encounter with the work of a chaplain came when I began lecturing at the University of Warwick, where my husband was a doctoral student. He was appointed as that university's first Muslim chaplain, and I spent much of my time in the chaplaincy with him. I was still working on my

PhD at the time, and I valued the opportunity to talk to students from all over the world about my topic. However, I quickly discovered that they also had difficulties and concerns that they wanted to talk to me about. These ranged from theological and Islamic jurisprudential concerns to practical health and welfare problems. Some of these were issues faced by female students which they might not have felt comfortable broaching in the presence of a man.

Historically, universities have been able to bypass a great deal of ecumenical debate by providing a range of Christian chaplains who are all supported by their respective churches. Many institutions have an Anglican chaplain, a Catholic chaplain and a Free Church chaplain, and part-time faith advisors may also be used to support the smaller Christian minorities such as Greek Orthodox, Quakers and so on. Muslim chaplains, however, are so few in number and poorly funded – if they are funded at all – that it is normal for a single Muslim chaplain to have to support Sunnis, Shi'as, Sufis and Salafis etc. and to ensure that each ISOC does not allow one particular group to dominate Muslim student life, leaving students of other persuasions feeling they do not have a voice or a spiritual home. As someone who has worked with a wide range of groups and studied with scholars from many traditions, I find this challenge both enriching and intellectually satisfying. I have found that few students or indeed chaplains are in fact aware of the eight agreed schools of thought that have been endorsed by the Islamic scholastic fraternity, knowledge of which can make individuals much more tolerant and accepting of the different ideas and practices of their fellows.

Aune et al (2019) highlight some of the differences in both needs and provision which demonstrates one of the challenges many universities are having to face to comply with the principles of their own equality policies. They cite the findings of Sophie Gilliat-Ray of Cardiff University that "while the general ethos affirmed by chaplains was inclusive, the resources accorded to them disproportionately favoured Christian students: 'Students claiming a Christian religious identity are the principal beneficiaries of any money spent on hospitality, entertainment, chaplaincy outings, missions, retreats, or preachers'" whilst also highlighting the specific need for prayer rooms for Muslim students. This difference in needs and provision can and does often create discord in some universities, with individual groups feeling they do not receive equal provision. It is important to remember here that equality does not necessarily require identical provision. Equity should be the overriding principle with appropriate provision being delivered in accordance with the actual needs of the different groups.

I was asked to take over the full duties of chaplain when my husband later took up a position in Cambridge. I was delighted to have received the invitation; supporting and helping people has always been an important aspect of what I understand to be good practice. My family raised me to place a high value on helping others, whether it be monetary or otherwise, and I grew up in a household where there was often an unexpected guest that had been invited for food after a chance meeting. Along with chaplaincy work I continued to teach an Arabic language module to students from different courses.

My appointment as a female Muslim chaplain was perhaps surprising to some, for many chaplains are seen as Christian clerics appointed to guide their flocks on campus. For them it would possibly make more sense for the Muslim chaplain to be an imam, which would exclude women from the role. This understanding overlooks the profound difference between a Christian minister and an imam. In the Muslim community, scholarship is honoured whether the scholar is a man or a woman, whereas the principal role of the imam is to lead the prayers. There is nothing in the role of a chaplain that makes a man more appropriate than a woman. In fact, as I will highlight later, there have been many times I have found my gender to be a distinct advantage.

Previously while working as a university lecturer, I had always given support to students I was teaching, but with the demands of preparing lectures, conducting research etc., my time for this was strictly limited. I enjoyed the intellectual development that the lecturing role provided and at first I saw chaplaincy work as not requiring the same intellectual depth. From the outside it just seemed to require a caring person who listens diligently and offers appropriate advice for any problems that students are facing. Later, however, when my family moved to Bristol, I was approached by the University of Bristol to work at the multi-faith centre. They were particularly interested in my in-depth knowledge of Islamic jurisprudence, theology and philosophy, as they already had two Muslim chaplains addressing pastoral concerns. I was duly headhunted specifically because of my studies and knowledge in the field of the Islamic sciences.

Chaplains as Theologians and Pastoral Carers

The published literature on chaplaincy that considers the two distinct roles of pastoral care and theological guide is quite varied. Megan Smith of the University of Nottingham proposes the development of Christian theology specifically oriented towards university chaplaincy to address her concern that their work becomes simply a form of well-being provision (Smith, 2015) whereas Asgar Rajput, a Muslim chaplain, makes the case for a distinctly Muslim approach to chaplaincy that emphasises the humanitarian aspects of care (Rajput, 2015). Indeed, I have found substantial differences in the culture of the chaplaincies in different universities. At Warwick, the Anglican chaplain was keen to discuss theology while the Free Church focused on Christian Mission and the Catholic chaplain sought to focus on the centrality of prayer in the life of the Catholic students. In some other institutions the chaplains are much more focused on issues of student welfare. Personally, I believe both aspects of the work of chaplains are important and would not want to see one over-emphasised at the expense of the other.

Presently I work at the University of Portsmouth (UOP). The UOP was first established as a college in 1970, becoming a university in 1992. It now has approximately 26,000 students, including a high proportion of international students.

The University of Portsmouth has published its 2030 vision statement (University of Portsmouth, 2023) in which it declares its aspiration to become the University of the Future. Targets it sets to enable it to fulfil that vision include becoming truly diverse through enhancing equality, diversity and inclusion. Through this it aims to 'respect and celebrate diversity and equal opportunity through an inclusive culture'. The university greatly values the work of the chaplaincy and the role of chaplains as it sees them as playing an important role in achieving these goals. Different universities have different models of operations. The UOP chaplaincy was initially directly under the university Executive Board but has now been placed under the Department of Curriculum and Quality Enhancement, where we work closely with the Student Wellbeing Service. This contrasts with other universities where I have worked where the chaplaincy fell under the department of student Services.

The chaplaincy has historically been a principally Christian chaplaincy with three full-time Christian chaplains representing the Methodist, Anglican and Catholic denominations. This had been the case in most universities in the United Kingdom as mentioned earlier. As there has been an increase in the number of Muslim students, the demand for Muslim chaplains has increased accordingly. In 2017 the UOP appointed its first part-time paid Muslim chaplain. The first Muslim chaplain was male, and he left after a year. I then joined the university as its first female Muslim chaplain.

New students are given information on all the support services that are available. Students sometimes are sent to seek help from the chaplaincy by their academic departments or by the Student Wellbeing Service. Many exploring the university campus visit the chaplaincy. When they walk into the chaplaincy, the chaplaincy administrator, who works part-time, or one of the chaplains shows them around the chaplaincy. We have a large social space where there are tea and coffee facilities, prayer rooms and the chaplain's offices. Presently there are five chaplains – an Anglican (full-time), a Baptist (full-time) and two Catholic chaplains (one working four days a week and the other working two); and one Muslim chaplain who works three days a week. Having seen the space, many students hesitatingly ask what a chaplain is as they are unfamiliar with the concept. I am then expected to define this term and my role:

The word 'chaplain' has Christian origins; today, however, it has a much more generic meaning, indicating someone who provides pastoral, spiritual and religious support. A chaplain was originally a priest or minister who had responsibility for a chapel, but the term later came to mean an ordained member of the clergy who had been assigned a particular ministry or service. Etymologically the word 'chaplain' is derived from the Latin word *capella*, meaning a cape. This came into use in the church in connection with a story of St Martin who is said to have given half of his cloak to a beggar in an act of pastoral care. The remnant of his cloak subsequently came to be revered and the tent in which it was preserved was called a chapel. This demonstrates the centrality of pastoral care to the concept.

Having explained the meaning of 'chaplain' I am typically then asked to explain the specific role I fulfil as a Muslim chaplain in the university. I tell them that I am here to support everyone – students and staff alike – pastorally, spiritually and religiously, as well as signposting other support services within and outside the university. I am here to welcome people and to listen. With the ice finally broken, students relax, and some are even astonished how much support is available.

Adopting Chaplaincy as a Profession

For me it was only when both spiritual/theological and pastoral aspects of chaplaincy became clear that I considered adopting chaplaincy as a profession. I find myself regularly approached for both pastoral and theological guidance and support. This makes the role of the chaplain distinct and unique in the university context and one that in a post-secular society will only increase in importance.

Chaplaincy work for me came as a natural progression of what I have always enjoyed, and a deeper level of study in the various Islamic sciences, both at Masters and PhD levels, gave me a sense of confidence working in the field of Muslim chaplaincy. I have always supported all the students and staff, whether they are Muslims or non-Muslims; however, I have seen that the more understanding that Muslim chaplains have of Islamic theology, the more they are valued. Many Muslim students struggle with maintaining their religious practice alongside their academic studies and want the support of someone with the knowledge to discuss with them issues of *fiqh* (Islamic law and legal theory).

I will highlight some examples of the work I do as chaplain. I have supported a number of students from non-Muslim backgrounds who chose to embrace Islam but who have subsequently found themselves in great difficulty. Many of these students I have supported over a long period of time, some over the whole duration of their course and some I have continued to stay in touch with even beyond that.

A student – we'll call him Babar – came to see me over his concerns about student loans and whether or not they are permissible for practicing Muslims, given the strong strictures against taking interest-based loans. For him it was fortunate that I had just attended a conference of the British Board of Scholars and Imams, of which I am an active member, where it was clarified that student loans are not in fact loans at all in the Islamic jurisprudential sense as one only has to pay them back if one has the money to do so and no debt is transferred to one's family should one pass away before the loan is paid.

Another student, Khadijah was concerned with her irregular menstruation and was unsure about whether or not she should be praying and how she should purify herself for the prayer. This was a good example of a case where a non-Muslim chaplain would lack the expert knowledge to answer her query, and had there only been a male chaplain available, she might have felt very uncomfortable discussing her concern.

Principles Underpinning my Chaplaincy Work

Much of my chaplaincy work is informed by the fundamental concepts of the Islamic theology of peace, dignity and compassion:

Peace is promoted daily through the greetings of peace. The sounds of *Assalaamu Alaykum* (peace be with you) and its response *Wa alaykum assalaam* (and peace be with you too) reverberate throughout the day around me as students and staff go in and out of the prayer rooms. Striving to create peace within oneself and around them is a duty of every Muslim.

At times of difficulty and calamity we are forced to examine our purpose and place in society. The philosophy of creating peace within me and around me is one which I use to help my students. How we find peace within ourselves may vary from person to person. It is guiding others to source that peace through creativity and service, whether it be working with animals or the environment or volunteering in a shelter home.

I also act as a peacemaker between the university and the student community, helping each side to understand the perspective of the other. Common examples of this include supporting students who request extra time for their assignments because they are struggling with fasting in Ramadan, or working with departments to schedule lectures so that Muslim students can fit the obligatory prayers into their schedules. Increasingly I have found colleagues within the university very open to such discussions and they are often only too happy to ensure their students can balance their studies with their religious observance.

In the Qur'an we are told:

> 'O humanity! Indeed, we created you from a male and a female, and made you into peoples and tribes so that you may 'get to' know one another. Surely the most noble of you in the sight of Allah is the most righteous among you. Allah is truly All-Knowing, All-Aware.' (Quran 49:13)

This 'getting to know one another' is at the core of my chaplaincy work.

Hania, an international student, highlighted the need for inter-cultural education. While looking for a job she found herself in a compromising position in a private meeting with the employer, thinking that this must be 'normal' here in the UK. She actually feared she might be raped but could not even discuss her traumatic experience with her family for fear they would tell her to leave her studies and return home. Hania needed both friendly and compassionate support and guidance on British culture and customs to ensure she does not allow herself to get into such a position again in the future.

Islam represents the culmination of the earlier Abrahamic traditions such as Judaism and Christianity as expressed in the Qur'an and the teachings of the last messenger Muhammad (PBWH). It is therefore only natural for Muslims to feel connected with those from the other Abrahamic faiths and so working in a multifaith chaplaincy to support people in need comes naturally to me. In fact, we are reminded:

> 'Indeed we have dignified the children of Adam…' (Quran 17:70)

Every human possesses dignity, and I do not have any right to undermine the dignity of another person. That God alone will judge on the Day of Judgement is at the core of the Islamic message. Throughout the ancient world humans were enslaved and abused by other human beings undermining their dignity.

We should therefore be in the business of liberating humans by enabling them to be responsible for their own learning and not blindly following others just because they are priests or scholars.

Harry was a student who came for support after he was accused of raping his friend and fellow student. For him it was crucial to have someone to talk to who did not assume he was guilty and did not stand in judgement on him.

It is also important that we do not take advantage of the vulnerability of others; consequently, treating service users with dignity also informs my practice. Listening without judgement enables the person to walk with me and speak about their fears and anxieties. Being compassionate and giving full attention, speaking a kind word, smiling at a person who may be feeling down and looking glum are all key to establishing a relationship and all are deemed meritorious charitable acts by the Islamic teachings.

A Muslim student, Khaled, came to me whilst suffering depression so severe that he desperately wanted to commit suicide but could not go through with because he knew that his faith prohibited it. For Khaled, like Harry, it was essential to sit with him and build a connection with him so that he felt that someone understood him. In his case, however, Khaled also needed reassurance from someone whose knowledge of Islam he felt he could trust to help him make sense of his conflicting thoughts and emotions.

While thoughts of suicide are there for many students, only a few actually make a serious attempt: some are unsuccessful while others go through with it. Islam forbids suicide but that should not prevent us from counselling and supporting those with suicidal thoughts or indeed the families of those poor souls who fall into despair and take their own lives. These tragic cases should also remind us of the need to always be proactive, educating and nurturing the students in our care to make them strong enough and confident enough to avoid such extreme feelings of worthlessness and the notion that they have been forsaken and are unworthy of forgiveness.

The Role of Chaplaincy in Holistic Education

Chaplaincy has the potential to play a major role in the holistic educational development of a student's intellect and character. Universities have lecturers with a wide variety of personal perspectives on issues such as faith, science or sexuality. This is a very healthy situation as they contribute to developing critical and independent thought. However, it can also lead an individual to suffer a personal crisis where they cannot reconcile the differing viewpoints with their own thoughts and feelings to their satisfaction. I have supported many students and helped them to work through these issues and this requires not just the patience of a counsellor to act as a sounding board, but also a breadth of knowledge in matters of faith. I have supported a number of students in coping with their personal crises, including clashes between their understanding of science and religion, issues of gender and sexuality, relationship issues, and so on.

Another Muslim student, Nafees, came to me concerned and conflicted about his gender identity. He did not have any intimate relations with others but dressed in a particularly feminine manner and had suffered a great deal of hostility from other Muslims who were completely intolerant of what they perceived as manifest homosexuality. Nafees was already aware that Islam condemns homosexual intimacy, and he was greatly relieved to find that I could talk to him and support him without his feeling judged and condemned.

As a Muslim chaplain, prayer is the single most important issue that I deal with day to day. Students approach me asking for departmental prayer space where, on a large campus, it is impractical for them to use a central facility. Friday prayers have also been challenging for some universities as they attract so many students that identifying a suitable venue can be difficult. In fact, all the universities I have worked with have provided a large hall for this purpose, with a beautiful, dedicated space being provided at Warwick University. And at the University of Portsmouth a large, dedicated space has also been provided which is much cherished by the students.

There can also be a need to vet guest imams to ensure their sermon or khutba adheres to the ethical principles of the university and is both inclusive and beneficial. Friday prayers do however provide an excellent opportunity for the Muslim chaplain to speak to students, provide generic guidance and highlight the services available for Muslims within the chaplaincy.

Islamophobia is an issue that no Muslim chaplain can ignore. The term was first coined in 1997 by the report of the Runnymede Trust which found that Islamophobia in Britain was becoming increasingly 'more explicit, more extreme and more dangerous.' However, as Allen (2010, p. 83) observes – 'At the time of its publication, an event of the magnitude of 9/11 could not have been comprehended'. Since the attack on the World Trade Centre there has been a massive increase in verbal and physical attacks on Muslims. The past twenty years have seen many initiatives to address this, yet a great deal of prejudice against Muslims still goes unchecked.

As a female Muslim chaplain, I have a unique opportunity to contribute to challenging distorted ideas or dispelling myths – particularly about Muslim women – and thus educate my colleagues both within the chaplaincy and in the wider university. My current university has welcomed my efforts in this area and I have been invited to present both to individual departments and at university-wide events to address the lack of knowledge and understanding amongst the wider university community. For Muslims too my role is effective in challenging cultural stereotypes. After the Friday prayer I address the congregation, which is typically the domain of male community leaders in Muslim countries. I have also established the provision of space for women in the main prayer hall as was the practice at the time of the Prophet, rather than their being segregated in a separate room.

Dispelling Myths about Islam and Muslims

Other common themes range from the hyperbolic 'Muslims are planning to take over the world' to local grievances such as 'Muslims always feel 'entitled and constantly make demands on the chaplaincy'. This latter is typically connected with the previously mentioned requests for prayer space. The policies promoting equality, diversity and inclusion that are present in all universities are now leading many to welcome in Muslims to their chaplaincies. This is very encouraging, but many chaplains have found that the old fears and prejudices remain. Long-standing Christian chaplains have developed their own way of working that is appropriate to their communities and so to make them realise that the needs of the Muslim community are distinct and different requires patience and fortitude. As the late Dr. Ataullah Siddiqui observed in his report on Islam at Universities in England, 'working in an inter-faith chaplaincy may sometimes be particularly trying'. (Siddiqui A. , 2007, p. 50). Despite years of interfaith work, I am still regularly surprised at the gaps in the knowledge and understanding I find in some Christian chaplains. To give a couple of pertinent examples, the idea that men and women become 'one' through marriage is alien to Islam, where marriage is through a 'nikah' contract that forms a partnership between two distinct individuals. Also, celibacy, far from being a devotional religious practice, is positively discouraged in Islam.

Despite this there are of course great benefits from being a part of a multi-faith team championing faith in an institution that may have some strongly secular elements.

Supporting Students Who Adopt Islam

One of the key issues particular to Muslim chaplaincy that I have dealt with extensively has been the situation of students from other faiths or none who have adopted Islam and become Muslim. They struggle with both the desire to learn and practice their newfound faith and with the problems of criticism, rejection and even open hostility from their family and friends.

Sarah was an international student who, after a number of years of personal research, decided to become a Muslim. Sarah came from a very devout, ministerial Christian family. Having a Muslim in the family was an embarrassment to them and they cut ties with her, including any financial support. As she had just finished her course the university was unable to help her. She was made destitute and homeless. I had to seek funds for her until she found a job and helped her with accommodation and other issues.

A home student, Anna, felt obliged to live at home as she had no source of income. She hid her new faith from the family and could not pray or eat halal food at home. Anna was struggling with her relationships with her family and believed her parents were both racist and Islamophobic. Some popular online speakers guide people like Anna to sever ties with their non-Muslim family, but I knew that this is not the teaching of the Prophet Muhammad (PBWH). Following his example, I supported her to be patient and to strive to maintain good relations with them:

> *He who believes in Allah and the Last Day, let him maintain good relations with kins.*
> (Sahih al-Bukhari and Muslim)

A European student, Jasmine, who had also embraced Islam, was distraught when her mother stopped speaking to her. She was also struggling to learn about her new faith.

In another case, Dipika, a girl from a Hindu family, became Muslim and asked me to look after her books when she went home during the holiday as she could not take any Islamic literature back into the family home. She could not speak to her family about her faith and felt that she had two identities.

In all these heartrending stories, I was caught in the middle, trying to give them a balanced understanding of their new faith. It is often difficult to find the relevant materials easily and it is a sad fact that a great deal of unhelpful guidance is readily available on the internet. Even good scholars sometimes give inappropriate advice because they are speaking about 'typical cases' whereas as a chaplain I can focus on the individual and their unique circumstances.

In all of these cases the students came under a great deal of stress and needed considerable emotional support to be able to continue effectively with their studies. It was also important to provide guidance to minimise any long-term problems with their families. Unhelpful advice is readily available through social networking and internet sites and this could have had a major impact had there not been chaplaincy support. This work has, however, been very rewarding and in each case the student in question expressed tremendous gratitude for the help I gave them. Moments like that are highlights that make the work of chaplaincy feel truly worthwhile.

For all the students and staff I support, the chaplaincy provides a refuge and a safe space where they can receive support and an opportunity to reflect and contemplate. It's a place where they can find a companion and sounding board that for a brief period will accompany them on their life journey. For some it is a spiritual or religious journey while for others it may simply be a waystation on a difficult path they are treading.

Other Aspects of My Role

Another area of practice I have become increasingly engaged in is the development of links with the wider community. This includes meeting with local mosque imams, schools and community organisations. This is in part to promote local student recruitment and also to cement the place of the university as a civic establishment that is in touch with local community issues and events. My engagement includes attending local meetings and events as a representative of the university and also to give presentations and speeches when required.

A final feature of my work which is perhaps unique to Portsmouth University is the out-of-hours service our Chaplaincy provides. The Chaplaincy team operates a rota ensuring that someone is always available 24 hours a day, 365 days of the year. This is working alongside the residential life team and student well-being service which fulfil this role at other universities, but we are at the front line receiving the calls from security about students in distress. This can mean going out to visit students in the middle of the night or simply providing telephone support. Depending on our assessment we may then bring in the mental health advisors from the student well-being service. This can be very demanding at times. However, it is reassuring to see the high level of trust the university places in the Chaplaincy team and of course from our perspective it can, where appropriate, allow a spiritual or religious intervention which would not otherwise be considered.

Concluding Remarks

Since I embarked on my career in chaplaincy, my journey has thrown up many challenges. Although it might have been easier to revert to my former career in teaching and lecturing, my belief in the importance and value of chaplaincy work and the rewards it brings has sustained me and given me the will to persevere. I cherish the principles of chaplaincy and its unique position within higher education establishments. Chaplains have the ability to comprehend and address the concerns of staff and students in a holistic way, considering both the secular and spiritual dimensions where academic departments can be more limited and under pressure to focus more narrowly on their particular area of expertise. The demands for equality, diversity and inclusion are increasingly being incorporated into university policies, and the ability to address these concerns places chaplaincies in a unique position. More and more universities are openly stating their desire to address the development of the whole person for their students. This means that in addition to pursuing academic excellence, character education and the spiritual development of each individual is catered for. University can better serve their student 'customers' by providing a safe space within which they can be nurtured and challenged to explore themselves and to ignite a passion for life.

Chaplaincies are in an excellent position to contribute to this holistic goal. Applying those same policies of equality, diversity and inclusion within the chaplaincy necessitates the development of multifaith chaplaincies that are truly multi-faith and challenge the traditional models of these formerly exclusively Christian domains. Simply providing a formulaic Muslim chaplaincy modelled on the established Christian model would be tokenistic and limited. Faithful inclusion can be deeply challenging as it requires expanding perspectives, reflecting on one's own assumptions and being willing to consider new ways of seeing things. Change is always difficult, as we are confined by our own cultures, and it can be painful. Muslim women chaplains are in a unique position to challenge some of the existing stereotypes as they cannot be confused with imams; rather, they offer support, particularly for female students, that goes beyond what most men would be able to achieve. This does not mean there is no place for male Muslim chaplains who can, for instance, lead the prayer and deliver the Friday prayer sermon, and some institutions are now choosing to employ both male and female Muslim chaplains to get the best that both can offer.

At the University of Portsmouth, I find that there is a genuine willingness to make changes to accommodate the needs of the wider Muslim student and staff community. We are in the process of opening a new prayer room, and a lot of effort has gone into ensuring that things are done in the best way possible. We know from history that great change has seldom come without an arduous journey. Muslim chaplains as representatives of the largest and most observant of the non-Christian faiths inevitably find themselves in the eye of this storm and may sometimes be seen as a source of trouble rather than as catalysts for change and growth. They therefore need to be highly resilient, patient and compassionate towards others, particularly those who may not understand that in order to move forward, old approaches may need to be challenged and, in some cases, discarded, in order to make way for new models. Muslim women chaplains are at the heart of this critical juncture, changing the face of the role and paving the way for new models of chaplaincy.

4

Mahshid Turner
Durham University

I realize now that my present chaplaincy role from one aspect had nothing to do with me at all. I can confidently say that contrary to the words of the song 'My Way', I most certainly did not do it 'my way'. Looking back, I see now how my destiny was already shaped and that the only things that I can own during my life's journey are my mistakes and my experiences of feeling lost whenever I chose to swerve off the path. I will therefore begin this chapter with my childhood experiences to show how I was gradually nurtured for my present job as Muslim woman chaplain.

Childhood Days in Iran

Although the work at school was really punishing for a six-year-old child, I was the best in class for English because I wanted to impress my teacher. I dreamt that one day I would become a teacher like her, with the power to use a red pen and mark over the children's neat writing, and to write on what was then called the blackboard. Our English teacher certainly stood out with her bouffant hair, her smart and stylish clothing and her stiletto shoes. Although I dreamt about being a teacher, I feared the task of failing certain students who were not up to the mark. It was sad to see some friends held back in the same class for another year just because they did not pass their exams. I consoled myself by promising myself that I would make sure all my pupils passed their exams.

My childhood days in Iran were over when I was told we were going on a thirteen-day journey by bus to England. We had an accident with a lorry high above a valley in Eastern Turkey. Our bus was rolling backwards, and the assistant driver could not help us. The German driver was also badly injured and could not move, as the steering wheel had penetrated his stomach. He was shouting in German for us to jump out as he could not help us and that at any moment our bus could fall off the cliff. However, I was oblivious to all that was happening, even when all the men in our coach were clambering over me and the rest of the women and children to get to the door of the bus and save their own lives. It seemed that at that age, things were much less complicated, as I did not pass on judgement or blame, or think much about the future or the past, and lived only for the present. I now realise that our feelings are also from God, and that I was saved from feelings of anger, and the apprehension of injury or death, and that it was Divine destiny that the bus did not fall over the edge and down into the valley; I somehow knew that its destiny was to crash into a small garage near the edge of the precipice: the only building on that steep and winding road. We all managed to disembark from the bus without any serious injuries, apart from the driver and assistant driver who were both badly injured. We heard later that the lorry driver who had crashed into the bus had died. The Turkish people in the village nearby were extremely friendly. Some girls from one family came and hugged me and showed sympathy. They took our family to their house and fed us and allowed us to sleep in their home while arrangements were being made for another bus to continue with our journey. Before we set off on the rest of our journey we went to a restaurant in the village for lunch. On my way to the bathroom, the restaurant owner came towards me and picked up something from the floor, he then offered it to me and asked me to eat it. Like an obedient child I took it and put it towards my mouth, when suddenly my father appeared and slapped it out of my hand. I later found out that it was hay. The restaurant owner began to laugh loudly at my stupidity. My father ignored him for fear of retaliation. In a short period of time, I had experienced both unkindness and extreme kindness; I had been shown compassion and generosity as well as selfishness. The kind family, however, were the ones who came to wave goodbye to us.

Childhood Days in England

Even though our journey to England was gradual, as it took thirteen days for us to finally arrive in Birmingham, I still felt as if I had been beamed down from one planet to a totally different world. One day I was on my bicycle in Tehran, playing with friends, the next day, I was transplanted into a place with a different climate, a different culture, a foreign language and a place where I knew no-one. However, children adapt very easily, and it was not difficult to find friends, for there seems to be an in-built common language between young people that draws them together. For me it was some of the adults who were the problem.

My father had rented a flat in a place called Walmley, part of Sutton Coldfield near Birmingham. On enquiring about purchasing the flat, he was informed that Walmley was a 'white only' area and therefore the flat could not be sold to 'coloured' people. This conversation seemed very strange to all of us since we were not familiar with the concept of racism. My father responded by asking whether the flat could be bought in the name of my mother, who happened to have very light skin. This proposal could not be rejected as my mother was deemed to be the right 'colour' for purchasing accommodation in that area.

I started school knowing only one full sentence in English and that was: "My name is Mahshid". However, it did not take me long to learn English as I was the only 'foreign' and 'brown' person in the school and the children crowded round me asking me all sorts of questions. Some of the children were very kind and helped me to adjust to the new culture. The only anger I ever encountered was on the face of the teachers. It seemed that they resented my presence in their 'white only' school.

I will never forget one particular incident. We were in the playground on the climbing frame, and for some reason most of my class friends climbed on to one side of the frame and I was on the other side. Owing to the imbalance and the fact that the climbing frame had not been securely placed in the ground, it collapsed. Happily, none of the children was hurt. The next day at assembly, the head teacher talked about what had happened at the playground and blamed the incident solely on me, pointing to me while he spoke. The whole assembly turned to me in disgust. I felt unwanted, excluded and was overcome by a feeling of being regarded as only worthy of being thrown onto the rubbish heap. I went to the headmaster, trying to express my innocence, but it was difficult for me to explain properly on account of my lack of English skills. In any case he was not interested to hear my side of the story. None of the children was ready to back up my story apart from one boy. After that incident the children were not so friendly towards me, apart from that one boy.

I had received no notification that the next day we were going on a school trip and so I had not prepared a packed lunch. The same boy who had been brave enough to back my story saw that I was sitting alone in the coach and with no lunch. He came over and sat next to me and offered to share his sandwiches with me. I will never forget my experiences of extreme kindness and injustice at that 'white only' school.

I soon became fluent in English and when it was time for the 11-Plus exam, I found it very easy. I had no doubt that I would pass and thus be able to attend a grammar school. However, on the day that the results were out, everyone received their results except me. I went to enquire from the head, but he just ignored me. I learned years later that my exam papers had been held back and that many non-white people had had the same experience.

My secondary education began at a secondary modern school where many of the pupils were classed as 'non-white'. My sister, my brother and I had to walk a long distance from the 'white only' area to our new school. Most of the teachers were very nice and tried their best to educate us in the best way they could. There was, however, one teacher whom everyone feared. She took a particular dislike to one black girl in our class and would hit her on a regular basis, most of the time without any reason or justification. The whole class hated that teacher and every single pupil acted as if they were part of a 'well-being' team, going out of their way to show kindness and compassion towards the girl who was being treated with such cruelty. My friend informed me later that physical violence was the norm for her at home too.

I put my experience down to Divine decree, and determining, for I came to realise that my 'life education' at that school was more important than actual education. However, I progressed well and climbed from the lowest stream to the highest, along with five other pupils from our girls' secondary school. We were considered the 'cream of the crop' and through prior arrangements and agreements were given the option to continue our education either at the local girls' grammar school or at a mixed-sex comprehensive school. Although we were greeted well at the grammar school, we chose the comprehensive school, purely because we were attracted to the idea of a mixed-sex school.

It was not surprising that none of us focused seriously on our education, since after five years at an all-girls secondary modern school we were suddenly let loose in a mixed school. I soon made friends with an Irish girl and another girl whose parents were originally from Italy. Somehow, I seemed to get on better with people from mixed cultures. There was one boy who followed me everywhere. One day during class registration, I opened my notebook to take notes, as I usually did, when I found a badly written sentence in Persian: It said, 'I love you'. I was shocked to hear that he had gone to the library to look for that sentence and had so carefully copied it out in actual Persian script. This same boy seemed to be searching to find meaning in his life and began a conversation with me and my Irish friend about God. My friend was a believing and practicing Catholic and what we had in common was that we both felt a close connection to God. On hearing that we both vouched for the existence of God and were certain about his existence, he became angry and frustrated as he could not understand how we could believe in a Creator who was not physically visible and palpable. But we did leave a lot of questions in his mind which he felt he really needed to answer.

Married Life

The boy at school who was searching for meaning eventually became my life partner, and we continued to question the purpose of our existence together. Belief in the transcendent Creator had very little to do with my upbringing or culture; it was just something very strong and unbreakable that was confirmed innately. But there were still so many unanswered questions, in particular the problem of suffering and evil. But my partner and I were now fellow travelers, questioning together the futility of a life that is lived without purpose, direction, meaning and justice.

Together we met people whose strong beliefs were manifested through their knowledge, their compassion and their kindness, which left a lasting and timeless mark in our hearts. But of course we also met people who lived shallow and pretentious lives. We met people who, as cultural anthropologist Ernest Becker (1924-1974) puts it, in their attempt to transcend the dilemma of immortality, invented their own 'immortality projects'.[24] This would manifest in various ways, such as ensuring that titles are inherited by their descendants after their death, or through the building of tall monuments in the hope of always being remembered. This construction of imaginary eternity projects in a transient world also manifests in other endeavours and stratagems, such as spending extensive amounts of money to keep oneself young by various means, including health drives, lotions and potions to keep wrinkles at bay, and spending millions on often very expensive cosmetic procedures.

It became so clear to my husband and me that the search for permanence and meaning was so evidently innate that everyone sought it. But the problem was that not everyone found it. This was inevitably because they were looking in the wrong place. They were expecting permanence from a transient world. Deep down they knew that this world could not give them the permanence they so desperately sought, but the refusal to acknowledge their own impotence and dependence made them cling on even harder to whatever they could grasp, engaging with as many people as possible in what was basically a 'shared pretence'. We had many dear friends and people we loved who were so much part of this 'shared pretence' that it made us both feel very uncomfortable. This does not mean that we also did not partake of it; indeed, we were also very much drawn to that way of thinking, but we considered ourselves fortunate to have been made aware of it.

My husband once pretended to tell a friend's fortune by reading her coffee cup. He is not a fortune-teller by any stretch of the imagination but was thoroughly enjoying himself making up stories about her predicted future, and my friend loved hearing them. The stories were becoming more and more outlandish, to say the least, so I interrupted his fun and told our friend that he was just making everything up. However, she did not want it to stop and in the end, she said: 'I know, just let him get on with it'. This astounded both of us. It was like a small window into the world of those who are happy to be part of a shared illusion, one which promises permanence when in fact ephemerality is its true nature.

We also took comfort by reading works of fiction such as *Moths* by Ouida,[25] in which skittish, capricious characters such as 'Dolly' confirmed our shared experience of the shallowness and futility that governs many human lives. We also read non-fiction books by authors such as Jalāl-al-Dīn Rūmī (1207-1273),[26] and Ibn Arabī (1165-1240)[27] and contemporary works which explain the nature of this world so clearly, such as the *Risale-i Nur* by Said Nursi (1877-1960).[28]

Working Life

Although my husband and I were both accepted to study at Durham University, I became pregnant and declined the acceptance, as I preferred to look after my baby myself. It was years later, when our three children started school, that I began my studies and working life in earnest. I was thirsty for knowledge after such a long time given solely to my children and so I decided to do a Social Sciences degree via the Open University. My degree opened my eyes to so many different worldviews. I then decided I wanted to extend my caring to the society in which I lived, and to help specifically those with mental health problems, and so did a second degree in Social Work (Mental Health). However, my experience showed me that social work was more about patching up people's lives rather than helping them not to become so entangled in the first place. Consequently, I chose to work in the community. I worked for Age Concern as a Project Office with ethnic minority older people. But I also worked with many young people, particularly refugees and asylum seekers, as part of many intergenerational projects that I led. It seemed that at that time, most of the issues that refugees needed support with were not part of the remit of the statutory institutions. Therefore, I began to recruit volunteers, including my husband and one of my sons, who gave their weekends to help refugees and asylum seekers with letters they needed to write dealing with legal issues or medical problems, as well as giving them English lessons and support with the use of computers.

My next job was with Sure Start as Community Health Development Specialist, where I gave support and guidance to young underprivileged families concerning all aspects of healthy living. While working, I also did an MSc in Public Health and Health Sciences. For my dissertation, I chose the title of 'Barriers to Healthy Eating'. My target audience comprised the families using the Sure Start centres in three different areas of the North-East of England. The open-ended interview questions enabled me to enter their world and uncover the symbolic meanings of food and its relation to so many feelings, particularly, love. Poverty or lack of food was not the main issue; for many the issue was not being together as a family and not eating together, not even for Sunday dinner. It was expressed by many that on numerous occasions as a child, either food was left for them to eat on their own or they had to prepare something for themselves. It was not the feelings of hunger which hurt them so badly, it was the symbolic non-acknowledgement of their existence which left painful scars. One young mum, who had expressed these feelings in detail, described the importance of Sunday dinner for her own family. She stated that although in the week they had to look for bargains as they could not always have the food they wanted, she made sure that Sunday dinner would be an exception. There would always be meat and potatoes, two or three different kinds of vegetables and, most importantly, gravy. And everyone would sit around the table together. She even described the ingredients of Sunday dinner with such passion as though it was love that she was placing on the plates – the love that she clearly craved as a child.

After the Sure Start projects were coming to an end, I was offered the opportunity to work for the NHS as a Specialist Stop Smoking Advisor. I seemed to have a high rate of success with helping people stop smoking. Many people wanted to come and see me even after they had given up. While working in hospital, I was helping a patient who was having treatment for cancer to stop smoking. She successfully gave up smoking and on my last visit I happened to compliment her on her beautiful dressing gown. She thanked me with a smiling face, expressing her gratitude and stating that 'my kind words would always remain in her heart'. A week later I meant to go and visit her again, but I was informed that she had passed away. I realised through this experience that our listening skills and non-judgmental stance are what people needed most.

Although I enjoyed my profession, I decided to take the opportunity of early retirement, as the NHS as an institution was becoming extremely bureaucratic, and people were being recruited from backgrounds – banking, for instance, or middle management – which seem totally incompatible with the needs of a caring role, with many nurses, teachers and social workers being pushed aside and basically forced onto the scrapheap.

After taking early retirement, I studied for three more degrees mainly in alternative therapies, as well as a degree in teaching. However, my main interest was to explore more how mental health can be impacted positively by religious belief, in particular from a Muslim perspective. So, I applied to Durham University again and was accepted by the Theology Department to do a PhD on the subject. And while doing my PhD, I also joined the Islamic Society Executive as Female Assistant President. This gave me the opportunity to mingle with many young students who experienced many problems in all areas. But there was no confidential space to give support. I therefore contacted the university and asked if I could become the Muslim chaplain for Durham University as such a position was very much needed. It took about a year to go through the official process for recruiting me as a non-contractual chaplain or volunteer for Durham University. Before I knew it, my picture was in the papers as I was the first Muslim woman chaplain to be recruited at a Higher Education Institution in the United Kingdom. It seemed that it was only after premature retirement that I had found the job that I was destined for. Although my journey in life, both experientially and academically, was devoted to the search for meaning, I still felt that I needed to find out more about the role of chaplaincy. So once again I became a student and did an MA in Muslim Chaplaincy at Markfield.

Chaplaincy at Durham University

I soon realized that the most difficult thing about Muslim chaplaincy was the fact that very few Muslims knew what Muslim chaplaincy was or what its role constituted. I therefore had to explain the role of chaplaincy to most people I encountered. I explained that while an imam's role is to lead prayers and give guidance on external religious queries, a chaplain's role was more holistic, as they are there for the whole person. In other words, a chaplain's role is to care for all aspects of student and staff well-being in their university community. This would include not only practical support by mediating between different departments, but also support with issues linked to physical, mental and spiritual health. Chaplains are different from other health care providers in that they are qualified to support with psycho-spiritual matters, since they have expertise in the relation between faith and physical and mental well-being. Doing a PhD for five years that focused conceptually on just one word – the word *ḥuzn*, which means 'grief as a consequence of loss' – from a Muslim perspective was something which prepared me to deal confidently with many issues that both staff and students experience as a result of loss. These issues range from loss of home life, after having moved away from the comfort of the family home, to loss of cultural security, for example, in the case of international students grappling with a new culture, language and environment. Other issues that stood out were those pertaining to breakdowns in relationships and, during COVID, loss of health and consequently its impact on mental health.

Building Trust

Another difficulty I encountered was getting others to know of my existence and obtaining the trust of the student and staff community at my institution. It seemed that all the odds were against me. Not only was there a lack of understanding of the role of Muslim chaplains, but I was also a woman, and a woman born in Iran. All these characteristics opened a huge gateway for assumptions.

Because Durham University is a collegiate university, it was difficult for Muslim students to meet other Muslim students from different colleges and departments. Although Durham Islamic Society has always been an active Society, some Muslim students tend to be hesitant to join the Society because they may not consider themselves to be 'religious enough'. I therefore organised many intra-faith, interfaith and intercultural activities which would enable students to get to meet Muslims from different colleges and departments, as well as like-minded people from different faiths and cultures. Also, I hoped that since I was the organiser of these groups, they would also get to know me and thus be able to slowly begin to break their assumptions and gain my support to deal with any issues that they may be having difficulty coping with. One example of the many activities we had was an environmental project led by one of the students, where students from all faiths got together to discuss what the environment meant to them from their own faith or cultural perspective. The group then linked in with the community and the council to organise a joint walk, picnic and litter-picking event. This event brought students and members of the community together and was lauded in the press.

Another long project, lasting around three years, was the joint intergenerational project with Durham University Interfaith Forum which I organised in collaboration with Durham Age UK. A Muslim student, who was passionate about working in the community, and supporting older people, led this project. We organised weekly visits for students from different faiths and cultures to a local older people's care home to get to know and chat to the residents. This project broke barriers at many levels. Not only was it beneficial for young people to mix with older residents in the care home, but it also spoke volumes to people who worked there, since they experienced, both visually and practically, that kindness and compassion is universal, despite differences in age, culture and faith. The feedback on this project was positive from all sides.

Students enjoyed and learned a great deal from their experience and the care home organisers were pleasantly surprised at the positive effect the students' visits had on the well-being of the residents. This befriending scheme won a coveted North-East Community Award.

Many other interfaith groups were organised and another group worth mentioning is the Inspirational Women's Group, where women students of all faiths and none get together to talk about inspirational women in history. In our group we had a mix of staff and students, both undergraduate and postgraduate, from Jewish, Catholic Protestant and no-faith backgrounds. Everyone in the group had the opportunity to research and then to talk about a woman who inspired them, from religious figures to women of fame and influence, or even women who were not famous, and who were not recognised or appreciated as much as they should be for the contributions they have made to society. After each talk there would be questions, followed by discussion. We discussed the attributes these women manifested and why we were drawn to them – attributes such as courage, compassion, equality and justice. Even though members of the group were all from different faiths, they were nevertheless drawn together by their passion and awe for the qualities the chosen figures manifested.

While universities provide many programs and activities for students in their institutions, unfortunately not all of these activities are suitable for practicing Muslim students. For example, many female students have informed me that they feel out of place wearing their modest attire and therefore choose not to attend formal dinners, for example. Small changes to invitations, which insist not just on the requirement of 'formal dress' but also give the option of 'own cultural attire' would be more inclusive and may signal that Muslim students are welcome too. Such small changes, including non-alcohol tables, would help universities not only to tick more Equality, Diversity and Inclusion boxes, but also to contribute towards real and much needed structural changes.

Universities also recognise the contribution of physical activity to general well-being, and so are excellent providers of sports activities. In our university, as well as a very large sports centre which is open to the public as well as students, every college also has its own sports activities, and most colleges have their own gyms. However, many practicing Muslim students are not able to take part in these activities owing to dress code and mixed sex issues. Therefore, I organised a 'women only' badminton group, with one student who happened to be very good at badminton taking the lead. We met once a week in Freeman's Quay sports centre in the middle of Durham. There, Muslim female students did not feel out of place in their modest clothing. Playing badminton was not just about sport, it was a social event where female students felt comfortable together and created a kind space where there were plenty of smiles and laughter and encouragement to gain expertise in the game. I also contacted St. Aidan's, one of the Durham colleges, to enquire about 'women only' time slots for gym. Hopefully this will be something that will be taken up by all universities. Unless these structural changes are made to accommodate the needs of all students, universities cannot claim to be truly inclusive.

Pastoral Care

Pastoral care is about helping students and staff with difficulties they may be experiencing and supporting them in their journey of healing and wholeness. Boundaries of confidentiality must be explained before offering guidance. A chaplain is required to have good pastoral skills. These include listening skills; empathy; compassion; and the ability to comfort and pray for people if they require it.

Sometimes pastoral care begins even before students or staff arrive at the university. Even at the enquiry stage, there may be some fear or apprehension. Much of my time is spent responding to enquiries from potential staff and students as to whether the university adequately provides for the religious needs of Muslims. Below is an example of such an enquiry:

> *I tried to search for the availability of Muslim accommodation, mosques, halal food and meat shops in Durham but unfortunately it seems like there are none. I really thought I was going to be the fish out of water until I saw your video. I am hoping that you would be able to help me. I am currently really anxious about moving there alone…*

Enquiries like these are followed by letters of reassurance that I am here to support them at every step of their journey in order to ensure they settle comfortably in their new home. The aim is to ensure students and staff are welcomed and to help to decrease the apprehensions they may have about certain issues pertaining to their faith needs. Pastoral care, therefore, often begins even before students arrive and in most instances has a positive outcome, as this response exemplifies:

> *Thank you for your reply and helpful information. I feel more at ease now because of you.*

In the first few months after arrival, many students face problems with settling into their new surroundings. These include problems with accommodation, catering, illness, work, relationship issues, financial issues, identity issues and specific issues related to faith, both in the area of belief as well as practice. Examples of some of these issues have been discussed in Chapter One.

Role as Mediator, Moderator and Educator

There are many practical issues that students and staff face, particularly in the first few months after their arrival. Issues include things such as inappropriate accommodation; the clash of exams with Ramadan or major festivals; experiences of Islamophobia; the lack of adequate provision of halal food, and many similar matters. I will give only one example here, namely the problems which attend halal catering, as I have already discussed some of the other problems – such as clashes of exams with Ramadan and my role as mediator – in Chapter One.

Food may not seem an important issue, but as discussed before, it is what food symbolises that is important. The body craves the nourishment of the soul much more than the nourishment of the stomach. I remember once I went to visit someone in a university and at lunch time I went to the canteen. Although there was no visible multicultural presence as far as one could presume, I noticed that behind the glass server some sandwiches were placed which were labelled: halal chicken and halal beef. Suddenly I felt very different, a feeling of being accepted, I could release the tension in my shoulders; I'd been accepted and included as a guest, just like everyone else. Even though I did not want meat and I opted for the vegetarian option, I could not believe that the sight of a 'halal' label would have such an effect on me. I realised that just as the Sunday dinner was so important to the lady I interviewed in Sure Start all those years ago because it conveyed messages of acceptance, inclusion and love, the provision of halal meat also helped me to understand and experience similar sentiments. The provision of meat spoke volumes to me. It said: 'Peace be with you. You are welcome here'. In my university, it was argued for many years that vegetarian food was provided for Muslim students. Unfortunately, vegetarian food sends that message of welcoming love to vegetarians and not necessarily to Muslims.

It is understandable that it is difficult to cater for the dietary needs of all students. However, careful consultation and planning is something that needs to continue. As someone who has listened to the dietary needs of students over the years, I have insisted that I should be included in the consultations. Also, the Muslim chaplain is the right person to consult with, not just for dietary needs per sae, but also regarding provision, to ensure the food is cooked in a halal way. For example, a spoon that has been used to stir the non-halal gravy, and which may contain oil from non-halal meat, cannot be used to stir the halal gravy. There are many such issues. In-house training can easily be provided to discuss provision of food, cooking methods, how to cut down costs and how all students, including vegetarians and vegans, Jews and Muslims and the like can be provided with the appropriate kind of food. There are many discussions to be had in this area, but unfortunately communication has been poor.

A main part of my mediating role has been to be the voice of Muslim students and staff and members and executive members of the Islamic Society. My role is to ensure that their voices are heard and their needs are met, especially since executive members are re-elected on an annual basis and it becomes difficult for them to take matters pertaining to Muslim students forward. Support and advice have to be given to the Islamic Society when requested, particularly on issues pertaining to liaising and mediating with various people in the university for arrangements concerning Ramadan, Eid and other such activities. Furthermore, advice has also been given in the past with regard to the training of a group of students to take the responsibility as prayer leaders (imams) for the Friday congregational prayers.

Prophetic Role

The prophetic role of a chaplain simply means being an advocate and champion for student and staff needs generally and one's own faith group in particular. Many practical needs of Muslim students are linked to both their physical and spiritual well-being. However, the status of a non-contractual chaplain makes it very difficult to help bring about changes which are both beneficial to students and staff as well as to the university as an institution. There are many reasons for this. Firstly, the opportunity is not always given to the Muslim chaplain to discuss issues which students and staff raise directly. The outcome of this often leads to either misrepresentation or a diluted version of the issues raised. In this way, a lot of time and energy is often wasted, as the desired outcomes will not have been achieved.

Another barrier to the prophetic role of non-contractual chaplaincy title holders is status. One is considered to be 'staff but not staff' and thus one is made to feel neither here nor there – a feeling of being in 'no man's land'. There are many responsibilities on the shoulders of the Muslim chaplain and trying to fulfil these responsibilities in the best way one can effectively, while one occupies the lowest rank – or even a 'non rank' – in the university has been very difficult. This could be because of the hierarchy within the institution and the powers associated with it, or because non-contractual chaplains have limited direct contact with service providers within the institution, or simply because they are not taken seriously because of their status as non-contractual chaplains. Moreover, the willingness of the university to appoint a paid position for an imam, whose only task is to lead the Friday prayers, devalues the work of Muslim chaplains, particularly when the chaplain is a woman. Despite the holistic work which contributes to the general well-being of students and staff, somehow the work of a Muslim woman chaplain is seen in a less favourable light than the work of an imam. In fact, if an imam is appointed, it should be the task of the Muslim woman chaplain to line manage him rather than a chaplain from a different faith, which is often the case.

A non-contractual chaplain also does not get an automatic right to access equipment such as laptops and mobile phones. During COVID and afterwards, when hybrid working became the norm, lack of access to necessary equipment made it very difficult for me to do my job as Muslim chaplain. My request for a laptop was turned down on the grounds that I was not 'paid staff'. My personal laptop had broken down and I had to rely on my personal mobile phone to deal with university emails. I had a few referrals requesting the support of the Muslim chaplain from students who were going through traumatic experiences and suffering severe mental health problems. Although counselling and social services were supporting these cases, they also requested spiritual support from the Muslim chaplain. Happily, St. Aidan's college understood the difficult situation I was in and gave me a college laptop for work purposes. I also requested a mobile phone, as for some cases I felt that using my own personal phone presented a confidentiality risk. But this request was also turned down. These are just a few examples of the barriers to effective chaplaincy work which, as a 'non-contractual chaplain', I have had to overcome.

Involvement in the University BAME Network

I received an invitation from one of the co-founders of the University BAME network to consider becoming a BAME co-chair. I felt that I shared the same passion for justice, equality and inclusivity as the BAME network and therefore considered myself suitable to join this group as co-chair. Not long after joining, many of the original co-founders left and one of the staff representatives also left later. He gave me the advice that since my knowledge area was the needs of Muslim students and staff, I could contribute greatly to the BAME network by being a voice for their specific needs. Following his advice, apart from supporting general BAME issues and taking part in the organisation of Black History Month activities and many other such duties, I used the BAME platform and network to raise issues about Ramadan and the needs of Muslim students which were not being accommodated. I believed that writing the *Ramadan Guidance* for the university would be a start to raising awareness of the needs of Muslim students. After many obstacles, eventually the *Ramadan Guidance* was approved. I received much helpful feedback, including from departments that were unaware of the needs of Muslim students generally and during Ramadan in particular. Despite the fact that I had the best interests of the university and students and staff at heart to bring about positive changes, sometimes I was seen as a rebel, made to feel guilty, or out of my 'place' by pointing out how small changes could bring about positive outcomes. As Sarah Ahmed points out, if you challenge anything, you run the risk of being labelled as 'challenging' yourself:

> *The more evidence she gathers to challenge their interpretation of the procedures, the more she is treated as being challenging.*[29]

Being a non-contractual chaplain has been very challenging; at times it has felt like being surrounded by sharp arrows pointing at me in order to make me feel uneasy. But among those arrows there have been a few which have carried compassionate messages of support and encouragement. This is what has kept me going as a Muslim chaplain, along with messages from students and staff such as this:

> *Thank you so much for always providing one solution or another every time I reach out to you, Mahshid! I never feel let down and I cannot tell you how much this means to me. Even though we may not meet quite frequently, just knowing that you are here for us has been a great source of comfort to me & so many other Muslim students at Durham. Lots of love* ♥

5

Rukia Bi
Keele University

Since its initiation seventy-four years ago, the unheard of became the heard – the first female Muslim chaplain entered Keele University – and it was clear that change was coming. With its growing Muslim student demographic, the university was finding itself short of the necessary resources to deal with the challenges arising – issues such as the lack of prayer spaces or the need to making reasonable adjustments to student services. Eventually it was agreed that a specialist role needed to be developed to bridge the gap – namely a Muslim chaplain. In this chapter, I will be sharing my personal experience as a Muslim chaplain at Keele University. I will discuss its successes and challenges, the unique and innovative services the role offers, and several key case studies which help to build a clearer picture of the role.

The Keele Chaplaincy team is unique in its own way, comprising a team of four, representing Catholics, Free Church, Anglicans and Muslims, catering to people of all faiths and none, for everyone is welcome. The chaplaincy team looks beyond labels and works according to the principle of the unity of 'faith' and basic morality; in other words, the principle of doing good, showing love and being open to accept and listen. The team works together on shared projects and campaigns to promote collaboration and coexistence between faiths, particularly with our 'pop-up' chaplaincy slots, where we visit departments across campus offering our support and service. Chaplaincy is not about the differing beliefs or opinions; it is about celebrating similarities while learning about differences, and always showcasing this unity to students and staff alike. This includes campaigns such as the 'Never OK' campaign, which ensures that students and staff are protected and supported on campus without fear of discrimination. Furthermore, we work together on interfaith events, including an initiative known as 'One Blessed Night', which is a showcase of monologues in which students share their personal journeys to faith, or explain what faith means to them. These events bring people of various backgrounds together and focus on the element of unity and shared learning.

The Christian chaplains are supported by both the Church and the university – this includes both religious and financial support. Staff salaries and housing are part-paid by the Church, which eases the burden on the university to facilitate these costs, especially at times of financial instability and redundancy. However, all three Christian chaplains are full-time in their roles, whereas the role of Muslim chaplain is part-time. The vision, however, is that, God willing, the Muslim chaplaincy will be full-time in the future. The Muslim chaplaincy differs in that it is funded directly by the university, which is a positive move in the direction of advocating for this much needed role.

Chaplaincy roles are often compared, but every role is unique in itself; it is not about the number of one-to-ones, or the numbers of young people reached, but about the difference that the role of chaplain brings to the university experience. Each chaplain role is created organically by the needs of the community. The role of Muslim chaplain differs slightly from that of other chaplains in that alongside pastoral care provided, many departments make student referrals to the service. The Keele Chaplaincy is all in all a strong, determined and comforting team: a force for good that makes a difference and brings about change little by little.

For some, the term chaplain connotes the 'God squad': those who spend their days praying, with the rest of their lives being a total mystery. However, beyond the assumptions and stereotypes, the role of a chaplain encompasses a range of higher education roles. A chaplain can be a one-to-one counsellor and a faith advisor; s/he can be a social activist and a giver of pastoral care, always with a listening ear and an empathetic heart. There is all of this and much more, and believe me, there is a lot. A Muslim chaplain therefore may have a somewhat generic job description, but s/he has multifarious roles and countless different duties. The question I repeatedly ask myself is whether the term 'chaplain' adequately encompasses what I do. The answer, I find, is that it does not, but then which term or title would? I am listed as a chaplain for "people of all faiths and none", and so is chaplaincy beyond religion? Again, I find that no answer is forthcoming.

Chaplaincy should, no matter how many times it is contested, be considered a crucial part of the university experience, for it is usually the first port of call for students of faith with issues to discuss or indeed anyone who is seeking a non-judgmental listening ear. Chaplaincy offers students a space for students who are ill at ease with the university experience – students, for example, who may be introverts in need of a safe group to help them settle. The role of chaplains is to listen, educate and bring people together for dialogue, socialising, worship and learning, while all the time centering the student. With their twin commitments to their faith and the higher education provider, chaplains seek the betterment of the university and the development of positive expressions of faith within it.

I chose the journey of chaplaincy following a tough personal experience at university, where I had no-one who could understand me, my context or my background. The advice and referrals I received were always generic, as though I was just another face in a crowd, and I felt that there was nothing which could help me individually as a person. Faith always played a crucial role in my life, but the support services were ill-equipped to support someonelike me. It was at this point that I gave up on university services and began the journey of becoming a chaplain – a Muslim chaplain – to help those with a similar plight to mine. With the growing number of female Muslim students in the higher education sector, the need for female Muslim chaplains is also growing.

I have studied Islam for over twenty years and have been a teacher of the Quran and the Islamic sciences for the last fifteen. I try to live and breathe Islam: it is my identity, my pride, my crown, my educator, my everything, and the role of Muslim chaplain allows me to freely practice this within a work environment. I think it is important to understand the difference between simply following a religion and actively believing in it. One can grow up in a religious family and follow one's parents' footsteps or one can grow up in with no religious upbringing at all and then discover religion oneself. No matter what the situation is, it is important to note that the only way you can truly follow a religion is by understanding, learning and listening. And chaplaincy allows the space in which one can do that. Because of this, I am better equipped to respond to student needs when it comes to spirituality and finding a path. From my own experience as a young female and a chaplain at a university, I have come to realise that generally, we as humans begin seriously asking questions pertaining to faith, the existence of God and creation around the time we are at university. Young people begin to find themselves at this age and having a chaplain at hand to explore this with and help where necessary is very much welcomed.

As a female Muslim chaplain, I realise the dynamics are unique – not only am I a role model to the Muslim and non-Muslim women on campus, but I am also accessible and more approachable in distinct ways. In Islam there is the notion of the *fitra* or 'God-given disposition', and I believe that the *fitra* of women tends to be more empathetic, approachable, caring and loving – all of which seem an ideal fit for the role of a woman chaplain. While both male and female students reach out to me for one-to-one services, this does not happen to the same extent in the case of my male counterparts within the chaplaincy network at Keele. This demonstrates the need for more females to enter chaplaincy, as the propensity of students to prefer female chaplains to males is quite pronounced. The question, however, is why this is the case. Do students feel more comfortable approaching a woman rather than a man and, if so, is that down to the innate nature – the *fitra* – of women?

However, given issues of privacy and anonymity which are key to the chaplain-client relationship, there are undeniably risk and safety concerns to be taken into consideration. Firstly, all one-to-one sessions with students take place in private and closed environments, with attendant risks such as verbal or even physical abuse for which there is no mitigation. Students want discretion in the safe space, but this comes with its own risks. In addition, owing to the sensitivity of the one-to-ones, sessions cannot be recorded or largely noted, which again leaves the risk of hearsay. In order to protect chaplains in this process, Keele University has developed a recording platform, which anonymizes the data inputted while serving as a data base for future referral.

In addition to the risks to the chaplains, there is also a risk from the perspective of the student when taking into account their disclosures or confessions. If a student discloses something which constitutes a considerable welfare concern, it is the duty and responsibility of the chaplain to actively report to the safeguarding teams at the university via student services. But does this not violate the notion of the safe space in which the disclosure was made? And does it not undermine the role? This is a contentious issue, but it is of the utmost importance to ensure that the 'Do No Harm' principle is taken seriously, and that students are supported and protected from harm, whether it be from themselves or other students. Chaplains have dealt with severe cases of bullying, sexual blackmail, forced marriage and sexual assault, among other things, and it is our duty to ensure that these are reported and the pathways to other services provided in order to ensure the safety of the students.

Having been in the role for over five years, I feel that I add to students' growth and personal journeys, helping them to find themselves at a crucial and often very challenging time of their lives. They call it the "time of uncertainty", as young people are full of ideas, desires, issues and problems while also trying to live their best lives. Young people at this stage of their lives are beginning to figure out where they will fit into the adult world. In the university setting in particular it is a time for big changes that comes with a lot of freedom and happiness, along with feelings of nostalgia and apprehension. It is a time when most young people are comfortable seeking advice from others, including their parents and support service, and when they most often realise that they may need some guidance to navigate their way through university. Sometimes, people need a safe space of guidance, and chaplaincy is just that, providing a space to allow students to be at ease.

The role of chaplain also provides a huge and much needed platform from which one is able to dispel misconceptions concerning Islam and Muslims which people may have, affording a golden opportunity to counter any negative impressions of the faith and its adherents that the Muslim minority often has to contend with. To this end, we have actually set up workshops in which such misconceptions and fears could be allayed.

The chaplaincy role also extends to dispelling unease in students who feel overwhelmed by their course and its requirements, particularly if they feel they are compromising their faith. This situation is particularly relevant to students of medicine who work on cadavers, which they understand to be disrespectful according to the laws of Islam. The Muslim chaplain is able to give such students informed answers and possible solutions to such problems, thus easing their anxiety and helping them to negotiate reasonable compromise situations with their departments wherever possible. There are also medical students who will feel considerable unease at potential compromises to modesty when learning to examine patients. Again, the Muslim chaplain's role is to help and highlight any exceptional provisions in Islamic law when it comes to providing intimate care, while at the same time seeking support from the medical school itself to help resolve problems. I am currently working with the local school of medicine, with medical students and with Manchester University's Muslim chaplain to produce a handbook to answer any FAQs and to serve as a resource for future students. It is to be hoped that this initiative will minimise any immediate unease for students as well as providing a source of information and clarification.

Another situation that requires the utmost attention of a Muslim chaplain is the occurrence of international crises. Many students on campus, both international and local, can be affected by a wide range of international crises, and the university's approach often draws huge criticism from Muslim students. The role of the Muslim Chaplain is to use the platform to lobby the university and the Vice-Chancellor to navigate a better approach that is inclusive of all, and for the university to have a wholesome and consistent response to any event that will affect any of our staff or students. Such an approach is always greatly welcomed and signifies a positive move in the engagement of Muslims within a higher education setting. In addition to this, the platform also provides a positive image when it comes to issues such as modest clothing (hijab) and charity-giving, to name but two.

Within the university setting, I come across a varied caseload, including issues such as: identity crises, cultural problems such as forced and arranged marriage; the breakdown or loss of faith; abuse, be it physical, psychological or religious; addiction to pornography; bullying; estrangement from family; religious restrictions; openings to faith and requests for information about Islamic issues. While I have knowledge of the given areas, it is impossible to have extensive specialist knowledge across the board, so the role of the chaplain is to listen, empathise and provide pathways to solutions, and not to be an expert in everything. Providing positive pathways allows the chaplain to pull in resources from other local services to ease the burden on the chaplaincy and find more effective solutions for the students. This includes using the local council mental health services, local mosques and madrasas (religious schools), anonymous groups, and volunteer networks, to name but a few.

Faith Societies

Another important area of work for a Muslim chaplain is working closely with different faith societies, particularly those within one's own faith. One of my roles is to work closely with the Islamic Society, and recently with the formation of the Ahl al-Bayt society also. The Muslim chaplain is usually the first port of call for such societies, and is accessed for support for various events, personal help or even issues concerning prayer spaces and issues pertaining to the society's resources. This aspect of the role is certainly one of those that I enjoy most: to see young adults committed to their faith and practice and to be looked upon as an older sister to give help when they need it most. Yet this part of the role has its challenges, too, not least in terms of managing their expectations of me and how they perceive the role and functions of a chaplain. The expectations can often go beyond one's role as chaplain, to the point where one becomes torn internally. Nevertheless, one has to remain committed to the role prescribed by the institute. However, over the years I have noticed a better understating of the role of chaplain, which has brought about great change and improvement to the relationship between the chaplain and the host institution.

Case Studies

Case studies are a crucial component in demonstrating the impact of chaplaincy, whilst providing detailed descriptions of outputs and outcomes. The following case studies look at student one-to-ones, based on real life situations. Names have been changed for safeguarding purposes, and cases slightly altered to maximise anonymity.

Student Case Study 1 – 'Showing an Interest in Islam'

During the Covid pandemic, an atheist astrophysics student approached me, showing interest in Islam and wanting to explore means of conversion. This led to an immediate dilemma with regard to my position: should I focus on my role as a Muslim and ensure they enter the fold of Islam, or should I focus on my role as chaplain and simply listen without bias? I chose the middle ground and asked the student to come to an understanding of the existence of God primarily, before finding any religion. Once he understood God, he would find the path that suited him. Over a period of a year, the student had weekly one-on-ones, questioning his conflicting thoughts between science and God, and what his ideal world looked like, but also why there was hurt, pain and death. For every question I gave no answer, but left him with more questions, to help him assess and reach his own understanding. In 2021, the student converted to Islam, having found God through his own path and reasoning. He felt comforted by the support I had provided, but ultimately the decision was his own. My role as a chaplain was successful: I played the non-biased listening ear, providing support and guidance as required.

Student Case Study 2 – Pornography Addiction

A Muslim student requested a one-to-one session with me after failing to find support through his own circle of friends, the local mosque or online forums. The student had struggled with a porn addiction for the last five years, following a failed early marriage and a high sex drive. The student was consumed by his addiction, having to take time out across the day to access content, followed by masturbation and the need for full ablution. The student wanted to understand how to break the addiction, as the guilt for violating the law of Islam was burdening him further. He wanted to gain this safe support without having to access external support, such as help from NHS groups. The student was so overwhelmed by all of this that it was leading to poor mental health and weight gain. He told me he began searching for support and noticed the university had a female Muslim chaplain, which he was comfortable with, as the thought of a male felt embarrassing and belittling. He began seeing me on a very regular basis. He initially did not disclose his pornographic addiction, but rather the breakdown of his marriage and the heartache he was experiencing. Once he became comfortable with me, he opened up a lot more about some underpinning issues. I provided tailored support to the student, mapping out his daily activities and creating a schedule for his day-to-day life, and fitting in new activities such as going to the gym, prayers, playing football, eating healthier and having 'no device' time – which in turn would help him overcome his boredom that had led to the addiction. I often reassured him that this safe space with me was available as long as he needed it. For his mental health issues, I referred him to NHS pathways to access further support and also to student services. Following this intervention, the student's addiction reduced, and he was extremely thankful for the 'non-judgmental' support he had received. He also showed appreciation for having been supported to reconnect with his faith again without guilt.

Student Case Study 3 – Bullying

As part of my regular one-to-one slots and visibility walks around campus, a student approached me quite cheerily, stating that she had not seen me before, and asking what role I played at the university. She ended up sitting next to me for over an hour, before revealing that she was being bullied by one of the faith societies. She said she felt isolated, alone and as a result had withdrawn from life and felt that she had nowhere to go. I asked if she would like to go somewhere a little quieter and more private to continue the discussion; she agreed and proceeded to share her story. The hurt she was going through was impacting her daily life, and in turn having a negative effect on her grades, leading to further disappointment at home. The student did not wish to report the faith society as she felt it would negatively impact its relationship with the university. She was worried that this would exacerbate the situation and so, she asserted, she simply wanted a listening ear and someone to whom she could express her feelings without being judged. She mentioned how she would not have opened up to me had I been a male as she felt that I was able to empathise with her and relate to the issues she was experiencing.

Over a period of six months, the student visited me regularly, sharing her burdens while I listened listening and responded with guidance from the religion and with referrals to university services where appropriate. The student eventually graduated with the acceptance and friendships she had been missing, feeling that the support I'd provided had made her feel that she had 'a big sister on campus' for which she would be forever grateful. Sometimes it's not the words you share; it's simply being there and being present. She is now an active alumna at the university and beams with gratitude, which is so heart-warming.

The role of chaplain is massively rewarding, and each day gives me a warm feeling, reminding me that I have made a difference in some way to the lives of others. It gives me personal satisfaction knowing that I have provided an avenue free from judgement to young adults who needed it most. I also end up meeting people I would never come across otherwise, and I accommodate and celebrate them as individuals. I have learned more from people than from books, and chaplaincy is a route to that. It also provides me with professional satisfaction, knowing that I am helping the wider university staff with students they would otherwise not know how to assist. Ultimately, it paints the picture that the chaplaincy is not a taboo, no-go area, but a group of individuals who will most certainly find a way to help you. Furthermore, the role expands from benefiting students to benefiting staff and colleagues at the university, giving them a more rounded view of the Muslim demographic on campus. This type of support cannot be placed into one category, as it ranges from academic support and timetabling to Ramadan workshops and social issues workshops.

Coffee, Cake and Contemplate – FGM, Forced Marriage, Honour Killing

As part of my role, I developed the 'Coffee, Cake and Contemplate' initiative to help tackle social issues on campus and in the wider area, without having to directly target the groups it was affecting, while at the same time dispelling any misconceptions anyone may have. The series looked into FGM, honour killings and the refugee crisis, to name but a few, and was supported by the local council, Staffordshire police, Keele Law and Criminology school, together with various NGOs. The events were attended by staff from the university, including academic heads and student services and support networks such as Karma Nirvana. The series was developed to shed light on taboo issues and provide a platform for support services to better flag their services to students. Following these sessions, numerous cases of forced marriage, FGM and potential honour killings have arisen as part of my one-on-ones, which demonstrates the need to tackle the issue further.

Ramadan Exam Timetabling and Prayer Allowance

As Muslims enter the holy month of Ramadan, they face challenges when exam coincides with their fasting schedule. This leads to numerous requests from students to have exams timetabled in a way that offers them the choice to sit the exam either in the morning or afternoon, depending on how the fast affects them. Supporting the timetabling team and different academic schools, I contribute to the setting up of exams, ensuring appropriate timings and also providing space for prayers before and after in temporary prayer spaces. I have advised all schools on campus of the mechanics of Ramadan and what reasonable adjustments can be made to facilitate better exam performance, as well as acknowledgment of religious obligations. This has been greatly welcomed by students and staff, as there is now someone in place who can navigate the space without discrimination or prejudice.

The feedback regarding this has been truly reassuring, with students feeling better equipped and understood across campus. Students' exam results have been extremely positive, which again highlights the importance of such input.

Medicine Course Human Anatomy

Keele University is one of the few universities in the country that allows students to access and work on cadavers (bodies donated to science) as part of its medicine course. While this is a revolutionary move in this era, it has drawn discontent from Muslim students. Muslims view humans, alive or dead, as sacrosanct, and some apparently believe that the body feels pain even after death. Therefore, having students dissect a body for the sole purpose of learning is not considered a necessity.

As a result of this unease, many students reached out to me as Muslim Chaplain to lobby on their behalf to the School of Medicine to allow a potential opt-out, with the added condition that they would be happy to learn using dummies. The students' defence was that once they became doctors, they would be operating on living people to save or improve their lives, but dissecting a body that had already died felt inhumane and painful. I began a conversation with a senior for this module, who responded with great concern and offered his ear immediately. I explained our religious view and why there was possible anxiety among students, also highlighting the timing of such classes, which begin shortly after students enter their first year. I was reassured that student feedback and concern was the top priority and that the course convenors would like to do whatever they could to make students comfortable. With great relief, I was told that students should definitely raise these concerns with their teachers at the time, but to feel at ease that their religious views would be respected and adjustments would be made to accommodate them.

Covid and the Spike of Mental Health Issues

The Covid pandemic period of my role was extremely challenging and daunting. There was a huge spike in mental health issues among staff and students at the university. I found that digital one-to-ones were being requested even more than before, both by students and the wider staff network. It was heartbreaking to see an increasing number of young female Muslim students desperate for one-to-ones, as things at home had become extremely intense. With an increased number of students now studying from home and being more visible in the eyes of their parents, I, as the Muslim Chaplain, saw a huge spike in potential forced marriages and concerns of this nature.

One case in particular was extremely difficult and heavy on the heart to listen to. A young female Muslim student contacted me as she was worried for her well-being at home. She had returned home owing to Covid-19 and noticed that the behaviour of her immediate family had changed drastically towards her. Her family had prepared for her to go to Pakistan on the pretext that she was to attend her brother's wedding. She knew something was not quite right, but told me she was looking forward to going, as she had not seen a lot of relatives for a while. After she left for Pakistan, I did not hear from her for a few weeks. All of a sudden, one weekend, I received an email with an urgent request for an immediate conversation. Due to the urgency, I arranged a call immediately. I was horrified to hear that she had been beaten quite badly in Pakistan by her parents for expressing an interest to marry someone there.

Given how intense the situation was, I spoke to the University Student Services and it was suggested strongly that the best advice was for her to return to the United Kingdom as quickly and as safely as possible, after which we would help her. The moment she returned to the university, we were able to secure accommodation for her and ensured her that its location would not be disclosed to her family. With the grace of God, she is now flourishing and has passed her degree with outstanding results. Her appreciation for my support and empathetic ear and understanding is truly humbling.

The resounding opinion of all students and staff who come to see me is that they come to me because they know I will be able to relate to them and understand their plight. However, there have been times where slight trepidation has stopped a student from approaching me, with the fear of my possibly knowing their family locally.

Ramadan Workshops & 'Our Shared Britain'

As part of the ongoing engagement with staff and students, I have developed a series of Ramadan workshops for colleagues to better understand their students and staff during the holy month of Ramadan. In these workshops, I share the concept of Ramadan, its meanings, the daily routine of one who fasts, how fasting affects students, and so on. I also give tips to help students through the holy month, including health, nutrition and revision techniques. These workshops have been greatly welcomed by staff, and the sessions are filled every year, including by members of senior management. This has proven to be a successful series that engages those not of the faith to better understand the need for support during Ramadan.

In addition to this, I developed 'Our Shared Britain' – a campaign to raise awareness of Muslim influences on Britain and British culture, and to create a shared tolerance and understanding. The series of workshops included storytelling of the origins of coffee; an evening session of stargazing and understanding the first Muslim influences on astronomy; a daff workshop introducing the ethnic beats in modern day music; algebra and its roots within Islam; and lastly, the English language and the influences on it from Arabic, Persian and Urdu. This was rounded off with a lunch menu tailored to take people's taste buds around the Muslim world and land back in the United Kingdom with a Chicken Tikka Masala. This drew huge attention from both national and local media, with the funders wanting to repeat the events as soon as possible. The concept remains one that I, Muslim chaplain at Keele University, developed, and it is hoped to repeat this initiative across many universities across the country in the coming years.

Islamic Centre, Faith Spaces & Security

Many Muslim chaplains across the United Kingdom do not ultimately possess stewardship of a building, but at Keele University, I was given full access and ownership of the Islamic Centre. This adds to the role of chaplain, as I must also work to maintain the building and its regulations, together with attending to all of the paperwork that comes with it. This, at times, includes boiler repairs, carpet cleaning, ablution facilities renewal, to name but a few. However, over the years, a new campaign has been developed to extend the Islamic Centre so that it can host more worshippers at the time of prayer, particularly on Fridays. This is also part of my remit, and so I have to participate in a number of working groups and management meetings to ensure that the university progresses with providing more access to its growing Muslim population on campus. Furthermore, as events unfold outside of campus, such as hate crimes or Islamophobia, I work with the security teams on campus to increase their presence at prayer times so that students feel safe and supported.

Usually, faith spaces are already established within the university setting, and we have been very blessed to have the Islamic Centre at the university for a long time. With Keele University being one of the largest campus universities in the country, it is often difficult for some students to attend prayers at the Islamic Centre owing to time constraints and the distances they have to cover in order to attend. Therefore during my time at the university I have helped to create further faith spaces in the School of Medicine and the CEC, with ongoing talks about the possibility of establishing prayer space in the library. This is a hugely rewarding part of the role of Muslim chaplain, to able to facilitate the provision of such spaces that allow students and staff freedom to practice their faith with ease.

International Crises: Palestine and Syria

The role of chaplain is not easy when a crisis hits and a faith group demands immediate action from a higher education actor. Each year, the challenging subject of Palestine arises from within the student demographic, which is usually a follow-up from potential attacks or arrests in Palestine. The university holds a firm yet neutral opinion, as would any academic institute, promoting the right to free opinion. However, this issue lands directly with me, the Muslim chaplain, from whom the students demand some sort of stance in favour of their cause. As a Muslim chaplain who understands the relevance of Palestine to the Muslim faith, it is hard to detach oneself from the politics and be seen as a neutral entity. As a way to move forward, I promote the idea of a free and open protest, petitioning the university in a peaceful manner, and raising funds for charities working in difficult locations, especially with young people. At times, students simply want to ensure that their voice is heard to some extent, and as a chaplain, I can help facilitate this.

A further example is that of the recent earthquake which hit Turkey and Syria. Students from both the Islamic Society and the Ahl al-Bayt Society all began individual campaigns to raise money for Syria and Turkey. To coordinate this effort and ensure it reached a wider audience, I contacted the Students Union and comms team to encourage them to better promote the work and also engage in the activities. Furthermore, I picked a charity that was vetted and had a 100% donation policy to ensure that the money raised was reaching those who needed it most and immediately. This was to ensure that any political views were left out and that no donation was a reflection of the university or its take on the Syria crisis.

With success and reward come plenty of challenges. The role of chaplain provides a platform for every student, staff member and volunteer within the university, but forgets about the person central to it all – the chaplain. Over the years, I have heard horrific stories in one-to-one sessions, many of which are emotionally and mentally draining – but to whom does the chaplain turn to for support and guidance? Coming home to a young family with a smile, when the day has been heartbreaking, is a challenge in itself. Who shares my burdens and who can help me process what I have heard? While helping others, a chaplain could compromise her own mental health and well-being. A safe space for chaplains needs to be developed, so that they too can offload in an informal manner, without having to feel judged.

At Keele University, I am in the process of developing a mechanism called the 'Safety Circle'. It is an anonymous link accessible to all chaplains, where they can share their thoughts, opinions and challenges of the week. The entire chaplaincy team and support staff will review this and respond anonymously, sharing thoughts, wisdoms or reflections, and offering support as required. But is this enough? Frankly speaking, I believe that this is at least a good first step towards solving a problem that is difficult to assess and resource, and that so much more can be done without the necessary needs assessment.

It does not stop there, however. Being a chaplain automatically provides you with a platform that sits centre stage, and with that comes criticism as you may be sitting too centre stage for some. Over the years there have been two extremes in the challenges I have faced: either I am seen as too religious or not religious enough, and every opportunity becomes an exercise to unpick. I am often seen as the religious one, so automatically I am deemed to be judgmental and heavily opinionated on matters such as hijab, modesty and opposite sex friendships. On the other hand, when an opinion is relayed according to the Islamic rulings as part of a seminar/session, my opinion is less revered, given that it is coming from a woman who is only 37 years old – which clearly cannot be right.

The best way to describe it is a crossfire, where the chaplain is always hit. It ultimately depends on meeting the expectations of the student population and whether we are doing enough that is relevant to their needs. No other role allows the flexibility for questioning or unpicking in higher education. It simply would not be an option, but why does this happen for chaplains? Some would suggest that chaplaincy is the most directly facing role to the students in the higher education space. Its personalization and privacy make it unique and hence open for more accountability and expectations. It is like having a negative experience at the GP's surgery. You would expect to complain, as you pay taxes, and there must be some sort of accountability.

The challenges continue in the religious realm and the highly male-dominated space, where the chaplain is expected to lead congregational prayers. But even wearing my chaplain's hat, it is clear from Islamic law that as a woman I am unable to lead congregational and/or Friday prayers. So what next? This creates some unwanted attention, as students may not see a Muslim female chaplain who cannot lead prayers as being fit for purpose. In particular, patriarchal attitudes among students can often be felt, and at times a certain sense of dominance and authority is demanded of their religious authorities, including the Muslim chaplain. However, what students may fail to see is that there is a strong woman leader present who has changed the mindsets of many and will do so again. I now actually encounter more males in the one-to-one pastoral service than females, a huge shift in both dynamics and attitudes. I can therefore be approachable by both sexes, and be one to empower all those on campus, to be the best examples of themselves. The key word one student used was "guide" when it came to understanding what chaplaincy offered him, and I feel that is a good generic term to describe the role.

The chaplain's role is a service for all in higher education, but it is not always seen this way as it is often unclear what chaplaincy has to offer. This is partly down to senior management not being involved at the ground level. They themselves do not engage in activities linked to chaplaincy, consequently failing to understand how some of these services are impacting university policy or student experience. Furthermore, no measurements are taken at the pastoral care level, i.e. impact figures, which would demonstrate the growing need for the chaplaincy service.

Furthermore, the funds allocated to the role are insufficient, with part-time hours offered for what is basically a full-time, out-of-hours role. This needs to be changed, given the growing demand for the service and the needs of Muslims students, who constitute the largest minority on the campus. This would also lean closely to what the other chaplains at the university are offered, as the service is over-subscribed when it comes to Muslim students. In addition to this, other faith groups, including the Sikhs, Hindus and the Buddhists, also reach out to the Muslim chaplain for support rather than to the Christian chaplains, perhaps on account of their greater understanding of the Islamic faith system.

But it does not stop there. The role of chaplain is involved in policy making of the university in various ways, from 'decolonizing' the curriculum to monitoring and improving race relations and partnership management. I often sit in meetings which involve EDI conversations, and my opinion is definitely sought and appreciated. I attend these meetings to ensure the right approach is being taken and for the right reasons. This then guides any further policy at the university, which in turn helps students thrive in a safe and engaging space. Impacting university policy and procedures through a faith lens is a new feature in the academic world, and it is within this space that Muslim chaplains can grow, develop and ensure that they are making a significant difference to the students and those around them. In generations to come, the role of Muslim chaplain will be an institutionally central one, and it will have greater impact than it does currently. My role as chaplain goes above and beyond the 'God squad' cliché and engages and intersects with many different departments and support services. And that is part of its uniqueness.

We could also ask the question of how far the role of chaplaincy can grow and where the limits of the role may lie. As a female Muslim chaplain, I feel that the role is constantly growing, changing and adapting, but at the core sits a person who lives and believes in change and will do whatever it takes to help others change. The future is bright for chaplaincy, and if universities, chaplains, religion and belief organisations work together and learn from each other, the positive impact of chaplains can become even stronger. I have learned that chaplaincy cannot be taught and must be experienced. No one chaplain's role will resemble another's. Each day is a new day with a new set of scenarios and learning opportunities. This keeps my role extremely relevant and rewarding. Chaplaincy has become a spark of hope for students, a safe space to help them through university life – and it is a pleasure to be part of that journey.

6

Sabiha Iqbal
Roehampton University

In the name of God, Most Gracious and Ever Merciful.

Linked to religious diversification, the field of chaplaincy has increasingly offered a vocational pathway to people belonging to world religions other than Christianity. Some in the role may have studied their way into the vocation, while many admit that it is a role they simply 'fell into'. Perhaps the expression, "I felt a calling" is one that may resonate more with chaplains across different faiths, with chaplaincy being something that they felt inexorably drawn towards.

The domain of Muslim chaplaincy is a relatively new one, particularly given the fact that the term 'chaplain' is not rooted or recognised directly in Islamic literature. Nevertheless, the notion of chaplaincy is very easily identifiable in Islamic practice in the three main foundational, text-based sources from which Muslims draw comfort and inspiration. These sources are the Holy Quran; the body of Prophetic Traditions known collectively as 'the hadith'; and the *sunna*, or the practices of the Prophet Muhammad (PBWH).

According to research cited in a book much referenced by Muslim chaplains called *Understanding Muslim Chaplaincy*,[30] there were approximately four hundred Muslim chaplains in the UK as of 2008.[31] There are many kinds of Muslim chaplain, from lay-workers and volunteers to full-time chaplains who work up to eight hours a day and seven days a week – and this may not include being almost by default 'on-call' round the clock to respond to incidents that require an immediate response, such as mental health crisis care, sudden homelessness, medical episodes and bereavement support, to name but a few.

The role of the Muslim chaplain, particular when in Higher Education (HE), is a prestigious one. It is a role that requires a great deal of compassion, empathy, patience, adaptability, durability, resilience, stamina and, most of all, time. It requires the kind of readiness and anticipation that serve to expand the term 'responding to change' to a dimension I certainly had never experienced in the five previous roles I had during fifteen years of service to HE in the United Kingdom.

The role of Muslim chaplain is a unique one, particularly as it is a role that has come about as a result of the existence of a protected characteristic, namely religion and belief. 'Religion' refers to any religion, including the lack thereof. Belief refers to any religious or philosophical belief and includes a lack of belief. Generally, a belief should affect one's life choices or the way one lives for it to be included in the definition. The role of a chaplain can cover a lot of ground, both literally and physically! It is a role that may require desk-time and administration, but it is also a role that often entails being on the move: walking or driving to visits, for example, and generally being hospitable. Chaplains usually have some treats up their sleeve, and will often know the best places for chai, coffee and chats!

My tenure in HE has lasted twenty years so far and has covered various roles and specialisms, including marketing and communications, conferencing, and, for the longest duration, international student support. Outside of HE, I have worked as a librarian, a barista, an environmental officer in waste management, a driver in the motoring industry, as well as a volunteer for an international NGO where I painted murals to transform classrooms in several countries, mostly in the Middle East and Africa. In my spare time, I work in radio, event management, and I enjoy doing research and development food security, community care and environmental sustainability projects. My hobbies include racquet sports, swimming, hiking, learning to cook, and, more than anything else, exploring God's gift to us – the earth on which we live.

So where am I now? I currently serve at the University of Roehampton (UR) in London. It is a unique institution insofar as it is the only one in the world that has an ecumenical relationship between three Christian traditions (Anglican, Catholic, and Methodist). The foundations of the University of Roehampton are built on four colleges, and these are set on two parkland campuses.

Back in the summer of 2018, the role of female Muslim chaplain was offered to me at the university. The role evolved largely in response to the inability of the university to find a suitable male for the role.

This chapter throws some light on my journey into chaplaincy. It elaborates on how the role has evolved to respond to demographic changes in HE, and in particular how one finds ways to address three main barriers for Muslims – language and communication; cultural expression; and religious practice.[32] The chapter also addresses how, through my role, and in the context of where I have worked, the physical, mental, and spiritual professional services within a university environment have evolved to accommodate religious practice institutionally, to help individuals prioritise their characteristics of faith and belief; and to create a sense of community so that people are able to express their faiths with freedom and confidence.

Journey to Chaplaincy

How does one get into chaplaincy? This is a question which is often asked – particularly from curious female Muslims – and it always makes me feel self-conscious when answering because the answer is not what most would think. There certainly was no degree in religious studies or attending an Islamic seminary involved. In fact, most of the journey which led to my becoming chaplain can be connected directly on a personal level to supplications made over the years: prayer requests to travel the earth and meet people from around the world; to deepen my understanding of the religion – Islam – into which I was born; to serve God Almighty, the Creator of all worlds; and to be used to fulfil my responsibility to God's creation in the best of ways.

No one individual will have had the same journey into chaplaincy as anyone else. The 'calling' to the role can be fed by different motivations and it would be wrong to assume that there is one route, or that everyone makes the same kind of journey. Indeed, at times even I can cross-reference different stages that became stepping-stones in my journey to becoming a chaplain – or whatever term is used depending on the sector or institution of service, e.g. faith advisor, spiritual advisor, and so on.

Prior to my current appointment, I spent time working in the capacity of an associate Muslim chaplain at an institution in Hertfordshire. Thus, my entry point into the world of chaplaincy really commenced in 2014, when I was 'head-hunted' and encouraged into the role on the basis that I frequented the prayer rooms a fair bit!

Academically, my route into chaplaincy has been somewhat unconventional. Having studied an undergraduate degree in geography, which was a subject I chose to study at school, then at college and finally in university, with a year spent in North America, I then did a Master's in Business Administration. Thus, I did not follow any obvious pathway to chaplaincy. In fact, bearing in mind the fact that my only C-grade at GCSE was in Religious Studies, I feel that most people would be forgiven for being flabbergasted to know me today as chaplain in a Muslim-majority university! Further to my degrees, during my initial role as associate chaplain, I did attend the Markfield Institute for Higher Education (MIHE) to study for a Certificate in Chaplaincy', attending once a month for several months. That experience to some extent became a marker of qualification – at least on paper, and in my conscience – for the role I perform today.

"What do you do as Muslim chaplain?" is another question that

always arises from perplexed prospective students, members of the public on Open Days, and even current students already embarked on their academic journey at university. Generally, most people will know who and what a Muslim is and, occasionally, what a chaplain is – but put the two together and 'Muslim chaplain' is a term that is alien to most. To tell the truth, I did not know what it was either when I was first asked if I would consider the role of associate Muslim chaplain. As my United Reform Church (URC) lead chaplain gently explained, the role would continue to cover what was already being done: tidying up the books in the prayer room; putting away the prayer mats considerately; frequently visiting the prayer room; maintaining the cleanliness of the facilities; participating in events held by faith-based student societies; feeding people and making lots of cups of tea; helping set up the Friday congregational prayers for Muslims; organising Eid festivals, and so on. It seemed that most of the things that the job specification might entail were being done by me anyway as Overseas Student Support Officer and a practicing Muslim at university. And so accepting the appointment seemed a simple enough decision to make, and that is how it all started.

Adding a bolt-on role to a full-time job is made so much easier when your manager and team recognise how your routine and day-to-day work are a balancing act which needs to be aligned with your commitment to your faith and to your worship. Living out faith can be challenging for many reasons, but striving to do so is something that can be worked on individually and collectively. And in my case, it led to life-changing outcomes. To practice one's faith as part of an inherent identity – like using your left hand if you are left-handed or using a wheelchair if you have a limited mobility – is a characteristic one should feel comfortable with expressing, and barriers should be lowered to allow for this to take place. A good manager encourages contentment at work, whilst a Muslim knows that:

> *Those who believe, and whose hearts find comfort in the remembrance of Allah.*
> *Aye! it is in the remembrance of Allah that hearts can find comfort;*[33]

On the macro level, pinpointing what a Muslim chaplain is expected to do and what may or may not be desirable is an area of personal and professional interest. Increasingly, the narrative in institutions is to be able to prove worth, and there is a fine line between that and proving one's value as an individual.

Much of this desire is driven by the strategic planning of resource allocation (finances, staffing etc.) in contrast to gain (growth in market, profitability, student retention, and so on). The request that we report through quantitative measures or those that seem suited to the work being delivered (qualitative measures, storytelling, testimony, etc.) has become an essential part of the role over recent years and it has really challenged the composition of chaplaincy, including how it is encountered and executed.

On the micro level, as a Muslim chaplain, one soon learns that no two days are the same, even if those days concern the same event which is celebrated annually. For example, one year Ramadan will be during the university assessment period and the next year it will straddle a vacation period. This then affects engagement in activities, or the number of requests for mitigating circumstances to complete assignments or take part in exams. In other areas of work, such as interfaith, for example, one year a variety of enquiries, ranging from faith festivals to social justice campaigns, land in one's inbox, while the next year, a whole different set of celebrations are marked. This shifting dynamic is symptomatic of the changing student demographic in the transient world of higher education. With three intakes of students a year, and ever-changing challenges for students encountering HE in the UK for the first time, chaplaincy almost needs to be continuously amenable and receptive. Most chaplaincy teams, including my own, contribute in earnest to the creation of a sense of belonging and to the building of community, both internally and externally, for students and staff through its day-to-day activities. The tagline for my chaplaincy is 'flourishing in faith and friendship', and this then serves to anchor the work we do.

The joys of my role are difficult to enumerate. There is joy in the anticipation of what a day might bring. There are joys in offering pastoral care, community building, and celebrating faith for all it offers. There is joy in the big things and even more in the small things. There is joy in the things you do which are hidden, that is, behind the scenes and between you and God, and there is also joy in those things which are manifest and witnessed by others.

If anyone says that there is absolutely nothing they don't enjoy about their job, then I believe they are either lying or their job is that of a Muslim chaplain. Joking aside, it really is a rewarding vocation. But for that reward, hard graft must be put in. Although it could be considered a contentious statement, if you are not fearful and you approach hard work with a sense of determination, then the likelihood is slim that you will not find some pleasure somewhere along the line in your role as Muslim chaplain. After all, it is evident from God's Word in the Holy Quran that there is ease after hardship:

> *Have We not opened for thee thy bosom,*
> *And removed from thee thy burden*
> *Which had well nigh broken thy back,*
> *And We exalted thy name?*
> *Surely there is ease after hardship.*
> *Aye, surely there is ease after hardship.*
> *So when thou art free, strive hard,*
> *And to thy Lord do thou attend whole-heartedly.* [34]

Challenges come from every direction, and this is evident when, in a 'chaplains world', despite every day beginning with a well-intentioned plan, the likelihood of the plan being compromised is always a possibility. Arguably that is what creates opportunities for growth, and helps bridge understandings between individuals, as well as challenging certain aspects of the status quo. Terms such as 'ministry of presence'[35] are often used and this ability to firefight and be ready to respond is a common feature of the role. But that is in line with the nature of our universe. After all, as we are taught in the Holy Qur'an:

> *And they planned and Allah also planned, and Allah is the Best of planners.*[36]

How the Role has Evolved to Respond to Demographic Changes in Higher Education

Anas relates that the Prophet Muhammad (PBWH) said,

> *None of you has faith until he loves for his brother what he loves for himself.*[37]

As someone who had made a conscious decision to develop in my faith and to learn more, and if possible, to dedicate my life to my faith, I consider this hadith to be of prime importance. For it reminds me that to have and grow in faith, I need compassion, empathy and the ability to understand others. The word 'brother' in the hadith does not only relate to fellow Muslims, but as Islam is a universal religion, it relates to our treatment of everyone we interact with, including those whom we have yet to meet.

The Golden Rule teaches us to do to others as we would have them do to us. But the teachings of Islam are superior to the Golden Rule. The Holy Quran commands Muslims to always treat others with justice, even if they act with animosity and injustice towards you or oppress you even.

If this is the premise of Muslim chaplaincy, then how has the role had to respond to the demographic changes in HE? As the data below show, our numbers have changed in terms of students professing no religion decreasing, Hindu students more than doubling, and the Muslim population increasing.

Religion

Religion	2020/21 (%)	2021/22 (%)
Not known	0.1	0.1
Jewish	0.4	0.4
Any other religion or belief	1	1
Buddhist	1	1
Sikh	1	1
Spiritual	2	2
Information refused	4	4
Hindu	4	9
Christian	29	2
Muslim	26	29
No religion	31	25

Table: Student Data for Religion at UR (Source: Annual Equality Report 2021-2022)[38]

Language and Communication

In my role as Muslim chaplain, some of my work has been dedicated to an exploration of how we can encourage the improvement of conversational skills among the student community. This has not been specific to Muslims only; rather, it is a stream of interfaith work that I am called to in order to respond to the demographic change of people of religion from different countries and cultures. The four colleges at UR have four great mottos, but seeking ways to create a narrative of coexistence with shared values in one place is important if we are to facilitate the increase of harmonious relations both on and off-site also.

The programme which developed that enabled bridge-building through conversation was called 'The Coexist Café'; this has gone on to become an actual physical space, with the same name, where people can gather for cross-cultural learning and sharing, as well as making and drinking complimentary cups of tea, coffee and hot chocolate. It is a space where all are welcome and bi-weekly discussion forums are held to discuss current affairs as well as issues of social justice and environmental campaigns.

Cultural Expression

Responding to the demographic change of the HE environment and enabling cultural expression to be shared and developed freely and confidently requires creating safe spaces and opportunities for knowledge exchange.

A series entitled 'Food, Fun and Friends' has been a fulfilling and fun initiative to roll out. While some eyebrows may be raised at a chaplain running cooking classes, it is in the act of coming together to share and to cook that cultural expressions can be exchanged, and inter-personal and inter-cultural understandings built holistically. How many different ways are there to bake biscuits, top a pizza or knead dough? I am no expert – even though my only A-grade GCSE was in Food Technology – but it is in the creative exchange, the skills development and the decision making, all of which are inevitably ingrained in cultural practice and tradition, that we can help build harmonious and dignified environments in which to study. We can learn so much from each other through the sharing of food. Indeed, building community through the sharing of food is rooted in many religions and belief systems, and it is also one of the things that we do best.

Another opportunity created which has become a common feature for many universities across the country now is the collective iftar during Ramadan. Breaking one's fast during Ramadan with friends, fellows and lecturers helps to create a sense of unity and humility that is difficult to find in other shared activities, although we do come together in a similar manner for events such as Remembrance Sunday, the commemoration of Holocaust Memorial Day and New Year celebrations. The feedback each year has been encouraging and so Iftar Together is now a permanent feature of the Ramadan activities each year. The catering provided at these events is a great way to bridge the cultural divide and to bring a sense of comfort and 'home' for many of our international students.

Religious Practice

The Muslim chaplain's role has evolved over the years in the context of responding to the needs of highlighting and teaching about religious practice in light of the demographic change within the HE environment – a change that is not limited to Islam, as we have seen. There is also an expectation, owing to my own ethnic heritage, that I speak to the needs of the Asian

Subcontinent students and staff too, and this also includes the needs of some students of the Hindu and Sikh faiths too, amongst others. In light of this, a social media strategy and a set of 'Religious Guidance Notes' has been put together to support the institutional response to the emerging communities of students recruited.

With regard to the Muslim community in particular, there has been the development of Ramadan Guidance notes, with sessions run on 'Preparing for Ramadan as a Student', as well as 'Ramadan Info Sessions for Staff'. Feedback from non-Muslim attendees is always uplifting:

> *Thank you so much again for the Ramadan information session yesterday, it was very clear and informative, and answered some of the questions I had about Ramadan.*

Much of my tenure has involved co-designing adequate facilities for Muslim worshippers, including the introduction of:

- six study spaces (three designated for sisters and three for brothers)
- five newly developed prayer rooms
- three ablution facilities
- two 'coexist' (open to all) spaces
- an Islamic Community Room

To help build university-wide understanding of the Islamic faith, and to share the teaching of religious practice, 'A-Z of Islam' sessions are run to answer questions that non-Muslim individuals may have and wish to learn more about.

Priority Area	Sub-Area	Further sub-area, if relevant	Activity	Frequency
Student-Facing Activities	Engagement with Societies		…	
	Wider Student Union Engagement		…	
	Provision for prayers, festivals, and other devotional activities	Friday Prayer	…	
		Dua-i Kumayl	…	
		Ramadan Iftar (Fast breaking)	…	
		Interfaith Week	…	
		Eid al-Fitr and Eid al-Adha	…	
		International Women's Day	…	
	Provision for vulnerable students not engaged in societies		…	
	Chaplaincy-led/ facilitated activities on campus		…	
	Non-alcoholic social events		…	
Estate Matters	Prayer Rooms and Ablution facilities	Maintenance	…	
		Furnishings	…	
		Ensuring adequate provision	…	
Pastoral Care	Staff and Students		…	
Team Formation	Contributions to chaplaincy team development		…	

Priority Area	Sub-Area	Further sub-area, if relevant	Activity	Frequency
Providing Expertise Matters relating to Chaplaincy, Faith, Islam, Muslims, and Culture	External	Offering contributions into network groups	...	
		Developing as a hub of expertise	...	
	Internal	Prevent Working Group		
		Specific advice to the university in the development of policy and strategy	...	
		Contribution to academic activities	...	
		BAME Network	...	
		Women's Network	...	

Table: Example of A Work Plan for Muslim Chaplaincy (Source: Author)

Evolution of Physical, Mental, and Spiritual Professional Services/Facilities within a University

It is important that the university environment is seen and felt to be somewhere safe where one can find and profess one's faith freely and confidently. This needs to happen not just through policy and practice, but through lived experience, real-life encounters and meaningful exchanges.

In my institution, the Student Well-being department sits as part of the university's central services and the Human Resources structure. Chaplaincy has not conformed, but rather continues to be housed within the collegiate structure of its faith foundations, i.e. with an Anglican chaplain appointed to Whitelands College; a Catholic chaplain appointed to Digby Stuart College; and a Methodist chaplain appointed to Southlands College. The exception is my role, since the Muslim chaplain is appointed to the university as a whole on a full-time contract. Furthermore, while I am affiliated with a Collage as all students and staff are, I do not serve only one College.

In the next section of this chapter, a carefully selected set of case studies is presented in order to elaborate on the different areas of my work and aspects of my role, showing how some of the methods used to develop the physical, mental and spiritual well-being agenda for members of the university, both Muslim and non-Muslim alike, have been implemented. The 'Areas of Work' category has provided a catalyst for change and a sense of improvement in the elements of well-being that constitute a whole person, and not just members of the Muslim community.

Area of Work (1): to Help University Adopt Religious Practice Institutionally

In my preliminary year as female Muslim chaplain, which was spent alongside a male Muslim chaplain, a thorough endeavour was made to identify a work plan for Muslim chaplaincy and all that it might entail. This highlighted the areas of individual and shared work responsibilities and areas of collaboration with colleagues in the chaplaincy as well as across the university as a whole. The institutional impact of this endeavour was to draw attention to the areas of high priority and lower priority and to invite inter-disciplinary working.

Building on that endeavour, a Muslim Student and Staff Experience Report was composed. A similar piece of work was carried out for my MBA dissertation (Looking at the Muslim Student Experience in Higher Education) and so that provided a platform to build upon too. This report for UR was a positive and constructive way of illustrating the areas of religious priority (i.e. having a place for ablution nearby a prayer room, providing halal catering options etc.) for departments such as Estates, Academic Services, Well-being Services and the like – departments where there may have otherwise existed a knowledge-gap regarding the needs of the Muslim community. This report streamlined conversations and funding streams to efficiently manage areas of previous under-development and, similar to the Work Plan, it helped prioritise institutional decisions.

Element Evolved: Spiritual Well-being

Context: One outcome of these projects has been a direct correlation between improvements made to the prayer room facilities and an increase in worshippers on campus who engage with those facilities, thus increasing their connection with spiritual well-being.

How: Doing the foundational work of writing a work plan and reporting on the experiences paved the way to systematically provide direction to the institution on how engagement could be increased. Furthermore, there are five mandatory prayers a day for Muslims and no data is captured on day-to-day use as it is not required and therefore would be unethical to collect. However, to provide adequate capacity of space and to fulfil specifications of the space needed, data for attendance is collected by the Muslim chaplaincy in collaboration with the Islamic Society (ISOC) of the Students' Union (SU) in the form of a headcount of attendees to inform institutional decision making on the allocation of spaces. The diagram below displays a snapshot of the incremental engagement at Friday prayers over a period of five years of my incumbency. When I joined the UR, Friday prayers were not organised on campus; rather, people were free to perform their own prayers in congregation using a prayer room, or they were instead sign-posted to a local community centre, which was increasingly in demand by the local community too.

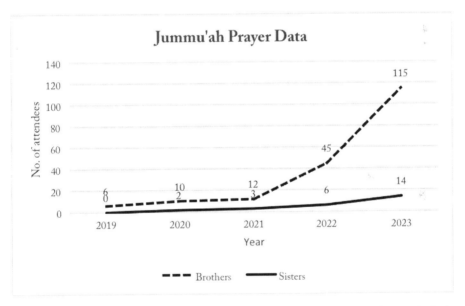

Diagram: Average Number of Attendees at Friday Prayers over A Five-year Period (Source: Author)

The number of attendees for Friday prayers, now approximately 130 in total, is a result of our providing the option to worship in congregation; providing bifurcation of spaces; introducing ablution facilities; and working in collaboration with the ISOC. Furthermore, the Friday prayer takes place centrally on the main campus of UR, and this makes it accessible in between breaks in the teaching timetable. The average attendance now would be difficult to sign-post elsewhere in the local community. However, during university vacation/closure periods, students and staff are encouraged to explore their local areas as well, in the hope of building a sense of belonging and brotherhood/sisterhood with a local worshipping community.

Area of Work (2): to Help Individuals Prioritise their Characteristic of Faith and Belief

This was one of the key reasons I explored chaplaincy as vocation and continued to stay in higher education. If asked how I would define Muslim chaplaincy, then I would say that it is service to God's creatures, that is, fulfilling the rights and responsibilities we have before God and His creation.

Having experienced how coming to university can feel like being thrown into the deep end, I wanted to do something to give something back – something which would enable a student transitioning from a school/college structure or, indeed, from any structure and community, to a new university environment, where they need to adapt and fit in, to do so more comfortably. I often noticed that the conventional university experience, including prior expectations of what such an experience would be like, created an identity complex predicated on the desire to want to 'fit in', e.g. in terms of how to dress, how to speak, how much to spend, and so on. In this process of finding community and also discovering one's own identity and skills set, e.g. discovering whether you can cook, do laundry or travel to university alone as a commuter, one often finds that one's faith remains on a constant forward and upward trajectory only with great difficulty, and that sometimes, one's faith actually plummets. Human beings are creatures of habit and thus when the environment changes, our ability to continue our habits, be they positive or negative, is tested.

Supporting the Muslim community to maximise opportunities at university to achieve academically and benefit from co-curricular activity is a core aspect of my work. After all, when a student funds his or her own degree, it is not just the teaching that comes with the package, but also all the services the institution has in place to help the individual to develop and succeed to the best of his or her ability. So, to find effective ways to help individuals prioritise their faith while they are with us continues to be an area of work that demands time and attention through strategic listening and observational data capture.

In some cases that I deal with, week-to-week, there is on occasion a thought which occurs to me that maybe a male Muslim chaplain would be able to fulfil certain aspects of the Muslim chaplaincy role better. Similarly, I often wonder whether there would be greater engagement pastorally if there were the option of a 'gender preference' given to users of the Muslim chaplaincy service. There are also certain aspects of my role (e.g. making announcements at the Friday prayer service) that do not sit comfortably with me as regards my own religious observances. While there is no male Muslim chaplain for me to work alongside, it is felt that such a role is needed, bearing in mind some of the needs of the Muslim community. To this end a detailed and evidence-based business-case to provide the Muslim chaplaincy team with a male Muslim chaplain has been submitted for consideration.

Nevertheless, the role of a female Muslim chaplain should never be considered secondary or subordinate to that of a male Muslim chaplain in the context of higher education. The Holy Quran (4:12) states:

> But whosoever does good works, whether male or female, and is a believer, such shall enter Heaven, and shall not be wronged even as much as the little hollow in the back of a date-stone.

An additional area that has been identified as being important to strengthen is the Student Well-being team, It is crucial that we ensure first and foremost that it is professional, and then that it is competent enough to address the three barriers identified for Muslims, namely language, culture and religious practice.

Element Evolved: Mental Wellbeing

Context: For this particular area of work, a business case has been made to address the need for a male chaplain and also someone to strategically listen to, and make knowledgeable observations of, the needs of the Muslim community, particularly around their mental well-being. My role was established specifically to support the female (72% of the 26% Muslim students at UR in 2018) Muslim community, but out of necessity my role has been to serve all Muslim students, whose numbers increased from approximately 1,600 in 2021 to over 2,100 in 2022, with Muslim staff increasing from approximately twenty-six in 2018, to fifty-three in 2021 and eighty in 2022). Data on staff gender are not available, but there still remains an absence of a male Muslim chaplain.

Student gender data are available, however, and recent intakes of students have dramatically shifted the balance of the male and female Muslim population of students. Back in 2018 it was 76% female and 24% male, but the 2021-2022 figures reveal the total percentage of students who responded to the question about religious identity by declaring themselves to be Muslim was 28%, of whom 55% were female and 45% male. Referring back to the dramatic increase in numbers of brothers attending Friday prayers in 2023, it is anticipated the that the ratio of females to males will at some point change, with males becoming the majority.

In an effort to allay the concerns and tend to the needs of the student population, I have been tasked by my institution to take the lead on a 'Roehampton Muslim Experience Project'. This initiative will broadly address a series of objectives aimed to enhance the experience of Muslim students. As it is an ongoing initiative, it is not possible to comment further on it at this time.

How: The attempt to enhance the mental well-being of the Muslim community has mainly involved lowering barriers to participation in all events and activities as much as is feasible. To this end, having peer-to-peer representation and support that is visible is key. Parallel to conducting the UR Muslim Experience Project and to alleviate the time spent on day-to-day tasks, the funding for Muslim chaplaincy has been increased and there is now a whole team of people whose remit it is to deliver Muslim chaplaincy to the Muslim student body

The team structure is as represented below:

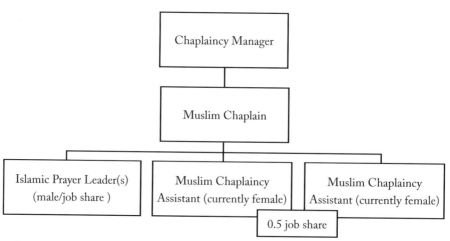

Diagram: Current Muslim Chaplaincy Team Structure at UR (March, 2023) (Source: Author)

These additional resources, including salaried positions, have significantly improved the complexion of Muslim community development, helping students to find friendships and build on them, and sign-posting students to the support they need internally or externally to UR. The roles managed by the Muslim Chaplain do not require pastoral support to be offered, but through representation of the Muslim chaplaincy team, who wear green hoodies with tags bearing their names and roles, the involvement of students who were previously not engaging, and of departments with majority Muslim cohorts, has increased. This much can be evidenced by the positive responses to events such as 'Food Fun and Friends for Brothers' which was an initiative that offered male students the opportunity to get-together to learn a new skill. There have also been opportunities taken up by Muslim Chaplaincy assistants to set-up a stall for World Hijab Day and to talk about mental resilience with regard to the adoption of the hijab. Other events have included Networking and Visibility sessions for sisters to address concerns around how to conduct themselves in a new work place; commemoration of International Women's Day; and, in 2023, a session on how to nurture an equitable mindset.

Area of Work (3): to Create a Sense of Community to Express one's Faith

Having previously worked in the office of International Student Support, I recognised the value of paying heed to the onboarding experience of students (orientation/induction); modelling good integration between students of different disciplines, countries, genders and ages; giving due consideration to values-based activity planning; and continually using up-to-date technology to respond to the challenges of connecting people and creating a sense of community.

Religion and belief can undoubtedly be one of the quickest ways to form community, but in practice, the assumption that all people of the same religion have the same set of beliefs can be dysfunctional to community building. Listening to the community and identifying gaps of communication is key.

In my first year at UR, having made observations of, and enquiries about, the gaps in communication within the College, I worked with a College head to pilot a College Community Leader's (CCL) project. The aim of the project was to review the current offering of student leadership roles, which was biased mostly towards the residential students, and to reimagine the offer of student leadership positions for the College. Below is an excerpt from part of the proposal that was submitted.

> One of the main objectives of creating the CCL role is to reimagine how College life is perceived, within a collegiate university campus. After reviewing the Flat Rep role and identifying the challenges that the College is facing, it is evident that there is a need for a more "professional" student peer leader role that exists to create an organic sense of belonging.
>
> A team of CCLs would be recruited, consisting of approximately 12 persons for the College. CCLs will be sub-divided to be responsible for the residential or commuting students; however, the expectations of the role will be mirroring. The training* for CCLs would be combined to ensure a CCL, regardless of their remit of care, has the ability to work across disciplines, levels/status of study, as well as for the commuting/resident community.

It is viable to consider providing rent free accommodation for resident CCLs; however, in the interest of team spirit as well as ensuring equality, it is recommended to have the CCL role salaried no matter the status (resident or commuting). Having a clearly defined role with remuneration is useful for CV building for the CCLs. Furthermore, it provides a platform for the College Team and the CCL role to forge a partnership, which is in line with the Student Engagement policy.

In the interest of equality and diversity, it would be advisable to recruit a balanced team of CCLs that was inclusive of different genders, races, ethnicities, nationalities, religions, as well as status/level of study (i.e. undergraduate, postgraduate, research, etc). At least one of the CCLs in the residential and commuting student team respectively should be postgraduate level. This will enable representation of a currently underrepresented group of students as well as encouraging the promotion and utilization of college spaces such as the Senior Common Room (SCR) that is designated for postgraduate students as well as staff.

Excerpt: Proposal for CCL Pilot Project (Source: Author)

This initiative was given the green light, funded generously by UR and rolled out successfully in 2019-2020. The pilot provided a platform for expanding the project to the sister Colleges and embedding the model of student leadership consistently in order to provide more commuters with opportunities on campus to work and to diversify engagement with the university experience. The project expanded during the response to the pandemic to include Southlands and Digby Stuart Colleges; however, with fundamental changes such as hybrid teaching and work patterns, the project did not expand to Froebel or Whitelands Colleges.

The project is now a well-embedded programme at Southlands College, and it continues to boast an ambitious and diversely representative CCL team.

Q1. Why do you want to continue being a student leader?

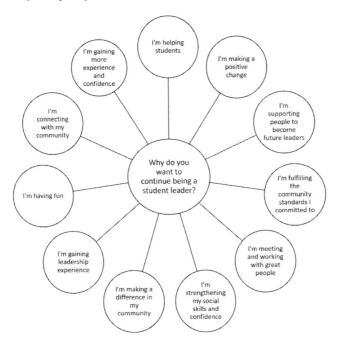

Q2. What does student leadership mean to you?

Q3. Why are student leaders important?

Word cloud of all the skills identified to have been developed by student leaders.

Data collected from College Community Leaders Programme (2021)

Element Evolved: Physical Wellbeing

Context: This area of work was very high on the institutional agenda in my initial year at UR, for we wanted to know how best to build a sense of community while also improving the metrics of student retention and outcomes of success or failure. Recognising that a sense of belonging is essential to the formation of the individual, one notices that students' sense of identity in the university context is manifested in the time spent in the classroom, on-campus and participating in activities, be they curricular or extra-curricular. Consequently, one is alerted to attendance and participation data; money being spent on food and drink; the foot-fall at facilities for physical and spiritual well-being; the use of services such as the library; and achievements with regard to counselling, well-being support and academic success.

How: Through the CCL project, the student leaders became ambassadors for the community. The team of CCLs developed a social media platform from which to raise awareness about events and activities in a somewhat quirky way – one that was evidently more successful than the humble posturing technique used previously. CCLs also played a vital role in delivering what was requested (the 'you said, we did' technique), which can create a sense of recognition in real-time that is invaluable.

I fondly recall the element of physical well-being being nurtured by opportunities for things such as women-only yoga, badminton for sisters, and the introduction of archery – activities that appealed to the Muslim community through their understanding of Hadith and *sunna*.

In addition to physical sports being introduced, opportunities for rambling in the local area were facilitated and kept free of any cost. This intervention lowered the barrier for the Muslim community to explore the outdoors and spend time in nature, something Muslims are encouraged to do in the Holy Quran:

Say, 'Travel in the earth, and see how He originated the creation.'[40]

Muslim chaplaincy for me requires service to others on the basis of the teachings of Islam.

Chaplains offer an institution a wholesome dynamic. It is within a chaplain's gift to offer physical, mental, emotional and spiritual attention; to be a Jack of all trades as some might say.

This chapter has attempted at some length to demonstrate the literal role as well as the practical steps that chaplains can take to help themselves and their institution live out and reinforce within its student and staff body the freedom and confidence to express one's faith identity.

Despite working hard in my role as Muslim chaplain for almost a decade, there still feels like there is so much more that needs to be done to make heard the voice of Muslim chaplains, particularly women, who have emerged relatively recently, in contrast to male Muslim imams who have played that particular role for much longer.

I believe that setting up stronger networks to build connections and learning from each other about how to build allyship within institutions and beyond would be a wonderful step to take in the near future, God willing!

Notes

1. IOK Chaplains 2022.
2. Ibid.
3. Gilliat-Ray, Ali, Pattison 2013, p. 5.
4. Ibid., p. 25.
5. Siddiqui 2007, p. 12.
6. BBC News 2011.
7. Siddiqui 2007, p. 48-50.
8. Siddiqui 2007, p. 44.
9. Gilliat-Ray, Ali, Pattison 2013, p. 5.
10. Quran, 35:24.
11. Quran, 2:160.
12. Quran, 3:89.
13. Quran, 3:135-136.
14. Centre for Media Monitoring 2021.
15. BBC News 2011.
16. Siddiqui 2007, p. 50.
17. When Umar Was Put To Explanation, n.d.
18. Siddiqui 2007, pp. 46-47.
19. Siddiqui 2007.
20. Siddiqui 2007, p. 53.
21. Sunan Abi Dawud 3641.
22. Sunan Ibn Majah 225.
23. Milton 1859, V1 and V2.
24. Becker 1973, pp. 47-66.
25. Ouida 2005.
26. For example, Chittick, W. C., *The Sufi Path of Love: The Spiritual Teachings of Rumi* (Albany: Sunny Press, 1983).
27. Ibn ʿArabī was an Arab Andalusian Muslim scholar, mystic, poet, and philosopher.
28. For more information on Said Nursi, see: Vahide 2011.
29. Ahmed 2021.
30. Gilliat-Ray, Ali, Pattison 2013.
31. Clines 2008,.

32 Lahaj 2011, p. 174.
33 Quran, 13:29.
34 Quran, 94:2-9.
35 Aune, Guest, Law 2019.
36 Quran, 8:31.
37 Al-Bukhari, Hadith 13, 40 Hadith an-Nawawi.
38 University of Roehampton 2023, p. 15.
39 Smith 2019.
40 Quran, 29:21.

Bibliography

Ahmed, S., *Complaint!* (Durham and London: Duke University Press, 2021).

Allen, C., *Islamophobia* (Farnham: Ashgate, 2010).

Aune, K., Guest, M., and Law, J., *Chaplains on Campus: Understanding Chaplaincy in UK Universities* (Coventry, Canterbury, and Durham: Coventry University, Canterbury Christ Church University, and Durham University, 2019).

Bang, H., Ross, S., and Reio, T. G., "From Motivation to Organizational Commitment of Volunteers in Non-profit Sport Organisations: The Role of Job Satisfaction." *Journal of Management Development*, 32,1 (2013), pp. 96-112. <https://www.emerald.com/insight/content/doi/10.1108/02621711311287044/full/pdf>

BBC News, *Prophet's Example Biggest Inspiration for Muslim Chaplains in Britain, Study Reveals* (2011). <https://www.lastprophet.info/home/news/100/prophet-s-example-biggest-inspiration-for-muslim-chaplains-in-britain-study-reveals>

Becker, E., *The Denial of Death* (New York: Free Press, 1973).

Al-Bukhari, *Forty Hadith of an-Nawawi*. Hadith 13, 40 Hadith an-Nawawi. <https://sunnah.com/nawawi40:13>

Burkhart, P. J. and Reuss, S., *Successful Strategic Planning: A Guide for Nonprofit Agencies and Organizations* (Newbury, London, and New Delhi: Sage Publications, 1993).

Caperon, J., Todd, A., and Walters, J. (eds.), *A Christian Theology of Chaplaincy* (London and Philadelphia: Jessica Kingsley Publishers, 2017).

Centre for Media Monitoring, *British Media's Coverage of Muslims and Islam (2018-2020)* (2021). <https://cfmm.org.uk/wp-content/uploads/2021/11/CfMM-Annual-Report-2018-2020-digital.pdf>

Chittick, W. C., *The Sufi Path of Love: The Spiritual Teachings of Rumi* (Albany: Sunny Press, 1983).

Clines, J. M. S., *Faiths in Higher Education Chaplaincy: A Report Commissioned by the Church of England Board of Education* (London: Church of England Board of Education, 2008)

Cran, C., *The Art of Change Leadership: Driving Transformation In a Fast-Paced World* (Hoboken: Wiley, 2015).

Dearden, L., "White Supremacist behind 'Punish a Muslim Day' Jailed for 12 Years", *The Independent* (2019). <https://www.independent.co.uk/news/uk/crime/david-parnham-court-punish-muslim-day-sentence-white-supremacist-trial-a9090186.html>

Gilliat-Ray, S., *Religion in Higher Education: The Politics of the Multi-faith Campus* (Aldershot, UK: Ashgate, 2000).

Gilliat-Ray, S., Ali, M., and Pattison, S., *Understanding Muslim Chaplaincy* (London and New York: Routledge, 2013).

IOK Chaplains, *From The Chaplain's Desk. Welcoming IOK Chaplaincy To MuslimMatters* (2022). <https://muslimmatters.org/2022/01/29/iok-chaplains-desk-intro/>

Kim, D. H., Fitchett, G., Anderson, J. L., and Garman, A. N., "Management and Leadership Competencies Among Spiritual Care Managers." *Journal of Health Care Chaplaincy*, 28,1 (2022), 1-10. <https://e-tarjome.com/storage/panel/fileuploads/2022-08-31/1661919291_e17154.pdf>

Lahaj, M., "End of Life Care and the Chaplain's Role on the Medical Team." *The Journal of Islamic Medical Association of North America*, 43,3 (2011), pp. 173-178.

Malik, A. and Wykes, E., *British Muslims in UK Higher Education* (London: Bridge Institute, 2018). <https://www.azizfoundation.org.uk/wp-content/uploads/2024/03/British-Muslims-in-UK-HE.pdf>

Marshall, S., *Strategic Leadership of Change in Higher Education: What's New?* (Milton Park, Abingdon, and New York: Routledge, 2019).

May, G. L., *Strategic Planning: Fundamentals for Small Business* (Hampton: Business Expert Press, 2010).

Milton, J., *The Poems of John Milton with Notes*, ed. by T. Keightley (London: Chapman & Hall 1859).

Office for National Statistics, *Religion, England and Wales: Census 2021* (2022). <https://www.ons.gov.uk/peoplepopulationandcommunity/culturalidentity/religion/bulletins/religionenglandandwales/census2021>

Ouida, *Moths*, ed. by N. Schroeder (Louisville: Broadview Press, 2005).

Parmenter, D., *Key Performance Indicators: Developing, Implementing, and Using Winning KPIs*, (Hoboken: Wiley, 2010).

Quran, Chapters 2, 3, 8, 13, 29, 35, 94.

Rajput, A. H., "The Role of Muslim Chaplains in Higher Education: Should They Be Doing What They Are Doing?" *Practical Theology*, 8,3-4 (2016), pp. 227-244.

Schuhmann, C. and Damen, A., "Representing the Good: Pastoral Care in a Secular Age." *Pastoral Psychology*, 67 (2018), 405-417. <https://link.springer.com/article/10.1007/s11089-018-0826-0>

Siddiqui, A., "Islam at Universities in England: Meeting the Needs and Investing in the Future." *Islamic Studies*, 46,4 (2007), pp. 559-570.

Smith, A., *Everyting Isn't Terrible: Conquer Your Insecurities, Interrupt Your Anxiety and Finally Calm Down* (London: Souvenir Press, 2019).

Smith, M., "Does University Chaplaincy Need a Theology?" *Practical Theology*, 8,3-4 (2015), pp. 214-226.

Sunan Abi Dawud 3641. *Book 26: Knowledge (Kitab Al-Ilm)*. English Translation: *Book 25, Hadith 3634*.

Sunan Ibn Majah 225. *Vol. 1: Book 1*. English Translation: *The Book of the Sunnah (Introduction)*.

Swift, C., Cobb, M., and Todd, A. (eds.), *A Handbook of Chaplaincy Studies: Understanding Spiritual Care in Public Places* (Milton Park, Abingdon, and New York: Routledge, 2016).

The University of Sheffield, *University of Sheffield Statement on Religious Activities on Campus* (2002) <https://www.sheffield.ac.uk/bnbr-life-centre/senate-statement>

UK GOV, *Equality Act 2010* (2010). <https://www.legislation.gov.uk/ukpga/2010/15/section/4>

University of Portsmouth, *Our Strategy* (2023). <https://www.port.ac.uk/about-us/our-ambition/our-strategy>

University of Roehampton, *Annual Equality Report* (March 2023). <https://www.roehampton.ac.uk/globalassets/documents/corporate-information/2021-22-equality-report.pdf/>

Vahide, Ş., *Bediuzzaman Said Nursi: Author of the Risale-i Nur* (Kuala Lumpur: Islamic Book Trust, 2011).

Part 3

Interviews

1

Ameira Abahadur Kutkut
Cardiff Metropolitan University

I work for a smallish university with just over 12,000 students spread over two campuses and I am employed full-time as coordinating chaplain. Our chaplaincy team is a little unconventional. I am a Muslim woman and the only chaplain who is employed by the university – the role of coordinating chaplain is typically held by Christian ministers in UK universities, although not always. We have two volunteer Christian chaplains, and I am trying to expand the team with more volunteer chaplains from other faiths. We are in a university city, so to speak, so everyone is after the same pool of people, which has its challenges. Our chaplaincy is a member of the Interfaith Council for Wales, so I have built up links with other faith leaders, whom I can refer students to if needed. If there are other faith-specific questions, support is available. We also have an Interfaith Working Group in the university which is a collaboration between the chaplaincy and the Student Union, and it brings together staff and students from across the university to discuss matters of faith and belief. This group informs some of the chaplaincy work and they advise us on what they would like in terms of faith on campus. For Friday prayers for Muslim students and staff, we currently have an academic staff member, who is not a chaplain, but volunteers to lead the Friday prayers. Acquiring these services and resources across the university enables us to use resources wisely and also allows for greater input to chaplaincy from a range of voices.

In terms of resources, the university provides us with a small but manageable budget every year which is helpful. Whenever we have wanted to do bigger events, we've been supported to tap into other areas of the university for funding, within reason. In terms of resources, I believe we are reasonably resourced. We have multi-faith prayer spaces on both campuses, including ablution facilities for Muslims. We are currently having a new prayer space built which is much bigger than the ones we have already. The university has been brilliant in making sure the prayer spaces on campus are adequate. Muslims make up roughly ten percent of the student population.

How would you describe Muslim chaplaincy?

We work in a multi-faith space. I see Muslim chaplaincy as spiritual care provided in a Muslim framework. I am a multi-faith chaplain. I did start off as a Muslim chaplain and even at that time I supported staff and students of all faiths. So I guess I was simply a chaplain who was a Muslim. The needs of Muslim students are often more apparent, mainly because of practical needs required by their faith, such as prayer space for example. Muslim students are as varied in their characters and practice as can be expected. University life presents many challenges for all students. It may be the first time that a young person is living alone and expected to make decisions for themselves and learn how to negotiate and question their own beliefs and what it is like to be a Muslim or any other faith without their parents telling them what to do. Chaplains can provide a safe space for non-judgmental support where students can discuss some of these issues

Are there any conflicts of interest given that you're a Muslim who is also an interfaith chaplain?

Not at all. The more I reflect on what Allah wants of us on this earth in spreading peace and harmony, the more I believe that multi-faith chaplaincy is an important part of my journey of faith. As Muslims, in what is an increasingly secularized world, for us to get what we need, we need to bring everyone else with us. There is no room for selfishness. We need to work to support the right of anyone of faith to be able to access the support they need. I think interfaith or multifaith working has a lot to teach the wider world. As different faith groups we often fundamentally disagree with each other's beliefs and yet can work together for the shared goal of ensuring we each have a right to hold those beliefs.

Why did you become a Muslim chaplain?

It wasn't something I planned for or aspired to be, mainly because I never really knew the breadth and depth of a chaplaincy position or how I could fit into the role of chaplain. I have been interested in Muslim philosophy and spirituality since I was very young. I remember being ten or eleven years old and reflecting on the verses of the Quran and what they meant for my life. When I was in my early teens, I persuaded my parents to send me to a boarding school to study Islam in depth. It was a six-year *'Alamiyya* course in a traditional seminary. During my studies I felt there was something of a disconnect between the theory and the spiritual practice of what I was studying and so with the support of my teachers, I set up an Islamic personal development peer-to-peer programme. I worked with other students to help deliver this across the college. When I graduated, all my work was focused on teaching Islam as a spiritual and theological guide. I loved studying and wanted to continue with it, and so I signed up for a Master's course looking at Islam in contemporary Britain at Cardiff University. That was the beginning of my adventure into higher education and at the time, I didn't realise how many doors this would open for me! Later, to further my understanding of supporting people with their personal spiritual development, I took a postgraduate counselling course and trained as a counsellor. In between studying, I was working in an organisation that supported ethnic minority communities through counselling, advocacy and other services. I was also involved with our local mosque, running Islamic study circles for university-age women, co-managing a Qur'an school, and I was involved in interfaith projects amongst other things. When this chaplaincy role came up, I was initially hesitant to apply for it, as I had never worked as a formal chaplain or in a university before and assumed that I wouldn't be the right person for the job. Looking back now, chaplaincy was and still is the perfect avenue for me to bring together all the fields I was working in. In other words, it was a natural progression for me.

I've come to realize there are many discrepancies with regard to the role of Muslim chaplain. Some places provide Muslim chaplaincy training in a few weekends spread over a few months. And there are other chaplains who have trained extensively for years. I think it is really important that universities do not take on just anyone as Muslim chaplain based solely on the fact that the person is a Muslim: a Muslim chaplain should have a level of expertise and experience appropriate for the role. In a Christian setting, hiring someone just because they were a Christian would never be acceptable. As for being a Muslim woman chaplain, well, that comes with its own challenges as many people, both inside and outside of Muslim communities, have different views on what a Muslim woman should or should not be allowed to do. This does also affect conversations on religious leadership. of which chaplaincy is part.

Why is it important to have a Muslim chaplain in university?

If there are Muslim students in a university, it is essential to have their voices represented and their support needs met. They should have someone to go to who understands them, without having to explain every little detail of the cultural and religious aspects of their lives. I don't necessarily feel that it is important for every university to have a Muslim woman chaplain, but it is important that women are not excluded from chaplaincy. Obviously, chaplaincy in the Muslim community is fairly new compared with chaplaincy in Christianity, and for a long time, Muslim chaplains were always male. In general, people over the years have come to expect that the Muslim chaplain will be a man, so they are always surprised when they see a woman Muslim chaplain. People are often surprised when they see me both as a woman and as a chaplain, which they regard to be a Christian concept. I do get people who consider the Muslim chaplain's role to be nothing more than leading the Friday prayers, but of course, the Muslim chaplain's role is much bigger than this. Thankfully, there is a lecturer in our university who is happy to take on the prayer-leading role. My work is so much more varied and involved than just that which happens on Fridays.

Can you list the jobs you do as a chaplain?

I give faith-based advice and support to both staff and students.

I support people from all faiths and none.

I deal with theological questions. And if a student or member staff wants to speak to someone from another faith about a particular question, I am able to refer them to the appropriate person. But most students are quite comfortable speaking to me, because they know that I do have a belief, and that it's okay to talk about faith, which is something they might find difficult to raise in other spaces. I actually had a student who asked me whether it was allowed for us to speak about God, which I found amusing. If you come to a chaplain, 'God-talk' is always welcome.

I am responsible for faith-based support to students and staff across the university, so if particular faith groups require specific considerations, I am there to support them as far as is possible. Such as festivals, etc.

I advise the university on faith matters. So, I sit on the EDI board. I sit on the PREVENT board also, as well as a few other committees like that.

I am responsible for organising a few large faith events that we have. We have an annual Iftar, a carol service and events for interfaith week. Our

Student Union holds a large annual Diwali event funded by the university too. These events are tied to particular religious celebrations, but we do invite all staff and students regardless of faith. I am also the university contact with other faith leaders, for involvement with other events for example. I also co-chair our interfaith working group and manage the multi-faith prayer rooms.

I organise the Friday prayers for Muslim students and staff, ensuring that provision is there every week.

In Ramadan, I work with the Islamic Society to support Muslim students' needs, ensuring that water and dates are available in prayer rooms etc.

I also offer bereavement support across the university to people of all faiths and none. Faith is discussed only if the individual concerned brings it into the conversation.

Students sometimes pop in to discuss all manner of problems, such as a breakup from a relationship, or feelings of loneliness and isolation, and so there is quite a lot of general pastoral care.

I also support victims of hate crime and racism. If they don't want to report it, they don't have to, but we encourage them to. Sometimes they just want someone to talk to in a safe space.

We are a university of sanctuary, and we provide annual scholarships every year for asylum seekers and refugee students, a few of whom I mentor every year. Refugee and asylum seeker students have different levels of need depending on their journeys. As a mentor, I am the first point of contact for support. Some may want to talk about what they have been through, and others don't. Other asylum seeker and refugee students may also come to see a chaplain, but not necessarily through the sanctuary route.

Also, if a student is in hospital and there is no one available to visit them, I would go and visit them.

I have been to prisons and to courts to provide victims with moral support.

So my role covers a whole range of things.

Normalising people's faith identity at every level in our institution is probably the most important part of the role of a Muslim chaplain. This can happen through support from EDI, through the big festivals we arrange, through advising the university, and through working on the ground and seeing students and staff one-to-one. To belong anywhere, we need to be able to bring our whole selves and every part must be embraced. Faith can be a massive part of a person's identity and chaplaincy work fosters a sense of belonging.

What percentage of your work is faith-based and what percentage practical?

It's hard to say exactly because I have so many varied roles. I would say that the majority of my initial one-to-ones are not faith-related, and not all of them go through a faith route, but all my other work is based on issues of faith. The majority of my one-to-one appointments are not directly related to faith. Faith is brought up later. It is not usually the first reason why they come to me, but faith will usually come up during sessions. I think they feel comfortable talking to me about their faith beliefs as they see me as a person of faith and know that they don't have to justify their own beliefs.

How is the value that you contribute to Muslim chaplaincy measured?

I have regular reviews with my line manager, who is very supportive. Seeing the changes in the university is itself an acknowledgement of the value of chaplaincy. Take our annual Iftar, for example. For the first one we held, I was planning to charge the students because I didn't know how we could pay for it, but my manager found the budget for it from elsewhere to cover the costs. And it went really well. Our Vice-Chancellor attended and saw the value in the event – so much so that funding was set aside to finance it every year. It was recognised that apart from being a faith event, it brings students together and is a means for positively impacting well-being. That first year we had a newish cohort of international students. It was their first year away from home and the atmosphere really helped them to settle in and give them a sense of belonging. And senior management acknowledged it by committing to making it an annual event. It shows that the Muslim chaplaincy work in the university is being acknowledged.

Also, when I started, Friday prayers was a men-only affair. There was a prayer room which was not even big enough for the men. Over time, I had many conversations with the university, and the university acknowledged that there was a need for a bigger space. And despite how tight we are for space in the university, they made sure we have a bigger space for Friday prayers. Now, men and women pray together in one big hall. The university has prioritized the prayer space and values it.

Do you record every activity?

We have an EDI annual report and I do feed into that to some extent. Our chaplaincy is part of the student services. And if a student is referred through student services, then they keep a record of that. But self-referrals are not collated.

What are the challenges that chaplains face?

Chaplaincy has been traditionally structured around Christianity. And that has come with certain elements of funding. And so a lot of chaplains are funded by their diocese rather than the university, which is a bit different for Muslim chaplains. Because we don't have that central funding source. So Muslim chaplains are often volunteers, which means they can't give the amount of time that is needed. Also, in terms of personal development, the opportunities are not always there. For Muslim women chaplains, getting into chaplaincy can be tricky because we don't have the same structures as Christian chaplaincy does: you can't work your way up a particular training ladder and turn out as a chaplain. But with Muslim men, training to become an imam serves as some kind of footing; Muslim women, I guess, don't necessarily have those kinds of titles in our community.

Thinking back, I have been a chaplain since 2016, but before then I would never have thought of myself as a chaplain, even though all the work I was doing before then was chaplaincy. I just hadn't put that label on myself. I was doing lots of different things for the Muslim community in a supporting role, but not really having that title. There is that kind of challenge. For Muslim women chaplains, there is the added challenge of being told: 'You can't lead Friday prayers, so how can you be a chaplain?'. And some people get really fixated on the idea of a chaplain not being able to lead a congregational prayer. I think there are two reasons for this. Firstly, in Christian chaplaincy, the chaplain can lead the services, and so within the Muslim community there may be the perception that the Muslim chaplain should also lead services. Consequently, there is the feeling that faith leadership should be for men. I was very fortunate to be supported by the local Muslim community and their recommendations helped. When you start working as a Muslim chaplain, you become more aware of the assumption that chaplaincy should be a typically male role. I trained for my role, but if I'd been a man, it would simply have been assumed that I already had all that knowledge. Sometimes people may say, I have this question, could you please ask your husband, or find an imam who can respond to it. And I'm thinking, 'I can just give you the answer myself'.

And these are the kind of assumptions that some people make. So I have to be a bit more vocal about my background in comparison to male chaplains. This can be frustrating at times.

Is there adequate knowledge out there about the work of Muslim women chaplains?

There is definitely not enough known about the work of Muslim women chaplains. Because Muslim chaplaincy itself is relatively new. So it was Christian chaplains, then Muslim men chaplains, and now we have a new wave of Muslim women chaplains emerging, which is brilliant. Not many people in the community even know that a Muslim woman chaplaincy role is even an option. Recently I was asked to talk about my journey to teenage Muslim girls at a career event. I thought that was really nice, especially since it wasn't an easy career to get into! For people to get to know more about it, routes to get into chaplaincy need to be spoken about much more. Also, the book that you are writing will, I believe, be a massive inroad to letting people know about our role as Muslim women chaplains. I think especially in academe, awareness of the important role of Muslim women chaplains needs to be raised.

2

Umm Issa
Manchester Metropolitan University

During the pandemic I was employed as a Muslim chaplain by the National Health Service Nightingale hospital in Manchester. After that, in 2021, the position of female Muslim chaplain came up at Manchester Metropolitan University, I applied and got the job. I work part-time, twelve hours a week, during term time. There is also a male chaplain who works sixteen hours a week. There are no Christian chaplains at our university. The Catholic church next to our university provides Christian chaplains as and when needed. Muslim chaplains are the only chaplains directly employed by our university. Jewish and other chaplains from other faiths are also contacted externally as and when needed.

Manchester Metropolitan University is very close to Manchester University. It is in the City Centre. We have a diverse range of students, both national and international. Around thirty-four per cent of the students identify as having a BAME background. Compared to the national average, our university has the highest percentage of Muslim students. The chaplaincy service at our university offers pastoral and well-being support on campus to all communities of faith.

Our chaplaincy team is run by the university pastoral support service. The pastoral lead manages the Muslim chaplaincy. He is non-faith aligned and he manages me and the male chaplain in our university. My main job is to offer Muslim students and staff pastoral support. My door is also open to others of different faiths and none.

Next door to our building is a Catholic church and the University of Manchester is only a five-minute walk from our campus. Christian chaplaincy is based at St. Peter's House (Manchester University), but many other faiths also use that building. We keep in constant contact with those services in order to give support to each other.

Tell me about your resources.

I have a physical space, my own laptop and phone. We have three large spaces with dividing doors, which is very useful. Having dividing doors allows us to change the prayer spaces in accordance with our needs and enable us to accommodate both men and women. So we have one room for men, one for women and one spare. We also have a large office space and two well-being spaces. Sometimes the three large spaces have to be given to the brothers because of the large number of men requiring space for Friday prayer. Friday prayer is not compulsory for women, but if women want to attend, we make sure we can accommodate them. For example, we may opt to do two or three different slots for Friday prayer, if there is not enough space for everyone.

How would you describe Muslim chaplaincy?

There is confusion about this term, especially among Muslims, as many people tend to link chaplaincy only to Christianity. Apart from an imam to lead the Friday prayers, Muslims also have pastoral needs, and that is where chaplains come in. Students and staff approach Muslim chaplains for so many varied issues. For example, issues linked to exams, financial support, negative interaction with other students, issues to do with religion, identity and so on. In fact, there are so many that it would take too long to enumerate. Chaplains are there to support them with all these issues, to listen and validate what they say and support them as well as they can. We are there not to preach to them or influence their decisions, but to help them not to be reactive, and to empower them to think things through before making decisions that they may later regret.

Why did you become a Muslim chaplain?

I feel that I have the skills and experience to support students and staff in our university. I started my chaplaincy career when I was a volunteer Muslim woman chaplain at the University of Manchester. That was in 2015. Students really needed an empathetic ear; they needed to be listened to.

Could you give us a case example?

We do encounter some difficult cases – cases which we aren't able to change or have influence on, but in such cases, it becomes especially important to give that extra emotional and faith support. One example is the case of a student and her sister rushing to catch their train home. As they didn't want to miss their train, they just managed to catch it with the intention of paying for their ticket on the train as they had no time to purchase it beforehand. However, they were really shocked and distraught that this was not permissible, and the conductor fined them. These young people had never broken the law in their lives, and the thought of having broken it – albeit unintentionally – affected them very severely. The student was filled with guilt, and the thought of being a bad example for her younger sister affected her mental health to such an extent that she was given medication. The distraught student was in much need of emotional support. I reassured her that it is the intention that matters and that, in this case, their intention was good and so they had nothing to blame themselves about. I tried to focus her attention on the fact that it was an innocent mistake, and I believe that this helped to remove some of the guilt she felt and empowered them to put this incident behind them.

Why did you choose to become a chaplain?

When I was a student of community studies, it was in my mind to go into a caring profession, such as social work. Also, I have been blessed with six children and a wealth of experience of dealing with issues affecting young people. I also had some tough times of my own to deal with, such as losing a child, enduring long hospital care, going through divorce and coping as a single parent. It was in 2013 that I experienced a major life change. My children's father left us. Without any reason or explanation, he decided that he no longer wished to be in this marriage. Consequently, I had to take care of six children by myself. I guess through these personal difficulties in life, I realised that if I can learn from these experiences and move on, then I can support others through difficult situations and life events.

Why is it important to have a Muslim chaplain in university?

I come across many students who cannot speak to their parents and loved ones about their problems for fear of being judged and controlled and forced to make certain decisions against their will. Some of the topics include 'forced marriage', 'cultural expectations' and so on. Chaplaincy offers that non-judgmental space in which informed decisions can be discussed and taken. In my experience, for these kinds of issues, both students and staff tend to seek a Muslim woman chaplain, as they perceive women chaplains to be less threatening. Muslim male students and staff specifically also seek the female Muslim chaplain in particular to talk about certain family issues, such as forced marriage. Also, female students and staff specifically ask for a female Muslim chaplain, as they generally feel more comfortable to talk to a woman, especially about issues pertaining to women. What they seek is a non-biased Muslim perspective on certain issues, so that they can work out for themselves what path to take, without being pressured and forced into a situation.

Can you list some of the jobs you do as a Muslim woman chaplain?

Pastoral care, practical and spiritual support, which I consider to be the most important, as we are there to help students and staff through their university life.

Supporting the ISOC team – giving talks, arranging workshops, training, and giving access to ISOC to our office as and when needed. We generally have a good relationship with ISOC, but sometimes boundaries are pushed. But we tend to deal with them as best as we can. ISOC organises Friday prayers in collaboration with the male chaplain.

How is your work measured and/or acknowledged?

I keep a record of all my contacts with students and staff and notes on the nature of these meetings. I share these records on the intranet so that colleagues are able to see them. The intranet is used to acknowledge and celebrate each other's achievements.

We have an annual award ceremony for staff, and the work of our team leader was acknowledged by being nominated and winning this award.

What challenges do you face as a chaplain?

One of the biggest challenges for us is the task of managing the prayer spaces. Although there are many mosques around, some community members whose businesses or workplaces are close to our university also use our prayer rooms. Sometimes this proves to be challenging, as we may need to limit the number of community members attending, owing to limited space. Students and staff have to be prioritized, and sometimes this causes tensions among our community.

One of the challenges for women chaplains is the image that some people have of women as being somehow timid and deficient in learning. But when they actually come to see you, their assumptions are dispelled. They see for themselves that the woman chaplain is confident and has the necessary skills and knowledge to give pastoral support to students and staff.

Another challenge is lack of awareness of the difference between the role of imam and that of chaplain. I have to remind people that I am not an imam and I usually have to explain my role as chaplain. If individuals ask about specific rulings, it is easy enough to look up the answers via many resources, as well as referring them to others who know the answers. The most challenging and important part of my role is pastoral care.

The problem is that people do not know about the work of Muslim chaplains generally and the work of Muslim women chaplains in particular. The work of Muslim women chaplains needs to be better understood and celebrated.

3

Farhat Yaqoob
Leeds University

Can you tell me a bit about your university and the chaplaincy team in your institution?

In our university we have around sixteen Christian chaplains and of those there are two main chaplains who are full-time. The chaplaincy team covers four different institutions of learning, so it's a broad area. Other faiths are not represented in the same chaplaincy format. But we do have connections with other faith links, for example places of faith such as Gurdwaras where people can be sign-posted. We have a Rabbi also who can be contacted and who works closely with the Jewish student community.

I'm not placed in the Christian framework because they have an ecumenical structure and they sit within the framework of their own particular church set-up. It has run for many years like this. I sit within a belief system outside of that. And I was the first of my kind at my institution being from the Muslim faith in a faith role. So technically we don't have a multifaith chaplaincy here. We have a Christian chaplaincy. Fortunately, I was put in a temporary department linked to the International Student Office in order to get paid. That was seven years ago, and I am still in that position as there is still no framework for multifaith chaplaincy as yet.

My position is full-time and is paid by the university, and my line manager sits in a team which is part of the International Student Office. I do have an extremely good relationship with the office however, and we work really well together especially when thinking about the needs of international Muslim students.

How would you describe the role of Muslim chaplains?

I would describe the role of chaplaincy generally as a companionship journey. To be a chaplain is to be an 'enabler'. That relationship is a relationship of trust. And the invitation to be invited to that place of companionship is important.

The Muslim framework of chaplaincy work sits within the faith of Islam, which becomes the Muslim chaplain's shade, their shelter, their roof. They are enriched by having the toolbox of tradition and the sayings of the Prophet (PBWH).

My Muslim chaplaincy role has been a very interesting one. Since Islam covers every aspect of life, my chaplaincy duties are also connected to every aspect of Muslim staff and student life on campus.

Many significant events occurred during my incumbency as chaplain: the Brexit referendum took place; Donald Trump entered the White House; and there were numerous terrorist attacks taking place. Consequently, there were a lot of anxious and, at times, displaced people who needed help and comfort, and a lot of the work I do has been about enabling people to feel safe again. This is done mainly through listening and having honest conversations. And there are no barriers involved: there is no-one with whom I will not speak, or who is not allowed or welcome to come to speak with me. Everyone is welcome to have a conversation, and everyone has the right to feel safe, both on campus and off campus, whatever their belief system or worldview.

Muslim chaplaincy is about a journey you take with a person who has invited you into their private space for support and guidance. And I am there simply to do everything possible to make life easier for them.

Why did you become a Muslim chaplain?

It was unintentional in many ways. I did not plan to become a chaplain. I genuinely didn't.

I worked in the voluntary sector for about six or seven years. In my job I came across many 'broken people'. In my community engagement work, where I was a communication specialist, I did a lot of outreach work and came across many 'broken' and 'displaced' people. These people were going through a really tough time and there did not seem to be many routes open to them for support. I was told very kindly but firmly that it was not my job to talk to people and help them in the way that I did. This made me feel very disillusioned as I felt that this was also part of my job. This, along with various other things, made my working with these charities very difficult and it eventually encouraged me to broaden my horizons.

At the personal level, my situation had also changed. I had lost a close relative and I realized that I wanted to do more in and with my life. At that time, I did not know anything about chaplaincy, but 'wanting to help people' served as a starting point for my future career. It was at this point that I realised there was a great need that was not being addressed. Chaplaincy was introduced to me by meeting the right people at the right time. I saw it as a vehicle for addressing this human service which I passionately wanted to undertake and that's kind of how the story began for me.

Did you undergo any training for chaplaincy?

In terms of chaplaincy training, I was not officially trained. However, by working for the charity sector, I had a lot of exposure to clinical environments and community mental health. I was also teaching at the local mosque, and as a volunteer for the magistrates' court I had done the essential thirteen-week training programme for volunteers. So, when I signed up for the short Muslim chaplaincy training course at Markfield, they said that it was not necessary for me, as I had already served a number of hours in the community in various settings.

Why do you think it is important to have a Muslim chaplain in a university and why is it particularly important to have a woman Muslim chaplain?

I believe university life for young people can be quite overwhelming: suddenly they move into a different life, with new interactions, new people, new ideas. And many people that I see, particularly from a Muslim faith background, come from very sheltered home backgrounds and are away from home for the first time. Universities are not about picking and choosing parts of who you are. Nor should individuals feel as though they have to leave their faith at the door, for it is about embracing all of you. Our service as chaplains should represent that holistic approach to the learning environment – an approach which does its best to see the multi-dimensional nature of all human beings. Universities offer many services to students, such as counselling, mental health services, accommodation support and so on, but where would a student or member of staff go if they needed spiritual support if there were no chaplains?

In the past seven or eight years I have seen many students who have come to me for spiritual support and demand is ever increasing.

Can you give examples of some of the jobs you do as a Muslim chaplain?

I offer pastoral care to both students and staff.

    I mentor the Muslim student societies as well as a number of cultural-based societies.

    I run training courses for staff: these can be ad-hoc or attached to issues of well-being.

    I provide advice and training on issues such as Ramadan.

    I facilitate activities around the Islamic calendar, including the Iftar program for Ramadan and the Eid events.

    I am part of many consultation groups which involve faith and race, helping to build up the university's religious literacy.

    I do much outreach work across faculties and services.

    My priorities have to be tailored according to circumstances or emergencies. For example, during exam times one realises that students require more one-to-one support on account of increased stress. On other occasions the focus could be on a world event such as the Turkish/Syrian earthquake. Events that call for chaplaincy are many, and no two days or cases are the same.

What proportion of cases focus more on faith/belief as opposed to practical problems?

A lot of things that people come to me for involve practical issues, but within those issues, the question of belief/faith is always there somewhere within the conversation. So, for a Muslim student, nine times out of ten, faith is a factor, because they know that to have a more stabilized life, they need to improve their faith, and they come to the chaplain for support with that. Everyone's journey and speed may vary, and we have to be extremely sensitive to this fact.

How is the value that you contribute to Muslim chaplaincy measured or acknowledged?

Historically, it was through data gathering and testimonials. Initially when I was a Muslim chaplain, it was on a voluntary basis. I was not paid. Consequently,

I had to build a business case from the first year. For the first four years I presented the statistical data and testimonials to the university annually as proof of the value and the need for my role as a Muslim woman chaplain. This was recognised by my institution, and that is why I am the only non-Christian chaplain who is in a full-time paid role as a Muslim chaplain.

Describe some of the challenges for Muslim chaplains generally and women chaplains in particular?

To be a Muslim chaplain in a secular institution has its own difficulties, but it was particularly difficult for me because there was no-one in the role before me, and so I had to start from ground zero. This meant literally building everything from scratch: my relationships with departments, my relationships with societies, my relationships with mental health services, my relationships with the Students Union, and so on. That was a real challenge as there was no mold or blueprint: I was the first person to be take on such a role. From one aspect it is a good thing, not having any precedent to follow, because you can make and shape it how you feel it should be, but the hard thing is that you have no reference point, and because you have no reference point, you cannot always justify the importance of what you are doing. Another challenge was that no one had been paid before in the role that I had undertaken. This meant I had the extra task of convincing the institution that I was a resource worthy of being paid for. This required a lot of determination and endurance because I had to gather data for over four years to convince my institution of the value I added to the well-being of students and staff.

I think as Muslim chaplains we have to fit into a mold that predates our entry of Islam into UK. So, there is a mold for Christianity, there is a configuration that they are used to, and it is very hard when it is not quite adaptable for Muslim chaplains, especially Muslim women chaplains. Christian chaplaincy has been part of the university for some time and Muslim chaplaincy is relatively new, and universities are only beginning to discover that Muslim chaplains are very much needed. But nevertheless, it is a role which is very difficult to fit into that mold. How do you locate yourself then, if you don't know what you are supposed to be or how you are supposed to be placed? We know we are needed, but the challenge is to prove this, and to align ourselves with the current model of services. And if one is not aware of how the institution is run, making a business case becomes a huge challenge – one that you have to do, on top of actually getting on with your role as chaplain. All of this is quite daunting, especially if you start off as a volunteer.

Therefore, the difficulty is finding your place within a spiritual welfare service that does not know how to locate you, and in which you don't know how to place yourself without stepping on someone else's toes.

Being from the minority community makes this especially hard. Female Muslim chaplains are generally few and far between, so you are often breaking new ground. You are creating a blueprint and that is hard because you are not sure what that is supposed to look like. The lack of peer support makes this role quite challenging. The loneliness of there being just one of you can be very hard.

Another big challenge is that the services provided by universities are not always representative of all faiths. This means having a dialogue with colleagues in order to bring the needs of students and staff to the forefront. This is by no means an easy task. In fact, it is extremely challenging, as it has not been done before, and you have to find the courage to be the first person to identify and point out to others the important issues that are of concern for Muslim students and staff.

More challenging than being a female Muslim chaplain has been the difficulty of operating in a secular institution. Having said that, dynamics-wise, power and gender dynamics do exist. In my role, I am very much on my own and I frame my chaplaincy in a way that I respond to need.

Muslim women chaplains are few in number. Male chaplains often come through the route of imam training or Islamic school education; this makes entry to this field more difficult for Muslim women chaplains. We are few in number and this is a disadvantage to us if we are looking to the future and hoping to have more women occupy these roles.

Muslim women chaplains are either not paid for their role or, if they are paid, they are not paid adequately. The importance of their role is arguably not acknowledged to the extent that it should be, possibly because they work differently from their male counterparts.

Do you think there is adequate knowledge about the work of Muslim women chaplains?

I don't think there is. When I first started working as a chaplain, I did not know where to draw information from for this role. I had to find my own way through contacts and networking. I think there is an absolute need for more information about the role of Muslim chaplains generally and Muslim women chaplains in particular. The work of Muslim women chaplains is often not appreciated and acknowledged as much as that of their male counterparts.

We do not have an institutional pathway to become Muslim chaplains. I know that Markfield does training for Muslim chaplains, but I am not sure if it is recognised across the board. So, a lot of us learn as we go along. We need resource banks, stewards and mentors, and we need some kind of work standard – best practice – to follow and for others to aspire to.

4

Concluding Remarks

There appears to be no adequately delineated or widely agreed-upon framework for the role of Muslim chaplains in Higher Education settings. Some chaplains are paid and are provided with sufficient resources to carry out their role, while others are appointed as volunteers.

The amount of time Muslim chaplain volunteers devote to their roles also differs from institution to institution. It often happens that volunteer chaplains work almost full-time because of the high demand in their institutions. Most institutions do not specify what kinds of experience or qualifications are needed for this role. Leading congregational prayers and teaching children how to read the Quran, for example, are not the functions of the Muslim chaplain. Within HE settings, the role of the Muslim chaplain is mainly to act as mediator, moderator, educator and advocate. Another key role is to provide the kind of psycho-spiritual support that contributes to the well-being of the university community. Muslim chaplains therefore need to have the right qualifications for this role. Often, Muslim chaplains are thrown in at the deep end and have to find their own way back up themselves. Through devotion to their work, they learn through experience, adapting and dealing with difficult situations as they arise.

Many Muslim chaplains who are experts in their field often feel that their voices are not heard because of the limitations imposed on them, such as barriers to direct contact with people and departments in their institutions. This causes a lot of frustration as they are then restricted with regard to the extent to which they are able to represent their student and staff communities adequately and efficiently. Often, the needs of the people they represent are either not heard or become diluted as a result of the vicissitudes of the various hierarchical processes operating in the institution in question.

To date, there has been no easily accessible, coherent and cohesive guidance on how Muslim chaplains can approach their role; there is no handbook, no chaplaincy *vade mecum* to help them perform their jobs. It is hoped that Part

One of this book will serve as a possible framework for all Muslim chaplains to use in their shepherding role. It is a framework grounded in Quranic theology in general, and in the lived experience of our many prophets – all of whom were 'shepherds of humankind' – in particular.

It is to be hoped that Part One of this work will serve as the kind of handbook that so many chaplains have said would be a Godsend to their vocation. This handbook provides a completely novel, yet deeply theologically grounded, six-step method of pastoral engagement, which can be adapted and applied to any aspects of a chaplain's role. It also doubles as a model for reflective practice that has a Quranic provenance, but which can also be used quite comfortably and confidently in a pluralistic context.

As for Part Two of this book, which focuses solely on the experiences of female Muslim chaplains in the HE sector of the UK, we have for the first time been able to gain some insight into the work of dedicated Muslim women 'shepherds' whose voices have hitherto been almost silent. It is hoped that their narratives will help to raise awareness about the work of Muslim chaplains in general and the crucial role played by female Muslim chaplains in particular.

About the Contributors

Ameira Bahadur-Kutkut is the Coordinating Chaplain and a PhD student at Cardiff Metropolitan University. Her interests include interfaith dialogue, community cohesion and women's well-being in Islamic ethics. She is a classically trained scholar of law and legal theory, a qualified counsellor and a developing academic.

Syyeda Midhat Batool, an English teacher by profession, embarked on the route of chaplaincy after being intrigued by the Christian concept of 'service', but was unable to forsake completely her passion for teaching and learning. Thus, while serving as Muslim chaplain at Loughborough University since 2011, she has also been teaching Academic English at the University of Birmingham. She has been a visiting lecturer at the Markfield Institute of Higher Education since 2012 and has supervised the training of Muslim chaplaincy students at her university. She has an MA in English Literature, an MA in Applied Linguistics & TESOL, a CertEd, a CELTA, a Diploma in Islamic Education and a Certificate in Chaplaincy.

Rukia Bi is Keele University's first Muslim chaplain. She is an educator, tutor and social activist, dedicating herself to the equality and justice of Muslim women globally.

Ameena Blake is a Muslim scholar with a Masters degree in Islamic Studies. Other qualifications include: a BA English Studies, a PG certificate in Teaching and an MSc in Leadership and Management. She currently serves as Muslim chaplain at the University of Sheffield and for South Yorkshire Police. She lectures in Islamic Studies at Markfield Institute of Higher Education and directs the EHUK women's refuge project.

Dr Amra Bone presently works as a university chaplain and an Associate Lecturer at the University of Portsmouth and the University of Chichester respectively. She is a researcher, presenter and regularly writes and reviews journal articles in the areas of Islamic law, Qur'anic ethics, gender, education and chaplaincy. She is the first woman in the UK to join a board of Muslim judges adjudicating on Islamic marriage and divorce. She has appeared on many TV and radio programmes.

Sabiha Iqbal serves as Muslim chaplain at the University of Roehampton. She has worked for over eighteen years in the HE sectors, with roles in recruitment, international student support and, most recently, in a multi-faith chaplaincy. She uses her work and learning to enhance the co-curricular experience for students and staff at her university, and has organised UK and EU excursions for students and staff to provide opportunities for learning in multi-cultural social contexts. During her tenure she has set up a variety of spaces for worship; established reflection spaces that enable peaceable coexistence; and has organised activities that encourage members of the community to venture into altruistic works, into learning or sharing a skill, or simply exploring their outdoor environment.

Umm Issa is a mother to six children whom she strives to raise to become upstanding, well-mannered contributors to society. Whilst in her nurturing phase, she volunteered as a Muslim chaplain for many years within a university environment and then with the NHS for many more years. Currently she is a paid Muslim chaplain at Manchester Metropolitan University and offers pastoral, spiritual and emotional support to students and staff on campus.

Dr Mahshid Turner is Durham University's Muslim chaplain and an independent researcher. She is the first female Muslim chaplain to be appointed in the Higher Education sector in the UK. She has undergraduate degrees in a number of subjects; an MSc in Public Health; an MA in Muslim Chaplaincy, Counselling and Pastoral Care; and a PhD in Muslim theology. She has also led many community projects, some of which have involved minority ethnic groups, as well as working full-time as the SEWA Project Officer for Age Concern's Minority Ethnic Community. She has also worked as Community Health Specialist as part of the Sure Start initiative. As well as her chaplaincy work for the university, Mahshid is Head of Education and Outreach at the International Foundation for Muslim Theology.

Farhat Yaqoob is the Muslim chaplain at Leeds University. She works full-time and is line managed by the International Student Office. She has worked in the voluntary sector for many years. Her voluntary work includes teaching at a local mosque and volunteering for the magistrate's court.